Aggies, Moms, and Apple Pie

Number Twenty-two:
The Centennial Series of the Association of Former Students,
Texas A&M University

Aggies, Moms, and Apple Pie

EDITED BY
Edna M. Smith

INTRODUCTION BY *John A. Adams, Jr.*

ILLUSTRATED BY *Mary Ann Flusche*

Edna M. Smith
12/87

TEXAS A&M UNIVERSITY PRESS
College Station

To Debbie and Bill —
Just reading all these
enticing Aggie recipes
and this crazy Aggie
love should whet
your appetites!
EMS

Library of Congress Cataloging-in-Publication Data

Aggies, moms, and apple pie.

Includes index.
1. Cookery.   2. Federation of Texas A & M University
Mothers' Clubs.   I. Smith, Edna M. (Edna Marie),
1932–   .
TX715.A246   1987   641.5   86-14565
ISBN 0-89096-267-7

Contents

Preface

If you're a mother with a son or daughter in college, you may find some distinctive new demands on your cooking skills, your time, *and* your recipe file. You may hear: "Mom, how can I get through finals week without something to munch on while I'm studying? Can't you send me something?" Or, "Mom, can you bring some food for my buddies to eat before the game? All the restaurants will be way too crowded for eating out." Or, "Mom, I can't stand one more can of chicken noodle soup. Can you send me a recipe for something else I can fix with a can opener?" Or, "Mom, a couple of carloads of us are coming through Friday on our way to the beach. What's for supper?" Or, the request that makes every mother's heart beat a little faster: "Mom, I miss you and Dad, and I'm coming home next weekend. Could you fix my favorite—please?"

Sound familiar? This cookbook is addressed especially to those people with college students—and also to those who are away from home attending college, perhaps living in an apartment for the first time and trying to solve culinary mysteries the hard way. Its appeal will not be limited to them, however. The busy mother with children still at home will appreciate the many quick and easy palate pleasers, and the active club member will value the various dishes that are so appropriate for luncheons, covered dish suppers, and parties. The book should also be a treasure to the newly married, who might be thinking about starting some of their own mealtime and holiday traditions.

The origin of this book is special—the recipes come from a very special group of people, Aggie moms. *Aggies, Moms, and Apple Pie* is a collection of nearly five hundred recipes submitted by members of the Federation of Texas A&M University Mothers' Clubs in Texas and Louisiana. Since many of these recipes focus on the needs of families with college students, there are cookies and other treats for the ever-popular "care packages" sent via mail or a friend returning to school. There are many simple (but tasty and nutritious) dishes that can be made with ingredients even a novice cook would have on hand. There are suggestions for foods to feed a crowd at a tailgate party in the shadow of Kyle Field. And for those weekends and holidays when Mom's favorite Aggie comes home, with or without a crowd of friends, there are casseroles and other make-aheads that will give Mom and student a chance to enjoy some together time.

Collecting these varied and delicious recipes from members of the Mothers' Clubs was not a difficult task. As usual, the Aggie Moms came through. To anyone familiar with the group and its history, this could hardly be surprising. Mothers' Club members have been coming through for Texas A&M since the 1920s. Anyone who is not familiar with this extraordinary "auxiliary" of an extraordinary institution should take a moment to read the brief history of the federation which follows. Some excellent books on the history of the university and its Association of Former Students are available, too, from Texas A&M University Press.

As I've said, variety is evident in these recipes collected from A&M Mothers' Clubs, which are supplemented by a few favorites from campus food services. Some feed two, others feed twenty (or one hundred, as you will see in the offerings from Cain Hall). Some have a regional flavor or ethnic origin. Others are time-tested versions of old standbys, whose gathering in one book can prevent frantic searches through your files and other cookbooks. I have tested many of the recipes myself, besides checking them all for clarity and completeness. In addition, many of the recipes have been reviewed and tested—and enjoyed—by various members of the staff of Texas A&M University Press. We think all the recipes are clear, and many of them are simple enough for a beginning cook.

Something I have learned in collecting recipes over the years for myself and for this cookbook is that they are very personal expressions. A treasured recipe may give insight into someone's heritage and family traditions. I especially enjoy reading personal comments that have been scribbled onto the recipes; in this book, the comments moms have offered are given in italics. When I see someone's recipe file, I want to copy those recipes which are dog-eared and food-stained. I *know* that those are the ones which have been used over and over and have been appreciated. They have become, in effect, family traditions. And who knows more about traditions than Aggies?

Let me now, as another mother of Aggies, share one of my own family's traditions, a recipe for a dessert that is itself almost the symbol of tradition, apple pie. This recipe came from grandmother to mother to me (although I was probably the first to write it down), and it has been modified a bit over the years. I will pass the recipe along to my own Aggie son and daughter, just as I have passed them many pieces of this pie. It's even requested for Thanksgiving dinner, when pumpkin is supposed to be "in."

Two-Crust Pastry

2 cups sifted all-purpose flour
1 teaspoon salt

⅔ cup plus 2 tablespoons vegetable
    shortening
¼ cup cold water

Combine flour and salt. Cut in shortening with pastry blender or two knives until mixture is the consistency of coarse cornmeal. Sprinkle on cold water gradually, tossing lightly and stirring with a fork. Dough should be neither sticky nor dry; do not handle any more than necessary after water is added. Shape into two smooth balls, and roll out on lightly floured surface.

Apple Pie

6–8 large firm, tart apples
    (about 2 quarts sliced), peeled
    and thinly sliced
⅓ cup sugar (or more to taste)
⅓ cup brown sugar, packed

juice of ½–1 small lemon,
    depending on tartness of apples
1 teaspoon cinnamon
1 tablespoon butter or margarine

Slice apples into bowl; add white and brown sugar, lemon juice, and cinnamon; mix well. (Do not expect to have the same results if you use canned apples.) Spoon into unbaked pie shell, heaping in center. Dot with butter or margarine. Top with crust that has been vented or pricked to allow steam to escape. (Or venting may be done after the crust is placed over the filling.) Seal and flute edges. Bake at 425° for 50 minutes. SERVES 6–8.

Aggie Moms from seventy clubs in Texas and Louisiana offer in this book recipes from their storehouses of edible traditions, recipes which can help ease the transition from child at home to independent young adult and which help keep the ties between campus and home strong. The

Moms share them, as we now share this book with you, out of a deep interest in Texas A&M University and its students, a contribution from the Twelfth Mom.

The Federation of Texas A&M University Mothers' Clubs

As far as I know, the Federation of Texas A&M University Mothers' Clubs is the only organization of its kind anywhere. This group of mothers of students and former students states as its purpose: "By individual and united effort to contribute in every way to the comfort and welfare of the students, and to cooperate with the faculty of the University in maintaining a high standard of moral conduct and intellectual attainment."

Currently seventy clubs strong, with some forty-five hundred members in Texas and Louisiana, the Federation—whose chapters are known as A&M University Mothers' Clubs, or Aggie Moms' Clubs—has been a viable service organization since 1928. The first A&M Mothers' Club was actually founded in February, 1922, in Dallas. Under the leadership of Mrs. H. L. Peoples, with support from eleven other mothers, the group was first formed as an auxiliary of the Dallas A&M Club. The Dallas Mothers' Club was quickly followed by groups in Fort Worth, Brown County (Brownwood), San Antonio, San Angelo, Houston, Bell County, and Brazos County. These groups became the nucleus of the federation, which celebrated its golden anniversary in 1978.

A past president (1973–74) of the federation, Mrs. Lewis Gross, explained her involvement in Mothers' Clubs: "We mothers feel we are a vital part of A&M; after all, without us there would be no university. Along with sending our sons and daughters to A&M to be developed into citizens of outstanding capabilities, we have sent love, tears, laughter—and cookies." Even this is an understatement, of course. Through the years, financial contributions have gone to numerous campus groups and facilities, and many more thousands of dollars have been given to scholarships and loan funds. During its first fifty years, members of the federation contributed $150,000 to A&M, and from 1980 to 1985 alone, the group gave a total of $456,695.

Each club plans its own fund-raising activities and decides which university programs it will contribute to. In the fall, members who attend the federation meeting listen to various organizations' requests for funds; at the spring meeting, they make their annual contributions. Throughout the year many of them meet for frequent workdays to create the original Aggie items sold at meetings and at the boutique held during Parents' Weekend in the spring. Many clubs send hometown newspapers to the Memorial Student Center's browsing library for the students to enjoy.

In addition to financial contributions—which have been considerable—there has also been other assistance, as Dr. Robert Walker, vice-president for development at Texas A&M, recently remarked. "Over the years there have been so many contributions for which we can't assign monetary value. There has been massive support for worthy causes." A&M Mothers' Club members have taken stands on issues affecting A&M whenever they felt the need, and they have been formidable lobbyists with the Texas state legislature. They have been vocal about campus concerns such as medical service, food service, and the library, to mention only a few.

As far as money is concerned, there are no "big" individual contributors. And many moms would say that they themselves are the biggest receivers, gaining much from the friendships and shared experiences that are an important benefit of federation membership.

EDNA M. SMITH

Introduction

Aggies and Food

While many generations of Aggies have complained about the monotony of campus food, most have made sure not to miss meal call. Aggies and food—a combination that almost deserves the status of "tradition." Three square meals a day have been available almost since the day A&M opened its doors, but there is nothing like a surprise survival package from home. During my fish year, we ate well and had access to plenty of snacks. However, about mid-semester I received a call slip from the postmaster to pick up a crushed box. I was informed I could put in a damage claim, but I declined. I was just happy to see a box from home, and I hurried back to Dorm 12 to sneak into my third-floor room. I had avoided all upperclassmen until I turned to open my door and two seniors yelled, "Hey, fish Adams what'cha got in the box?" I was caught. The seniors informed me with a smile that it was their solemn duty to check my box to prevent any illegal items from entering the dorms. Upon opening the box, they found the crushed remains of three dozen large brownies. In their inspection process the seniors picked out and ate the big chunks and sent me to find three spoons, whereupon the three of us finished off a half a box of powdered crumbs. They informed me that the box (now empty) passed inspection and advised me to write a thank-you note to my mother . . . asking her to send more brownies. The seniors signed the letter and made me pay the postage to mail it home! Such were the trials of a hungry "fish."

Cuisine on the Brazos has had its own colorful, unique significance and flavor from the earliest days of the fledgling college. During the past one hundred ten years there have been only a handful of stewards in charge of subsistence and the dining halls. Former Confederate General Hamilton P. Bee was the first such steward, hired in 1876 at $500 per year. The original mess hall was set up on the first floor of Gathright Hall and was known as Steward Hall. General Bee was getting ready to leave A&M in late 1877 when a New Orleans–trained chef and hotel entrepreneur named Bernard Sbisa was in town from Galveston to visit friends in Bryan.

Sbisa (correctly pronounced SBEE-ZA not SA-BEE-SA) had been saddened by the loss of his 125-room hotel and restaurant, the Grand Southern, in Galveston during a fire that gutted the town in June, 1877. His friends in Bryan informed him that the new college could use someone like him. Thus, in January, 1878, after fourteen years in the commercial food and hotel business, he joined the college as its second chief steward and manager of the Subsistence Department. Having no housing available at the college for his family, he moved them into a home in Bryan while he lived and worked in Gathright Hall, the college's first major building. During the late 1870s and early 1880s, Gathright served as the mess hall, dorm, and classroom for the cadets.

The remoteness of the pre-1900 campus did not diminish Sbisa's desire to provide the best of basic foods for the students and faculty. Sbisa maintained a "poultry yard," annually canned tremendous amounts of "cooked down" fruits and jams, and encouraged the college to provide funds for a facility to make cheese. In September, 1886, he boasted to George Pfeuffer, chairman of the board, that he had produced 421 pounds of butter.

Sbisa's greatest delight was to stage marvelous banquets. His flair for the distinctive tastes of the Old Quarter of New Orleans helped spice up the menu. Early menus attest to the richness of Sbisa's taste and his particular zest for perfection. Such gatherings as class balls, the senior banquet, and Christmas dinner were always well attended and the social highlights of each school year, although the lavishness of such events was directly related to how much of the budget remained at the end of each semester. At one dinner, Sbisa treated the diners to such appetizers as oyster cocktail, green sea turtle mikado, consommé imperiale, and broiled rockfish maître. The main course consisted of fresh lobster Newburg on petit fours, imported smoked tongue, fresh stuffed tomatoes, and pineapple fritters covered with romain sauce. Accompanying his gourmet meals were Vienna rolls, snowflake crackers, and croustades of sweetbreads à la Creole. While no recipes have survived, it is obvious that all who tasted his cuisine must surely have been well fed. W. Ray "Quebie" Kerr '26 of Houston, Sbisa's grandson, recalls visiting the campus as a youngster and being treated to a dinner with all the trimmings in the private dining room of the mess hall. Kerr remembers Sbisa as a "real food expert."

His dedication to serving daily well-planned meals was but once interrupted during Sbisa's near half-century of stewardship. During the early morning hours of Saturday, November 11, 1911, the mess hall was destroyed by fire. Only the cold-storage plant and a few items of dining room furniture were saved. By mid-morning of "11-11-11," however, Sbisa was in complete command of the situation. Ernest Langford '13, then a student, recalled that Sbisa in his white linen suit was "straight as a ramrod and walked with the precision of a metronome." Sbisa mustered local boiling pots from the community to the lawn of the president's home in order to prepare breakfast. The Corps supply officer issued field gear and mess kits, and a temporary shelter was set up to feed more than 450 cadets and staff. By ten o'clock all had been served breakfast, and Sbisa was already planning for both dinner and supper in the crisp November air.

Construction was begun on a dining hall in May, 1912, but the new one-acre facility was not complete until 1920. This massive new building at the north end of Military Walk to this day boasts one of the largest open dining rooms in America. For three decades prior to World War II the entire student body was seated there family-style for each meal. The "modernized" facility was the delight of Mr. Sbisa, for whom the hall was named. Sbisa, who died in Moron, Cuba, in 1928 while visiting relatives, passed along a rich tradition of stewardship to the college. He outlasted eleven Texas A&M presidents, two wars, and forty-three classes of Aggie cadets.

After the departure of Sbisa in 1921, W. A. Duncan became the director of subsistence. As the college grew, so did food service. The challenge of feeding more students each year led to a variety of novel improvements during the 1930s. Emil H. Schmidt of College Station worked as a baker during this era and recalls that the bakery formulated pre-mixed cake mixes long before they were commercially available. He explained that problems in getting all the dry ingredients when they were needed led the crew to devise the mix. The bakery also experimented with self-cleaning ovens in the 1930s. Schmidt observed that "most fruit pies would boil over while baking, leaving a sticky mess in the oven." So after one such occurrence they experimented with turning the oven up to about 600° to char and clean the inside. This method worked and was in use long before the introduction of the home self-cleaning oven in the mid-1960s. Moreover, since time was always critical and so that the cooks did not have to stay over all night to prepare dough, the Sbisa bakery developed a "40 minute donut." The bakers accomplished this by raising the mixing temperature from about 75° to 95° and adding extra yeast, thus shortening the time it took the dough to rise. The doughnuts were a smash hit among the students and faculty who frequented the old Aggieland Hotel across the street from Sbisa. Need is often the mother of invention; it led Schmidt to develop an ice-box pie that caught the fancy of President Franklin D. Roosevelt.

During May, 1937, Roosevelt visited the Texas A&M campus while returning by train from an ocean fishing trip off Galveston. The president's advance men had been to the campus and eaten in Sbisa. One item they particularly liked was an orange chiffon pie. The secret of the pies, which brought Schmidt a lot of local notoriety, was the "cornflakes crust and the use of freshly squeezed orange juice." In order to please the president, his advance men ordered fifty pies to be put on the train when it arrived. Fruit pies were the normal dessert of the time; ice-box pies were both a delicacy and a rarity because of the lack of refrigeration. The A&M carpentry shop worked through the night to build a special insulated pie "safe" to hold the fifty ice-box pies. After a brief tour of the campus by President Roosevelt highlighted by a twenty-one-gun salute, the staff carefully loaded the pies onto the train.

A story some time later in the local Bryan paper posed the question: "Who made that pie?" In response, Schmidt freely provided the recipe:

Orange Chiffon Pie

1½ teaspoons gelatin	4 egg yolks
½ cup orange juice	4 egg whites
¼ cup water	½ teaspoon salt
1 cup sugar	

Soak gelatin in half the orange juice. Cook egg yolks, water, and half the sugar in a double boiler until a custard consistency. Add soaked gelatin and stir well, then add the remaining orange juice and sugar. Chill, stirring occasionally, until mixture mounds slightly. Beat egg whites with salt until glistening, stiff peaks form. Fold gently into gelatin mixture. Fill crust and chill.

For an unusually rich pie crust, roll or grind 4 cups cornflakes to yield 1 cup fine crumbs. For each pie use ½ cup fine cornflake crumbs. Mix thoroughly with 4 ounces of melted butter and press the cornflake pastry firmly into pan. Chill while filling is cooling.

It must have been real good, because FDR did not forget Texas A&M. In 1938 he approved $2 million in funds to build twelve new Corps dorms and a dining hall, which was named for Duncan. That amounts to about $40,000 per orange chiffon pie!

"From the time I left A&M in 1943 until my return in 1965 there was very little change in dining," says Col. Fred Dollar '44, present director of the food services department. The number of meals prepared actually decreased after the war. But by the late 1960s the trend was a rise of over 5 percent per year. Over the past two decades, 300 million meals have been served. To meet the needs of the growing campus, new methods have been developed to serve more students. In the late 1960s, Dollar worked closely with Swift and Company to develop precooked bacon. Swift invested over a quarter of a million dollars in the new process, which maintained quality, reduced shipping weight by two-thirds, and required no refrigeration thanks to new, vacuum-tight containers. In another innovation, the "accordion-style" layout, featuring several identical serving lines, was developed in the mid-1970s to allow students quicker access to a wider selection of foods. During dining hours 120 people a minute can be served in Sbisa. A multimillion-dollar renovation is on the schedule for Duncan Hall, which will facilitate the serving of 270 meals per minute.

In addition to choosing from a wide selection, Aggies today have an opportunity to concoct and bake their own pizza, make their own morning waffles, and dine at varying times during the day. The variety and quality envisioned and maintained by Bernard Sbisa is alive and well at A&M.

To handle fifty thousand meals per day at seventeen locations and numerous special events requires train-carloads of supplies. One hundred years ago Sbisa produced 421 pounds of butter for the full 1886–87 school year. That amount today would last about two days, since over 90,000 pounds of butter and oleo products are used annually. In a normal year Aggies consume 267,919 pounds of hamburger; 43,392 pounds of catsup; 95,232 pounds of green beans; 185,400 pounds of lettuce; 310,750 pounds of flour; 42,673 pounds of fresh bananas; and 10,000 gallons of apple juice. A&M boasts a 62,000-square-foot commissary and processing facility, which is nearly self-contained. Everything from fresh salads to 3,000 pounds of barbecue brisket per day can be prepared for dining halls around the campus. Where there is an appetite, there is a lot of food.

And Aggies do like food. Any kind of food—on or off campus, fast food, hot food, or a midnight snack! If there is an opportunity to eat, it isn't hard to find willing Aggies to meet the challenge. This book of recipes has been prepared with these hungry Aggies in mind.

And don't be surprised if someday you receive an urgent letter: DEAR MOM, SEND MORE BROWNIES. GIG 'EM!

—John A. Adams, Jr. '73

Part I

On Campus

1

Handle with Care

A coffee can packed with candy or cookies or granola—a "little" package that shows someone cares. The box may arrive labeled "Homesickness Helper," or it may come tagged as a "Finals Week Survival Kit." It may hold late-night munchies, basics for quick breakfasts, or instant lunches to eat right in the dorm room. This gift is a part of Mom that travels well and is always welcomed.

There is also another type of special delivery that comes each year from moms in the A&M Mothers' Clubs—cookies for Aggie Bonfire workers. In the autumn of 1985 the cookies didn't stop coming until 125,000 dozen (yes, 1,500,000) cookies had arrived. This care package could have been renamed Mt. Aggie. Obviously, even the Aggie Bonfire doesn't have quite enough helpers in the work crews to consume all those, so some of the donated cookies were packed away in freezers to be brought out for many other student activities during the school year.

Everyone loves to receive a package; that part of us never grows up. And homemade treats—especially those made by Mom—are important links in love chains that can cover many miles.

In case you're a new sender of care packages, you will find in this chapter, along with recipes for favorites, a number of suggestions concerning types of foods that can be mailed successfully and some tips on packing the goodies. The first rule is not to send anything that will crumble, melt, or spoil during shipping. Then packing carefully is important in avoiding crumby catastrophes (although I'm willing to bet even the crumbs will get eaten).

MAILING TIPS

1. Select cookies that are good travelers: most brownie types, most bar cookies (especially the moist varieties), soft cookies, refrigerator cook-

ies, sugar cookies, filled cookies. Crisp cookies will crumble easily, so they must either be made a little thicker than usual or be packed extremely well. Soft and crisp cookies should never be packed together, as moisture from the soft ones will make the crisp ones soggy.

2. Other good foods to send include: instant drink mixes, instant soup, popcorn for popping, muffins, and quick breads.

3. For best results, pack homemade goodies into tins, coffee cans with lids, or sealable plastic containers or bags. Pack these into heavy corrugated cardboard packing boxes, with packing material on the bottom, sides, and top.

4. Crumpled newspaper or styrofoam pellets may be used as packing material around the food containers. Inside the container itself, crumple some waxed paper on the bottom. Pack heaviest cookies at the bottom.

5. Wrap flat cookies in pairs, back to back, in moisture- and vapor-proof material, with waxed paper in between if they're sticky or fragile. Wrap other cookies and candy snugly; tape well. Edible packing material works very well for packing between layers of cookies and adds to the fun of the package. Puffed cereal, popped popcorn, or miniature marshmallows are all good "crevice fillers."

6. Before closing the container, top with more crushed waxed paper or folded paper towels. Add more cushioning on top of the container, tape the box shut, and label "Fragile—Handle with Care."

7. Caution: Never wrap anything until it is completely cooled, or the food will mold.

No-Bake Fudge Oatmeal Cookies

3 tablespoons cocoa	½ cup milk
2 cups sugar	1 teaspoon vanilla
¼ cup (½ stick) butter	3 cups quick-cooking oats

In heavy saucepan, combine cocoa, sugar, butter, and milk. Boil for 2 minutes. Stir in vanilla and oats, and mix well. Quickly drop by teaspoonfuls onto waxed paper. *Good recipe for Bonfire cookies.* MAKES 2 DOZEN.

—*Yvonne Butler, Montgomery County Club*

Chewy Chocolate Cookies

1 package (12 ounces) semisweet
   chocolate morsels
½ cup (1 stick) butter
1 can (14 ounces) sweetened
   condensed milk

1 teaspoon vanilla
1 cup all-purpose flour
½ cup finely chopped pecans
   (optional)

Melt chocolate morsels and butter in top of double boiler; add condensed milk and vanilla. Measure flour into large mixing bowl, and gradually pour in hot chocolate mixture while beaters are running. Add pecans and stir well. Allow to set for 10 minutes. Drop by teaspoonfuls onto cookie sheet that has been well greased or sprayed lightly with nonstick cooking spray. Bake in 350° oven for 9 minutes, no longer. Cookies will look soft and shiny. Leave on cookie sheet for about 2 minutes, and then carefully remove them. *This is a family favorite and a good Christmas gift, too.* (Ed. note: slightly different version follows.) MAKES 60 COOKIES.

—Mrs. Shirley Winterrowd, Williamson County Club

Fudge Cookies

¼ cup (½ stick) margarine
1 large plus 1 small package (18
   ounces total) semisweet
   chocolate morsels
2 cups all-purpose flour

2 cans (14 ounces each) sweetened
   condensed milk
1 teaspoon vanilla
2 cups chopped nuts

Melt margarine and chocolate morsels over low heat; set aside. In large mixing bowl, combine flour and sweetened condensed milk. Add chocolate mixture, vanilla, and nuts, and mix well. Drop by teaspoonfuls onto greased cookie sheet. Bake at 325° for 8–10 minutes. Do not overbake— these are chewy. *These pack and mail very well.* MAKES 8 DOZEN COOKIES.

—Jo Ann Robison, Pasadena Area Club

Chocolate Crinkle Cookies

4 squares unsweetened chocolate, melted

½ cup vegetable oil

2 cups sugar

4 eggs

2 teaspoons vanilla

2 cups all-purpose flour

2 teaspoons baking powder

½ teaspoon salt

1 cup powdered confectioners sugar

Combine melted chocolate and oil; add sugar, and beat well. Blend in eggs, one at a time, beating until well blended. Add vanilla. Stir in flour, baking powder, and salt. Cover and chill several hours or overnight. To form cookies, drop teaspoonfuls of dough into powdered sugar, covering each completely. Roll into balls in palms of hands. No need to flatten—just space 2 inches apart on greased baking sheet. Bake 10–12 minutes at 350°. MAKES 50 COOKIES. —*Carol Ireland, Fort Bend Club*

Buffalo Chips

2 cups (4 sticks) melted butter

2 cups brown sugar

2 cups sugar

4 eggs

2 teaspoons vanilla

1 teaspoon salt

4 cups all-purpose flour

2 teaspoons baking soda

2 teaspoons baking powder

2 cups quick-cooking oats

2 cups cornflakes

1 package (12 ounces) semisweet chocolate morsels

1 cup chopped pecans

1 cup coconut

Using large bowl, blend butter and sugars. Stir in eggs and vanilla. Sift salt, flour, soda, and baking powder together. Add to bowl. Mix well. Stir in oats, cornflakes, chocolate morsels, pecans, and coconut. Use an ice-cream scoop to place six cookies on lightly greased cookie sheet. Bake for 12–15 minutes at 350°. Cookies will be soft and chewy if you don't bake until brown. *These are the greatest!* MAKES ABOUT 36 VERY LARGE COOKIES (4–5 INCHES).

—*Inga Barrett, Titus County Club*

Crispy Rice Cookies

1 cup vegetable shortening

1 cup white sugar

1 cup brown sugar

2 eggs

1 teaspoon vanilla

2 cups all-purpose flour, sifted

1 teaspoon salt

1 teaspoon soda

1 cup coconut

2 cups quick-cooking oats

2 cups crisp rice cereal

Cream shortening; add sugars, and blend well. Add eggs, one at a time, and beat for 3 minutes after all are added. Add vanilla. Add salt and soda to flour; stir flour into creamed mixture. Stir in coconut, oats, and crisp rice cereal. Blend well. Drop by tablespoonfuls onto ungreased cookie sheet. Bake at 350° for 10–12 minutes, or until lightly browned. Cool on racks. Store in tightly covered containers. *Son was on the Aggie football squad in 1976–80, and these cookies went to the athletic dorm often.* MAKES 6 DOZEN.

—*Mary Louise Giamfortone, Mainland Club*

Snickerdoodles

1 cup vegetable shortening

1½ cups + 2 tablespoons sugar

2 eggs

2¾ cups all-purpose flour

2 teaspoons cream of tartar

1 teaspoon baking soda

½ teaspoon salt

2 teaspoons cinnamon

Mix together thoroughly shortening, 1½ cups of the sugar, and eggs. Sift together flour, cream of tartar, soda, and salt; add to shortening mixture. Chill dough, if desired. Pinch off bits of dough and roll into balls about the size of small walnuts. Roll in mixture of 2 tablespoons sugar and cinnamon. Place about 2 inches apart on ungreased cookie sheet. Bake at 400° for 8–10 minutes, until lightly browned but still soft. (These cookies puff up at first, and then flatten out with crinkled tops.) *These keep well for Bonfire cookies.* MAKES ABOUT 5 DOZEN 2-INCH COOKIES.

—*Cora Hartman, Austin Club*

Peppernuts

½ cup (1 stick) butter, softened

2 cups sugar

1 teaspoon lemon juice

1½ cups light corn syrup

1 teaspoon soda dissolved in 1 cup cream

6 cups all-purpose flour

1 teaspoon cinnamon

¼ teaspoon ground cloves

1 teaspoon allspice

½ teaspoon salt

¼ teaspoon black pepper

Cream butter and sugar. Add lemon juice and corn syrup. Sift flour and spices together. Alternate flour and spice mixture with soda and cream mixture in adding to the butter-sugar dough. This will be very stiff. Chill dough several hours. Take chilled dough and make several long rolls about the circumference of your thumb. Lay these rolls on cookie sheet covered with waxed paper and chill 2 more hours. Cut rolls of dough into small pieces—½–1 inch in length. Bake on greased cookie sheet at 350° for 10 minutes. These cookies are soft when removed from the oven but become hard. *They make an excellent snack for those late nights of studying. I pack them into "zippered" bags for mailing.* MAKES 100+ COOKIES.

—*Billye H. Martin, Corpus Christi Club*

Fast Moist Cookies

1 package (18.25 ounces) yellow cake mix

½ cup (1 stick) margarine, softened

2 eggs

1 teaspoon vanilla

1 package (6 ounces) semisweet chocolate morsels

Combine cake mix, margarine, eggs, vanilla, and chocolate morsels. Mix well. Pour into greased 15-by-10-inch baking pan. Spread very thin. Bake at 350° about 10–12 minutes. Cut with pizza cutter. *This makes a quick, moist cookie, good for mailing.* MAKES 36 SQUARES.

—*Mrs. Warren K. Bell, Orange County Club*

Hermits

1⅓ cups margarine, softened

2 cups brown sugar, packed

4 large eggs

5 cups all-purpose flour

2 teaspoons baking powder

2 teaspoons cinnamon

1 teaspoon salt

1½ cups broken pecans

1½ cups raisins

Cream margarine and brown sugar. Add eggs and beat. Sift together flour, baking powder, cinnamon, and salt; gradually add to margarine-sugar mixture. Beat; then stir in pecans and raisins. Drop by teaspoonfuls onto lightly greased cookie sheets. Bake at 375° until browned, 12–15 minutes. *Many dozens of these have been delivered and mailed to our Aggies and to the Bonfire builders. This was my Mom's recipe back in Detroit.* MAKES 5 DOZEN.

—*Mary Lou Coleman, Austin Club*

Ice Box Cookies

1 cup (2 sticks) butter, softened

1 cup sugar

1 cup brown sugar, packed

3 eggs

3½ cups all-purpose flour

1 teaspoon baking soda

2 teaspoons cinnamon

½ teaspoon salt

1½ cups broken pecans

Cream butter, sugar, and brown sugar. Add eggs, one at a time, beating well. Sift and measure flour. Add flour, soda, cinnamon, salt, and pecans to butter mixture, kneading into a stiff dough. Make into rolls, wrap, and place in refrigerator overnight. Cut into thin slices and bake in a 450° oven 5–10 minutes. MAKES 4–5 DOZEN COOKIES.

—*Mrs. Roy Birkhead, Pasadena Area Club*

Pumpkin Cookies

1 cup vegetable shortening

2 cups (16-ounce can) pumpkin

2 eggs

2 teaspoons vanilla

2 cups raisins

1 cup chopped nuts

4 cups sifted all-purpose flour

2 teaspoons baking powder

2 teaspoons baking soda

2 teaspoons cinnamon

1 teaspoon salt

2 cups sugar

Cream together shortening, pumpkin, and eggs. Add the other ingredients, in the order given, and mix thoroughly. Drop by teaspoonfuls onto greased cookie sheet. Bake 10–12 minutes at 350°.

ICING:

1 box (16 ounces) powdered
   confectioners sugar

1 teaspoon cinnamon

1 teaspoon nutmeg

⅓ cup butter or margarine,
   softened

1 teaspoon vanilla

milk to make spreading
   consistency

Combine powdered sugar, cinnamon, nutmeg, butter, and vanilla. Add milk, by the teaspoonful, to make a spreading consistency. MAKES ABOUT 8 DOZEN COOKIES.   —*Carol Ireland, Fort Bend Club*

Mom's Oatmeal Cookies

1 cup vegetable shortening

1 cup sugar

1 cup brown sugar

2 eggs, beaten

1 teaspoon vanilla

1½ cups sifted flour

1 teaspoon baking soda

½ teaspoon salt

3 cups quick-cooking oats

In one bowl blend shortening, sugar, and brown sugar (dark brown is best). Add beaten eggs and vanilla. In another bowl, sift flour, soda, and salt over oats. Add to first mixture, and mix well. Drop by spoonfuls (size of spoon will determine size of cookie) about 2 inches apart on cookie sheet. Bake about 8 minutes at 375°. *Warning: Make these when no one is home; otherwise dough may be eaten raw or cookies may be eaten by the handful, and the cook will never know whether she has made 1 or 6 dozen. These may be substituted for an on-the-way-to-class breakfast.* MAKES ABOUT 5–6 DOZEN COOKIES. —*Bebe (Mrs. David) Combs, Wichita County Area Club*

VARIATION: My Children's Favorite Oatmeal Cookies: Substitute ½ teaspoon almond flavoring for ½ teaspoon vanilla. Decrease oats to 2 cups and increase all-purpose flour to 2 cups. Follow mixing method for Mom's Oatmeal Cookies. Bake at 350° about 12 minutes. *These have been favorite care-package cookies in our family.* MAKES ABOUT 5 DOZEN COOKIES.

—*Martha Rutherford, Deep East Texas Club*

Pop's Oatmeal Cookies

2¾ cups all-purpose flour

1 teaspoon baking soda

2 teaspoons salt

1½ cups (3 sticks) margarine or
    butter

2 cups brown sugar, packed

½ cup sugar

½ cup honey

2 large eggs

2 teaspoons vanilla

½ cup water

6 cups quick-cooking oats

2 cups chopped nuts

2 cups golden raisins

Sift together flour, soda, and salt; set aside. Cream together margarine or butter, brown sugar, and sugar, until light. Add honey and eggs, and beat until smooth. Add vanilla, and blend well. Add flour mixture alternately with water, ending with flour mixture. Stir in oats, nuts, and raisins. Drop by tablespoonfuls onto greased baking sheets. Bake at 350° for 15–20 minutes, or until light brown in color. *Although Carl is not an Aggie Mother, his oatmeal cookies are excellent and a great favorite of family and friends.* MAKES 7 DOZEN COOKIES. —*Carl E. and Marie Lidell, Williamson County Club*

Handle with Care

Oatmeal Lace Cookies

½ cup (1 stick) margarine, melted

1½ cups instant oatmeal (3 individual packages)

1¾ cups sugar

1 tablespoon all-purpose flour

½ teaspoon salt

1 teaspoon baking powder

1 egg

1 teaspoon vanilla

½ cup pecans, chopped fine

Melt margarine in small saucepan; add oatmeal, stirring constantly. Mix sugar, flour, salt, and baking powder in mixing bowl. Beat in egg and add margarine-oatmeal mixture. Add vanilla and pecans. Line baking sheet with foil. Drop about ½ teaspoonful of dough for each cookie. Do not place too close to each other, as they spread out flat. Bake at 350° for 11 minutes. Cool completely and peel from foil. (Ed. Note: The secret to making these cookies "lacy" is to pull the foil off the baking sheet as soon as you take the cookies out of the oven. Then cool completely before removing the cookies from the foil. Use new foil each time. They are also lacier if you substitute butter for margarine. They taste good either way.) MAKES 48 COOKIES. —*Lola Repschleger, Mainland Club*

Ranger Cookies

½ cup (1 stick) margarine

1 cup sugar

1 cup brown sugar

1 egg

1 cup all-purpose flour

½ teaspoon baking powder

1 teaspoon baking soda

¼ teaspoon salt

2 teaspoons vanilla

1 cup oats

1 cup crushed cornflakes

½ cup chopped pecans

½ cup coconut

Cream together the margarine, sugar, and brown sugar. Add the egg, and beat until smooth. Sift together the flour, baking powder, soda, and salt; add to creamed mixture. Stir in vanilla, oats, cornflakes, pecans, and coconut; mix well. Drop by teaspoonfuls onto greased cookie sheet. Bake at 350° for 15–20 minutes. MAKES 4 DOZEN.

From Hungry Aggie Cookbook, *Kingsville Club*

Oatmeal Carmelitas

½ pound (approximately 32) light candy caramels

5 tablespoons light cream or evaporated milk

1 cup all-purpose flour

1 cup quick-cooking oats

¾ cup brown sugar, firmly packed

½ teaspoon baking soda

½ teaspoon salt

¾ cup (1½ sticks) margarine, melted

6 ounces (1 cup) semisweet chocolate morsels

½ cup chopped pecans

Melt caramels in cream in top of double boiler. Cool slightly; set aside. In large bowl, combine flour, oats, brown sugar, baking soda, salt, and melted margarine. Mix well. Press half of this mixture into ungreased 11-by-7-inch or 9-inch-square pan. Bake at 350° for 10 minutes. Remove pan from oven; sprinkle with chocolate morsels and pecans. Spread carefully with caramel mixture. Sprinkle with remaining crumb mixture. Bake 15–20 minutes. Chill 1–2 hours. Cut into squares. MAKES 12–16 SQUARES.

—*Miriam Womack, Midland Club*

Coconut-Pecan Squares

1 cup (2 sticks) margarine, softened

3 cups brown sugar

2 cups plus 4 tablespoons all-purpose flour

2 eggs, beaten slightly

1 cup coconut

1 cup chopped pecans

Cream margarine and 1 cup brown sugar. Add 2 cups flour and mix thoroughly. Press into bottom of 15-by-10-inch pan. Bake 20 minutes at 350° (or until slightly firm to touch). Meanwhile beat eggs very lightly with a fork; add 2 cups brown sugar. Toss the 4 tablespoons flour with coconut; add pecans. Combine with egg mixture, and spread over first layer. Bake 20 minutes longer at 350°. Cool, and cut into small squares. *These are delicious—very durable for mailing—and they stay fresh for some time if kept in a sealed container. If I had a hundred dollars for every one I have sent for bonfire, in care packages, etc., I would never have a budgeting problem!* MAKES UP TO 8 DOZEN TINY SQUARES.

—*Mrs. Rex (Beth) Robinson, Wood County Club*

Double Chocolate Brownies

¾ cup all-purpose flour

¼ teaspoon baking soda

¼ teaspoon salt

⅓ cup butter

¾ cup sugar

2 tablespoons water

1 package (12 ounces) semisweet chocolate morsels

1 teaspoon vanilla

2 eggs

½ cup chopped nuts

In small bowl, combine flour, baking soda, and salt; set aside. In small saucepan, combine butter, sugar, and water. Bring just to a boil; remove from heat. Add 6 ounces (1 cup) of the chocolate morsels (real chocolate recommended) and vanilla. Stir until morsels melt, and mixture is smooth. Transfer to large mixing bowl. Add eggs, one at a time, mixing well after each addition. Gradually blend in flour mixture. Using a spoon, stir in remaining 1 cup chocolate morsels and nuts. Spread into greased 9-inch square baking pan. Bake at 325° for 30–35 minutes. Cool completely. Cut into squares. *The disposable aluminum pans, 8 inches square, are just right for baking this recipe and for making the trip to A&M, either by car or mail. Baking time may be a little longer.* MAKES 16 BROWNIES.

—*Loretta Franke, Midland Club*

Special Brownies

1 package (23 ounces) brownie mix

¼ cup milk

3 eggs

½ cup sour cream

1 package (12 ounces) semisweet chocolate morsels

½ cup chopped pecans

Combine brownie mix, milk, and eggs; beat by hand. Stir in sour cream, chips, and pecans. Pour into 13-by-9-inch greased baking pan. Bake at 350° for 25–30 minutes. When cool, cut into bars. MAKES 20 BARS.

—*Sharon Preston, Montgomery County Club*

Candy Orange Slice Bar Cookies

2 cups all-purpose flour

2 cups brown sugar

¼ teaspoon salt

¼ teaspoon baking powder

1 teaspoon cinnamon

4 eggs, well beaten

1 pound candy orange slices, finely chopped

2 cups coarsely chopped pecans

Combine flour, sugar, salt, baking powder, and cinnamon; mix well. Add the beaten eggs, and beat well. Fold in orange slices and pecans. Bake in greased 15-by-10-inch pan (jelly roll pan) for 30 minutes at 350°. Test with toothpick for doneness. Cut into squares. *This cookie is a family favorite, a tradition begun by our Aggie's grandmother.* MAKES ABOUT 35 BARS.

—*Phyllis Biggar, Austin Club*

Brown Sugar–Chip Bars

10 tablespoons (1 stick plus 2 tablespoons) butter, melted

1 package (16 ounces) brown sugar

3 eggs

2½ cups all-purpose flour

2½ teaspoons baking powder

1 cup semisweet chocolate morsels

1 cup pecan pieces

Melt butter in saucepan; pour into large mixing bowl. Add brown sugar, and beat well. Add eggs, one at a time, beating well. Add flour and baking powder; beat until smooth. Stir in chocolate morsels and nuts. Turn into buttered 13-by-9-inch baking pan. Bake in 350° oven approximately 30 minutes, or until a cake tester inserted in center comes out clean. *These bars bake with a wonderful satin finish on top and keep very well.* MAKES 24–36 BARS.

—*Jesilin Rigano, Titus County Club*

Congo Bars

1 cup (2 sticks) margarine, melted

1 box (16 ounces) brown sugar

2½ cups all-purpose flour

2½ teaspoons baking powder

1 teaspoon salt

3 eggs

1 cup chopped pecans

1 cup semisweet chocolate morsels

1 teaspoon vanilla

Melt margarine; mix in brown sugar, and set aside. Sift together flour, baking powder, and salt. In large mixing bowl, combine margarine mixture and dry ingredients. Beat in eggs. Stir in pecans, chocolate morsels, and vanilla. Pour into greased 13-by-9-inch baking pan. Bake at 350° for 30 minutes. Cake will appear not done, but after cooling will become chewy. Cut into bars. MAKES 30–35 BARS.   —*Bobbie Yauger, Austin Club*

Caramel Fudge Bars

1 cup butter

2½ cups light brown sugar

½ cup sugar

4 eggs

2 cups all-purpose flour

1½ teaspoons baking powder

1½ teaspoons vanilla

1½ cups chopped nuts (optional)

2 tablespoons powdered
    confectioners sugar

Using a very heavy 2½ quart pan or double boiler, melt together the butter, brown sugar, and sugar, stirring constantly. Remove from heat; cool. Pour into mixing bowl. Add eggs, one at a time, beating well after each addition. Add flour, baking powder, and vanilla. Stir until well blended. Stir in nuts, if desired. Bake in greased and floured 13-by-9-inch baking pan at 350° for 45 minutes. Don't overbake—the sides should not get too hard. Sprinkle with powdered sugar while still warm; sprinkle again after it has cooled. Cut into 2-inch squares. *These are nice, moist, brownie-type bars that mail well and stay fresh for quite a long time. They are great for morning coffees, afternoon snacks, or midnight study sessions.* MAKES 20 SQUARES.
    —*Sandee Gehler, West Bell County Club*

Apricot Bars

1 cup all-purpose flour

¼ cup sugar

½ cup (1 stick) butter, softened slightly

Combine flour, sugar, and butter in bowl, cutting in the butter with a pastry blender until particles are the size of small peas. Turn into a 9-inch square baking pan and press firmly to make an even layer over the bottom of the pan. Bake at 300° for 15 minutes, watching carefully that crust does not get too brown.

FILLING

⅓ cup all-purpose flour

½ teaspoon baking powder

½ teaspoon salt

2 eggs

1 teaspoon vanilla

1 cup brown sugar, firmly packed

1 cup snipped dried apricots

½ to ¾ cup chopped walnuts

Blend flour, baking powder, and salt; set aside. Beat eggs with vanilla; add brown sugar gradually, beating until thick. Stir in the flour mixture, apricots, and walnuts. Remove pan with crust from oven; spread apricot layer evenly over it. Return to oven, and continue baking 30 minutes at 300°. Cool completely on a wire rack before cutting into small bars. *These bars are good mailers; they stay moist for several days. They also freeze well.* MAKES 16–20 SMALL BARS. —*Margie Lee, Midland Club*

Strawberry Nut Bread

3 cups all-purpose flour

1 teaspoon baking soda

1 teaspoon salt

1 tablespoon cinnamon

2 cups sugar

4 eggs, beaten

1¼ cups vegetable oil

1 cup chopped pecans

2 cups frozen strawberries and juice, thawed

Mix flour, soda, salt, cinnamon, and sugar. Add eggs, oil, pecans, and strawberries, blending well by hand (do not use electric beater). Pour into two greased loaf pans. Bake at 350° for 60–70 minutes. MAKES 2 LOAVES.

—*Harrison County Club*

Handle with Care

Banana Nut Bread I

2 cups all-purpose flour

1 teaspoon salt

1 teaspoon baking soda

3 large, ripe bananas

½ cup vegetable shortening

1 cup sugar

2 eggs, beaten

½ cup chopped pecans

Combine flour, salt, and soda; and set aside. Mash bananas well with a fork and set aside. Cream shortening, and add sugar gradually. Add beaten eggs, and cream until mixture is fluffy. Gradually add flour, salt, and soda, mixing well. Stir in mashed bananas and chopped nuts. Line one bread pan (8½ by 4½ inches) and a smaller loaf pan (6½ by 3 inches) with waxed paper. Carefully pour in batter, filling each pan half-full. Bake at 300° for 45 minutes (small pan) and 1 hour (large pan). Test for doneness by inserting a toothpick in the center. Cool on a rack. This bread can be served warm or cold, but be sure to cool completely before wrapping for mailing. Stays moist for days, if it lasts that long! *I have been baking this bread for over 30 years and sent it literally all over the United States. It's fast, easy, delicious, and nutritious—my sons request it constantly in a "care package." Small loaves make good Christmas gifts, too.* MAKES 2 LOAVES.

—*Mrs. Neal Corbitt, East Bell County Club*

Banana Nut Bread II

3 medium bananas, mashed

1 cup sugar

1 egg

1½ cups all-purpose flour

¼ cup melted butter or vegetable oil

1 teaspoon salt

1 teaspoon baking soda

¾ cup chopped nuts

½ cup chopped maraschino cherries (optional)

After mashing bananas (ripe ones have more flavor), stir in other ingredients, in order listed. Mix by hand. Pour into greased loaf pan (8½ by 4½ inches). Bake 1 hour at 325°. *I double the recipe to make 3 smaller loaves—then there are a couple to freeze.* (Ed. note: If making smaller loaves, check for doneness after 50 minutes.)

—*Iris Bowler, Orange County Club*

Banana Nut Bread III

1 cup ripe bananas, mashed

¾ cup vegetable oil

½ cup sugar

1 box (18.25 ounces) yellow cake
mix

5 eggs

1 teaspoon vanilla

3 tablespoons brown sugar

½ cup chopped pecans

1 teaspoon cinnamon

Combine all ingredients, in order given, in large mixing bowl. Mix well. Pour into two greased loaf pans (8½ by 4½ inches). Bake at 350° about 1 hour, or until loaf tests done with a toothpick. *Banana nut bread freezes well.* YIELDS 2 LOAVES.   —*Irma Wall, Panola County Club*

Zucchini Bread

2 cups sugar

1 cup (2 sticks) margarine,
softened

3 eggs

2 cups shredded raw zucchini

1 teaspoon vanilla

3 cups all-purpose flour

¼ teaspoon baking powder

1 teaspoon baking soda

½ teaspoon salt

1½ teaspoons cinnamon

1 teaspoon ground cloves

½ teaspoon allspice

½ teaspoon nutmeg

¼ teaspoon ginger

1 cup raisins (optional)

1 cup chopped nuts

Blend sugar and margarine; add eggs, and mix well. Stir in zucchini and vanilla; add flour, baking powder, soda, salt, and spices to egg mixture. (If mixture seems too dry, add a few drops of water.) Stir in raisins and nuts. Pour into two greased and floured loaf pans. Bake at 325° for approximately 1 hour. Test for doneness. Cool 20 minutes in pan; turn out on rack. When completely cool, wrap in plastic wrap or aluminum foil. *I usually leave out the raisins—students prefer just the nuts. These freeze well.* MAKES 2 LARGE LOAVES.   —*Jo Ann Robison, Pasadena Area Club*

No Egg Banana Bread or Bars

1 cup vegetable oil

2 cups sugar

6 ripe bananas (2 cups, mashed)

1 teaspoon salt

2 teaspoons baking soda

4 cups all-purpose flour

1 cup chopped nuts (optional)

6 ounces semisweet chocolate morsels (optional)

In large mixer bowl, blend oil, sugar, and mashed bananas. Combine salt, soda, and flour, and add to banana mixture. Mixture will be stiff if bananas were not really ripe. Add nuts or chocolate morsels (or both) if desired. Bake at 350°; cooking time varies with pan used. For 9½-by-5½-inch loaf, check at 1 hour; for 13-by-9-inch oblong pan, 50 minutes; for 2 smaller loaves, 7⅜ by 3⅜ inches, 45 minutes; and for 15-by-10-inch jelly roll pan, 20 minutes. May also be used for cupcakes. *As bars, this recipe with chocolate chips makes my son's favorite care package. They keep well in his dorm refrigerator.* MAKES 1 LARGE LOAF, 2 SMALL LOAVES, OR 30–36 BARS.

—*Mrs. Homer L. (Van) Cox, Jr., Fort Worth/Tarrant County Club*

Pumpkin Bread

3 cups sugar

1 cup vegetable oil

4 eggs

⅔ cup orange juice

1 can (16 ounces) pumpkin

3½ cups all-purpose flour

2 teaspoons baking soda

1½ teaspoons salt

2 teaspoons cinnamon

1 teaspoon nutmeg

1 cup chopped nuts

1 cup raisins

Combine sugar and vegetable oil in large mixing bowl; blend well. Add eggs, one at a time, mixing well. Add orange juice and pumpkin. Blend in flour, baking soda, salt, cinnamon, and nutmeg. Stir in nuts and raisins. Pour batter, evenly divided, into four 1-pound coffee cans that have been well greased and floured. Bake 1 hour at 350°. Test for doneness with toothpick; longer baking is sometimes required. *This is our daughter's favorite holiday bread. I begin making pumpkin bread at the first sign of fall and continue through the holidays. Also a good mailer.* MAKES 4 LOAVES.

—*Martha Rutherford, Deep East Texas Club*

Cranberry-Pumpkin Bread

3½ cups all-purpose flour

2 teaspoons baking soda

1 teaspoon salt

1 tablespoon pumpkin pie spice

3 cups sugar

½ cup vegetable oil

4 eggs

⅔ cup milk

1½ cups pumpkin

1 cup whole raw cranberries

1 cup nuts, chopped

Combine and blend flour, soda, salt, and pumpkin pie spice. Stir in sugar, oil, eggs, milk, pumpkin, cranberries, and nuts. Beat well. Pour into two greased and floured 9-by-5-inch loaf pans. Bake at 325° for 45 minutes or until done. MAKES 2 LOAVES.

—*From* Hullabaloo in the Kitchen, *Dallas County Club*

Pineapple Banana Bread

1 cup vegetable shortening

2 cups sugar

4 large ripe bananas, mashed

1 small can (8 ounces) crushed pineapple, drained well

4 eggs

2¼ cups all-purpose flour

2 teaspoons baking soda

1 teaspoon cinnamon

1 teaspoon allspice

½ teaspoon ground cloves

½ teaspoon nutmeg

1 cup chopped pecans (optional)

1 teaspoon salt

Cream shortening (butter-flavored is good) and sugar. Thoroughly mash bananas, and add to creamed mixture, along with drained crushed pineapple. Add eggs, one at a time, beating after each addition. Sift together the flour, salt, soda, and spices. Add to banana mixture, blending thoroughly. Add pecans, if desired. Spread into three or four greased and floured 8-by-4-inch loaf pans, or several smaller pans. Bake at 350° for 45–50 minutes. Check small pans for doneness at 30–35 minutes. Let cool in pans for 10 minutes; remove to racks and completely cool before wrapping and storing. Refrigerate or freeze. *Delicious as tea sandwiches—spread with softened cream cheese. Aggies like pineapple banana bread with a glass of milk when they come home, and they enjoy taking some back to the dorm.* MAKES 3 OR 4 LOAVES.

—*Helen Putnam, Brazos County Club*

Granola

4 cups quick-cooking oats

3 cups whole wheat flour

1 cup all-purpose flour

1 cup soy flour (optional)

1 cup wheat germ

1 cup coconut (optional)

1 cup chopped nuts

1 teaspoon salt

1 cup vegetable oil

1 cup honey

1 cup brown sugar

½ cup water

Mix oats, flours, wheat germ, coconut, nuts, and salt. Then add oil, honey, brown sugar, and water; mix well. (It works best to mix with the hands.) The mixture will be crumbly; more water may be added to make larger chunks. Put into two large, flat jelly roll pans and bake in slow oven (250°–300°), turning every 20 minutes to keep from becoming too brown around the edges, for about 1½ hours, or until crisp and golden brown. Cool and store in air-tight container; it will last for several mornings' breakfast cereal. It is also good with raisins, bananas, or other fruit on it with milk. *Sunflower seeds or other seeds are good in this. Our college daughters like to eat it dry as a snack when they are studying—so they prefer the larger chunks. This has been the most called-for care package from our girls.* MAKES ABOUT 3 QUARTS. —*Doris Smith, Amarillo Club*

Exam-Time Granola Snack

6 cups old-fashioned oats (not quick oats)

1⅓ cups dry powdered milk

1 can (3½ ounces) coconut

2 cups chopped nuts

2 cups raisins (optional)

¾ cup honey

¼ cup *hot* water

1 tablespoon vanilla

¾ cup vegetable oil

1 teaspoon nutmeg

1 teaspoon cinnamon

Mix together the oats, powdered milk, coconut, nuts, and raisins in a large bowl. Put honey in a smaller bowl; add hot water and vanilla and mix. Add oil, nutmeg, and cinnamon to the honey mixture; stir well. Pour liquid mixture over dry mixture and mix well, preferably with hands. Place mixture in a large flat pan, or cookie sheet with sides. Bake in 250° oven for 1 hour, turning mixture every 15 minutes. Allow to cool completely at room temperature, and break into chunks. *Snipped dates, apricots, or other dried fruits may be added to this mixture, too.* MAKES ENOUGH FOR A 3-POUND COFFEE CAN.   —*Sandra B. Lydahl, West Bell County Club*

Survival Snack

4 cups honey graham cereal

2 cups thin pretzels

1 cup peanuts

¼ cup butter, melted

¼ cup peanut butter

Combine all ingredients in baking pan. Bake at 350° for 10 minutes, or until snack mixture is well coated with butter and peanut butter. Cool and store in airtight container. MAKES ABOUT 6 CUPS.

—*Virginia Saldua, Fort Bend Club*

TV Niblets

½ pound (2 sticks) margarine, melted

½ cup bacon drippings

1 tablespoon garlic salt

1 teaspoon savory salt

1 tablespoon Worcestershire sauce

¼ teaspoon Tabasco sauce or ¼ teaspoon red pepper

1 package pretzel sticks

1 package rice cereal squares

1 package wheat cereal squares

1 package O-shaped oat cereal

½ pound pecan halves

½ pound cashews

½ pound peanuts

Combine margarine, bacon drippings, salts, and Worcestershire and Tabasco sauces; set aside. In 2 large, shallow pans, mix the remaining ingredients. Pour sauce over cereal-nut mixture and stir to coat well. Bake at 225° for 1 hour. Stir often. Store in airtight container. MAKES ABOUT 8 QUARTS.   —*Milam County Club*

Cheese Crisps

1 pound cheddar cheese, grated
½ pound (2 sticks) margarine, softened
2 cups all-purpose flour
2 cups crisp rice cereal
¾ teaspoon red pepper
½ teaspoon Tabasco sauce
½ teaspoon garlic salt

With mixer, blend grated cheese and margarine at low speed. Add remaining ingredients and blend by hand (literally). Form long rolls 1 inch in diameter. Wrap in waxed paper and chill. Slice in ½-inch slices, and bake at 400° for 10 minutes, or until golden. Store in airtight container or freeze. MAKES 60–70 WAFERS. —*Pat McCorstin, Garland Club*

Caramel Candy

1¾ cups sugar
1 small can (5 ounces) evaporated milk
3 ounces water
additional ¾ cup of sugar, for carmelizing
½ cup (1 stick) margarine
2 tablespoons vanilla
1½ cups chopped nuts

Put 1¾ cups of sugar and evaporated milk, and water into a double boiler. Bring to a boil. Put ¾ cup sugar into a heavy skillet and brown, stirring constantly. (This will become a caramel-colored liquid.) Gradually add hot sugar-milk mixture to skillet, and cook until a fairly hard ball will form in water (250°–260° if you use a candy thermometer). Add margarine, and beat well. The secret of the candy is to stir and beat constantly. Add vanilla, and beat until very thick. Add nuts, and pour onto buttered plate. If you have trouble getting it to harden, place in freezer for about 30 minutes. Mark into squares or form candy into small balls. MAKES ABOUT 1½ POUNDS. —*Joyce Worley, Panola County Club*

Peanut Patties

2½ cups sugar

1 cup milk

2 cups raw peanuts

⅔ cup light corn syrup

½ cup (1 stick) margarine

1 teaspoon vanilla

3 shakes red food coloring

1 small bag (7 ounces) shredded coconut

Combine sugar, milk, peanuts, corn syrup, margarine, vanilla, and food coloring in large heavy saucepan. Cook to soft ball stage (240° on candy thermometer). Remove from heat, and beat until cool. Add coconut and mix well. Pour into buttered 13-by-9-inch pan. Cut into squares when cool. MAKES ABOUT 100 SMALL PIECES. —*Carol Ireland, Fort Bend Club*

Evaporated Milk Pralines

2 cups sugar

2 tablespoons light corn syrup

1 small can (6 ounces) evaporated milk

⅓ teaspoon soda

2 cups chopped pecans

1 teaspoon vanilla

Mix sugar, corn syrup, and evaporated milk; cook to a soft ball stage (240°). Remove from heat and add soda, vanilla, and pecans. Return to heat and let come to a boil. Remove from heat again and beat until thick. Drop by spoonfuls on waxed paper. Wrap individually when cool. *This recipe has been in my family for years. It was handed down to me from my 90-year-old aunt.* MAKES ABOUT 25 PATTIES. —*Ann Henry, Victoria County Club*

Peanut Brittle

2 cups sugar

1 cup light corn syrup

½ cup water

2 cups raw Spanish peanuts

Pinch of salt

1 teaspoon vanilla

1 tablespoon butter

2 teaspoons baking soda

Combine sugar, syrup, and water; and boil until almost hard ball (250° on candy thermometer). Add peanuts and salt. Cook to brittle stage (295°) or until it turns golden brown. Add vanilla and butter and mix. Add soda and beat. Pour on large buttered surface to cool. Break into pieces, and store in tightly covered container. MAKES ABOUT 2 POUNDS.

From Another Hungry Aggie Cookbook, *Kingsville Club*

English Toffee

1 cup butter or margarine

1 cup sugar

1 package (6 ounces) semisweet chocolate morsels

Combine butter and sugar in a small, heavy saucepan. Cook over moderate heat, stirring constantly, until a candy thermometer registers 310°. At this point the candy should be caramel-colored. Quickly pour candy into buttered 9-inch square pan, and spread evenly with a spatula. Cool until hardened. Melt half of the chocolate morsels; spread over hardened candy. Cool until chocolate is hardened. Turn candy out onto waxed paper, chocolate side down. Melt the remaining chocolate morsels; spread on candy. Cool again until this layer of chocolate is hardened. Break toffee into pieces and store in tightly covered tin for at least 2 days to develop flavor. MAKES 1 POUND.

—*Mrs. J. W. Wade, Williamson County Club*

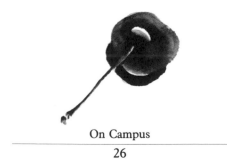

Friendship Tea Mix

1 jar (18 ounces) orange-flavored instant breakfast drink

1 cup sugar

½ cup presweetened lemonade mix

½ cup instant tea

1 package (3 ounces) apricot-flavored gelatin

2½ teaspoons cinnamon

1 teaspoon ground cloves

Combine all ingredients in large bowl, stirring well. Store mix in airtight containers. To serve, place 1½ tablespoons of mix in a cup. Add 1 cup boiling water, and stir well. MAKES ENOUGH MIX FOR 50 CUPS.

—*Shirley McCutchen, Milam County Club*

Instant Hot Chocolate Drink

1 pound chocolate-flavor drink mix

1½ cups powdered nondairy creamer

½ cup powdered confectioners sugar

8 cups powdered milk

Mix all ingredients until well blended. Store in tightly closed container. Use ¼ cup mix per cup of hot water. MAKES 12 CUPS OF MIX (48 SERVINGS).

—*Geneva Miller, Orange County Club*

Cocoa Mix

1 box (8-quart size) nonfat dry milk

1 jar (13 ounces) nondairy creamer

1 box (1½ pounds) chocolate-flavored drink mix

3 tablespoons cocoa

2 cups powdered confectioners sugar

Mix all ingredients thoroughly. Place in jars or self-sealing containers. To prepare a single hot chocolate drink, stir 3 heaping teaspoons of this mix into 1 cup hot water. *Good to take to school!* MAKES 20+ CUPS OF MIX.

—*Pat McCorstin, Garland Club*

2

Survival Made Simple

The college student faced with finding something for Sunday supper, when the campus cafeteria is closed, or the one who has to "sandwich" supper back in the apartment between the last class of the day and a long evening in the library, needs recipes that are quick and easy to fix. Survival is the name of that menu—satisfying the "eating-to-live" instinct—and this chapter offers recipes that make survival simple.

It could also become one of your own most frequently used sections of this book, simply because time is precious not only to collegians but also to everyone else who seems to come up with less than twenty-four hours a day. Ease of preparation is something we're all looking for; shortcuts are welcomed most of the time. Making something palate-pleasing with just a few ingredients is good for the budget and rewarding to those who hate grocery shopping.

I'm sure all of us have looked through the foods sections in newspapers or at food preparation articles in magazines hunting for something new and easy. I've even heard people say, "If it takes more than one side of the recipe card, I'm not interested." The college student who does occasional or even frequent cooking is even more dependent on simple recipes than most of us. He or she probably does not have a well-stocked kitchen, much less a full pantry. Sometimes everything must be done with a minimum of utensils in just one or two pans.

The seemingly unending array of products in the supermarket can be bewildering. Thousands of frozen foods, mixes, and semiprepared foods are available. Look at these products as first-aiders. With just a little creativity, you can prepare some very good combinations that are less expensive than fast food, tastier than the heated contents of a can, and more appealing than something thawed on a plastic tray. Coming to our rescue are many time and labor savers: partially prepared foods, premeasured mixes, and versatile canned and frozen foods, which can be used in many ways beyond their original purposes. I'm sure the early food-processing companies never dreamed their staffs and consumers would develop so many recipes with simple cans of soup.

SEASONING SURVIVAL (Basic spices, herbs, and seasonings that are useful to have on hand)

chili powder

dried onions

dried parsley

garlic salt
  and/or powdered garlic

ground cinnamon

ground mustard

ground pepper

Italian herbs mix

lemon pepper

onion salt

paprika

salt

seasoned salt

Spices and herbs need to be kept tightly sealed and are at their fullest flavor if used within a year or two.

Easy But Good Chicken

1 can (10¾ ounces) cream of
  mushroom soup

½ pint (1 cup) sour cream

½ cup semidry white wine

1 frying chicken (approximately
  3½ pounds), cut up

paprika

Mix soup, sour cream, and wine together in bowl. Place chicken pieces (boned, if you prefer) in 13-by-9-inch baking pan. Pour soup mixture over all, and sprinkle generously with paprika. Bake uncovered at 350° for 1½ hours, or until tender. *The sauce thickens better if casserole is cooked ahead of time, allowed to cool, and then reheated for serving. Macaroni or noodles may be served as a side dish with the sauce.* SERVES 4. —*Maureen Thode, Fort Bend Club*

Easy Barbecued Chicken

1 package chicken wings, cut in
two, with tips removed

1 can (12 ounces) cola drink

1 cup catsup (or ½ cup catsup and
½ cup barbecue sauce)

Put chicken in frying pan. Pour cola over and cover; simmer until tender. Pour catsup (or catsup and barbecue sauce) over, and continue to cook without cover about 10 minutes longer. A cut-up fryer will also work, or any combination of chicken parts. SERVES 4–6.

—Nancy Mayor, Montgomery County Club

Chicken Casserole

2 large chicken breasts (or 1–1½
pounds leftover turkey)

1 small box (8 ounces) process
cheese spread, cubed

1 can (10¾ ounces) cream of
mushroom soup, undiluted

1 can (10¾ ounces) cream of
chicken soup, undiluted

1 small onion, diced

2 packages (10 ounces each) frozen
chopped broccoli

3 cups cooked rice

Cover chicken breasts with water, and simmer until tender, 30–40 minutes. Remove chicken from bones while still warm; cut into small pieces. Combine cheese, mushroom and chicken soups, stirring until cheese melts. Add onion. Cook broccoli in separate pan until tender; drain. Combine all ingredients; mix well. Pour into greased baking pan or casserole and cover. Bake at 350° about 45 minutes, or until bubbly. SERVES 6.

—Mary Perez, Laredo Club

Chicken and Rice Casserole

1½ cups uncooked rice

1 envelope dry onion soup mix

6 chicken pieces, seasoned to taste
(use breasts or thighs)

1 can (10¾ ounces) cheddar cheese
soup

1 can (10¾ ounces) cream of
chicken soup

1½ cans water (use soup can to
measure)

Spray 13-by-9-inch baking dish with nonstick cooking spray. Layer rice, soup mix, and seasoned chicken pieces. In separate bowl, combine cheddar cheese soup, cream of chicken soup, and water. Pour over chicken. Bake for 1½–2 hours at 350°. SERVES 6.   —*Lynn Ryan, Liberty County Club*

Chicken Broccoli Casserole

1 package (10 ounces) chopped
broccoli

1 cooked and diced chicken (may
use 1 50-ounce can)

½ cup mayonnaise

3 tablespoons lemon juice

1 can (10¾ ounces) cream of
chicken soup

1 cup shredded cheddar cheese

½ cup bread crumbs

Cook and drain broccoli, according to package directions. Arrange on bottom of oblong baking dish. Top with cooked and diced chicken. Combine mayonnaise, lemon juice, and soup; spread over chicken. Sprinkle with cheese and bread crumbs. Bake 30 minutes at 350°. SERVES 4–6.

—*Abilene Club*

On Campus

Mother's Casserole

1 small box (7 ounces) ready-cut
  spaghetti

1 pound ground beef

1 small onion, diced

1 small box (8 ounces) process
  cheese spread, cubed

1 small can (8 ounces) tomato
  sauce

salt and pepper to taste

Cook spaghetti according to package directions; drain. In large casserole, break up ground beef, add spaghetti, diced onion, cubed cheese, tomato sauce, salt, and pepper. Mix well. Bake in 400° oven for 45 minutes to 1 hour, or until cheese has bubbled and formed brown ring on top of casserole. *Serve with a tossed salad and hot rolls. Fills the stomachs of those growing Aggies!* SERVES 4.   *—Joan Dowell, Lubbock Area Club*

Easy Stroganoff

1–1½ pounds round steak, cut
  into thin strips

1 can (10¾ ounces) cream of
  mushroom soup, undiluted

1 envelope onion soup mix

1 cup Burgundy wine

vegetable oil for browning

Brown strips of meat in small amount of hot vegetable oil in skillet. Add soup, soup mix, and wine; cook over very low heat for 3 hours. Add a small amount of water if mixture gets too dry. Serve over cooked rice. SERVES 4.   *—Nancy Mayor, Montgomery County Club*

Easy Hot Dish

1 pound ground beef

2 cans (10¾ ounces each) vegetable
  beef soup, undiluted

1 package (16 ounces) frozen
  potato nuggets

salt and pepper to taste

Brown ground beef; drain if necessary. Add soup, salt, and pepper. Place in ungreased casserole dish, and top with potato nuggets. Bake covered at 350° for 45 minutes. SERVES 4–5.   *—Linda Hand, Garland Club*

Monterrey Casserole

1½–2 pounds ground beef

1 can (10¾ ounces) cream of mushroom soup

1 can (10¾ ounces) cream of chicken soup

1 can (10 ounces) enchilada sauce

1 can (4 ounces) taco sauce

¾ teaspoon lemon pepper (optional)

8 tortillas

Brown ground beef, and drain off grease. Combine cream of mushroom soup, cream of chicken soup, enchilada sauce, taco sauce, and lemon pepper, and mix well. Add to ground beef. Cut tortillas into quarters, and place some in the bottom of a greased 2-quart casserole. Add some of meat mixture. Add more tortillas and meat mixture until all is used. Bake at 350° for about 30 minutes or until bubbly. SERVES 4–6.

—Marilyn Matusek, DeWitt–Lavaca County Club

Hamburger Casserole

1 large onion, chopped

1 pound lean ground beef

1 can (23 ounces) chili-flavored red beans

1 can (26¼ ounces) spaghetti in tomato sauce with cheese

Brown chopped onions and ground beef in skillet. Stir in beans and spaghetti. Stir until hot, and it's ready to serve. As a variation, place hot mixture in casserole or cast-iron skillet; cover with a tube of biscuits and bake in oven (at temperature listed for biscuits) until biscuits are done. *Talk about quick—this is it! Add a salad and dessert, and you have a speedy meal.* SERVES 6.

—Averill Johnson Walters, Corpus Christi Club

On Campus

Vegetable Burgers

1 pound ground beef

1 cup quick-cooking oats

¼ teaspoon salt

¼ teaspoon pepper

2 tablespoons water

1 can (10¾ ounces) of *one* of these soups: vegetarian vegetable, cream of celery, or cream of mushroom

¼ cup water

Mix ground beef, oats, salt, pepper, and water. Form into 4–6 rather thick patties. Brown on both sides in a large skillet, medium heat, about 4 minutes. Pour can of soup, undiluted, over browned patties; add ¼ cup water, and simmer 15 minutes. *This is good served over a slice of toasted bread or over rice.* MAKES 4 LARGE PATTIES OR 6 SMALL ONES. —*Velma Lemons, Tyler Club*

Hamburger-Beans Rancho

1 pound ground beef

1 small onion, chopped

1 can (16 ounces) chili-flavored red beans

chili powder to taste

Brown ground beef in skillet; add chopped onion and cook until soft. Drain fat before adding beans and chili powder. Simmer 15–20 minutes. SERVES 3 OR 4. —*Inez L. Marx, East Bell County Club*

Burritos

1–2 pounds ground beef

1 envelope burrito seasoning mix

1 can (15 ounces) refried beans with sausage

1 package (12 ounces) flour tortillas

1 package (16 ounces) block chili process cheese spread, melted, for topping

Brown ground beef in skillet; add burrito mix. Mix in refried beans and sausage. Put mixture in tortillas, and roll for burritos. Serve with heated chili and melted cheese, which can be spooned over the burritos as sauces. SERVES 6–8. —*Joyce Simpson, Titus County Club*

Barbecued Pork Chops and Bean Bake

2 cans (16 ounces each) pork and beans

5 or 6 lean rib pork chops

salt and pepper to taste

prepared mustard, about 1 tablespoon per chop

brown sugar, about 1½ tablespoons per chop

catsup, about 1½ tablespoons per chop

5 or 6 slices of onion

5 or 6 slices of lemon (optional)

Lightly grease 13-by-9-inch baking dish, or spray with nonstick vegetable cooking spray. Add beans. Prepare chops by dashing each with salt and pepper. Spread with prepared mustard; sprinkle with brown sugar; spread with catsup. Arrange chops over beans. With toothpick, attach a piece of onion and lemon to each chop. Bake in a slow oven (325°) about 1½ hours, or until the pork chops are fork tender. Garnish with parsley. *If you are a rib fan, substitute loin back ribs for the pork chops. Cut into serving-size pieces, and prepare according to directions above. This may be served with crisp relishes or a tossed salad and hot garlic bread; add a fruit compote or fresh fruit for dessert.* SERVES 5 OR 6.

—*Jane Boehm, Past President (1984–85) of Federation, Brazoria County Club*

Cheese Toast

6 slices French bread, about ¾ inch thick

6 ounces muenster or mozzarella cheese, shredded

1 egg

¾ teaspoon prepared mustard

½ teaspoon Worcestershire sauce

butter or margarine

Butter both sides of French bread. In 10-inch skillet, brown bread on both sides over medium heat. In medium bowl, combine cheese, egg, mustard, and Worcestershire sauce. Spread equal amount of mixture on one side of each piece of browned bread. Place bread cheese-side up on cookie sheet. Place about 4 inches from broiler, and broil until cheese bubbles (about 2–4 minutes). If no broiler is available, return to skillet (cheese-side up), cover, and heat over medium heat until cheese bubbles. *May be served with salad, or with Italian food.* SERVES 2–3.   —*Eva Chaloupka, Fort Bend Club*

Clam Sauce for Linguine

½ cup butter or margarine, melted

4 cloves minced garlic, or ½ teaspoon powdered garlic

4 cans (4 ounces each) sliced mushrooms, drained

2 cans (6½ ounces each) minced clams

¾ cup chopped fresh parsley

salt and pepper to taste

½ teaspoon oregano (optional)

1 package (8 ounces) linguine or spaghetti, prepared according to package directions

grated Parmesan or Romano cheese for topping

Sauté garlic in melted butter for 1 minute over low heat. Add mushrooms, and cook 5 minutes. Stir in clams, parsley, salt, pepper, and oregano (if desired). (If using garlic powder, add now.) Cook linguine; drain. Mix with sauce and heat thoroughly. Serve with grated cheese. (Ed. note: If you have a food processor, try using it for chopping parsley—makes it simple.) *Very quickly prepared; easy main dish for a hurry-up dinner. Can be expanded easily. Except for linguine, can be prepared in microwave oven.* SERVES 4–6.

—*Mrs. W. A. Reiter, Jr., Bi-Stone Club*

Sheri's Pat-a-Pizza

1 can (7.5 ounces) refrigerated biscuits

1 can (6 ounces) tomato sauce

cheddar cheese, grated, for topping

sliced stuffed olives or sliced ripe olives for topping

Pat each biscuit flat in the palm of your hand. Place on cookie sheet, and spoon about 1 teaspoon of tomato sauce onto each biscuit. Sprinkle on grated cheese and sliced olives. Bake according to directions on biscuit can. (Ed. Note: Canned or bottled pizza sauce is now available and may provide more pizza flavor.) MAKES 8 SMALL PIZZAS.

—*Mrs. Ednita W. Lane, Beaumont Club*

Jalapeño Pie

1 small can (11 ounces) jalapeño
  peppers (nacho slices, mild or
  hot)
1 cup grated cheddar cheese

3 eggs, slightly beaten
salt and pepper to taste

Line bottom of baking pan with sliced peppers; cover with cheese. Combine beaten eggs, salt, and pepper. Pour over cheese. Bake at 350° for 20–30 minutes. Allow to cool slightly before slicing. *If you use a deep dish, use 2 cups of grated cheese and 5 eggs.* SERVES 8.   —*Mary J. Scroggins, Fort Bend Club*

Fat Fighter Mushroom Crust Quiche

3 green onions, chopped
1 4-ounce can mushrooms, drained
  (or fresh mushrooms, if
  preferred)
4 tablespoons margarine

25 saltine crackers, crushed
8 ounces grated Swiss cheese
3 eggs
12 ounces cottage cheese

Sauté green onions and mushrooms (chopped or thinly-sliced, if fresh) in margarine. Combine with cracker crumbs, and press into 10-inch pie plate, forming crust. Sprinkle grated Swiss cheese over crust. Blend eggs and cottage cheese together in blender. Pour over cheese. Bake at 350° for 35 minutes or until set and light brown. *This quiche has only 244 calories per slice.* SERVES 6.   —*Gerry Allen, Garland Club*

Open-Faced Sardine Sandwiches

1 can (3¾ ounces) sardines
mayonnaise and/or butter
bread

3–4 slices onion
3–4 slices tomato
3–4 slices American cheese

Toast bread slices lightly. Put sardines on bread spread with butter and/or mayonnaise. Top sandwiches with 1 slice each onion, tomato, and cheese. Broil until cheese is melted. MAKES 3–4 SANDWICHES.

—*Dorothy Lunday, Laredo Club*

Breakfast Casserole

1 tube (8 ounces) refrigerated
crescent rolls

1 pound breakfast sausage,
browned

2 cups grated mozzarella cheese

4 eggs

¾ cup milk

Flatten crescent roll dough into 13-by-9-inch baking pan. Brown sausage, drain, and spoon over roll dough. Sprinkle grated cheese over sausage. Mix eggs and milk until well blended and pour over cheese and sausage. Bake at 425° about 20 minutes or until center is set. *This is a favorite of my college kids and their friends.* SERVES 6–8. —*Karen Hicks, Montgomery County Club*

Baked Beans Plus

1 large can (31 ounces) pork and
beans

1 small onion, chopped

1 small green pepper, chopped

2 or 3 strips bacon, cut up

2 tablespoons brown sugar

2 tablespoons syrup

1 heaping tablespoon prepared
mustard

Put beans in baking dish. Sauté onion, green pepper, and bacon. Combine with brown sugar, syrup, and mustard and stir all into beans. Bake about 20 minutes at 325°. SERVES 4. —*Inga Barrett, Titus County Club*

Fancy Fruit Salad

1 can (20 or 21 ounces) peach or
apricot pie filling

2 large cans (20 ounces each)
pineapple chunks, drained

1 package (10 ounces) frozen sliced
strawberries, partially thawed

1 or 2 bananas, sliced

Combine all ingredients and chill. *This salad keeps in the refrigerator for several days.* SERVES 6–8.

VARIATION: Substitute 1 can (11 ounces) mandarin oranges for 1 can of the pineapple chunks.

—*Gerry Allen, Garland Club, and Inga Barrett, Titus County Club*

Orange Pancakes

1 cup self-rising flour

½ teaspoon baking soda

1 egg

1 cup (or more) orange juice

vegetable oil

Mix together slightly, and drop onto lightly oiled skillet. Turn when bubbles form. Serve with syrup and jelly. *This is good and easy college survival food.* MAKES 10–12 PANCAKES.   —*Nancy Mayor, Montgomery County Club*

Oven Pancake

¼ cup (½ stick) butter

2 eggs

½ cup all-purpose flour

½ cup milk

powdered sugar, if desired

Melt butter in iron skillet in oven set at 425°. Meanwhile, beat eggs in large measuring cup; add flour and milk. Beat by hand a few seconds to break lumps in flour. Pour mixture into hot skillet, and bake 15–20 minutes or until golden brown. Cut into pieces. Sprinkle with powdered sugar if desired, and serve with honey or syrup. *A favorite of my son's—very easy to prepare.* SERVES 2–4.   —*Betty Barnard, Hays County Club*

Beer Bread

3 cups self-rising flour

2 tablespoons sugar

1 can (12 ounces) beer, at room
   temperature

1 egg white, for topping

Mix flour, sugar, and beer together until well blended. Spoon into greased loaf pan. Brush top with slightly beaten egg white, and bake at 350° for about 1 hour, or until brown. SERVES 6–8.

—*Marian W. Prihoda, Lafayette, Louisiana, Club*

Beer Rolls

3 cups buttermilk baking mix   1 can (12 ounces) beer

3 tablespoons sugar

Combine baking mix, sugar, and beer; mix well. Batter will be thin. Spoon into well-greased muffin tins, filling about ⅓ full. Bake at 375°–400° until brown, approximately 25–30 minutes. *These are slightly sweet, and may be used for breakfast or other meals.* MAKES 18 ROLLS.   —*Abilene Club*

Whuffins

2 cups buttermilk baking mix   1 egg

1¼ cups milk   1½ cups wheat flake cereal

¼ cup sugar

Combine biscuit mix, milk, sugar, and egg. Gently fold in cereal. Fill well-greased muffin cups ⅔ full. Bake 20–25 minutes in 400° oven, or until tops are golden brown. MAKES 1 DOZEN MUFFINS.

—*Maureen Thode, Fort Bend Club*

Too Easy to Be Good Coffee Cake

24 frozen cloverleaf rolls   ½ cup chopped pecans

1 cup brown sugar   ½ cup (1 stick) butter or

1 package (3½ ounces)   margarine, melted
   butterscotch pudding (not
   instant)

Place one layer of frozen rolls in greased Bundt pan. Combine brown sugar, dry butterscotch pudding, and pecans; sprinkle half of mixture on rolls. Add another layer of frozen rolls and remainder of pudding mixture. Pour melted butter on top. Cover with towel, and let rise overnight. Bake for 35 minutes at 350°. Remove from oven, and invert on serving plate. *This makes a delicious, easy, do-ahead company breakfast. Serve with bacon and coffee or milk, and invite me over!* SERVES 8–10.

—*Barbara Tompkins, Midland Club*

Cinnamon Pull-Apart Coffee Cake

3 cans (10 biscuits each)
  refrigerated biscuits

1 cup sugar

¼ cup brown sugar

2 tablespoons cinnamon

½ cup (1 stick) margarine, melted

Lightly grease Bundt or tube pan. Cut each biscuit into quarters with knife or scissors. Combine sugar, brown sugar, and cinnamon in medium-sized bowl. Dredge biscuit pieces in sugar mixture and drop in pan. Pour melted margarine over biscuits. Top with remaining sugar mixture. Bake at 350° for 30 minutes. Remove from pan immediately. Add powdered sugar glaze, if desired. *Best eaten while warm.* SERVES 8–10.

—*Joan Smith, Baytown Club*

Pineapple Stir Cake

1 purchased or home-baked pound
  cake (loaf-pan size)

2 cans (20 ounces each) crushed
  pineapple, with juice

1 large container (12 ounces)
  frozen whipped topping, thawed

With hands, crumble cake into a layer in bottom of a crystal bowl or oblong cake pan. Pour crushed pineapple and juice over cake; add a layer of whipped topping. Repeat in layers, or just stir it up until you have used all of the ingredients. Chill in refrigerator. Best made the night before, but it can be made and served within the hour. *A very simple dessert to make, but good. Serve with spoons.* SERVES 8–10.

—*Russie Lynn DeZengotita, Mainland Club*

Easy Cobbler

¼ cup (½ stick) margarine

½ cup all-purpose flour

½ cup sugar

½ tablespoon baking powder

½ cup milk

1 can (approximately 20 ounces)
  fruit of your choice

Melt margarine in 9-inch square baking pan. Combine flour, sugar, baking powder, and milk. Pour into pan. Spoon fruit over dough, but do not mix. Dough will come to the top during baking. Bake at 350° about 45 minutes, or until top looks done. SERVES 4–6.

—*Mrs. Warren K. Bell, Orange County Club*

Peanut Butter Bars

¾ cup (1½ sticks) margarine, melted

1 jar (18 ounces) peanut butter

1 box (16 ounces) powdered confectioners sugar

1 chocolate bar (8 ounces)

3 teaspoons margarine

Melt margarine and mix into peanut butter. Add powdered sugar and mix well. Press into 13-by-9-inch pan; chill about 20 minutes to set. Break candy bar into sections and combine with 3 teaspoons margarine. Melt to spreading consistency. Spread thinly over peanut butter mixture. Score chocolate into the size bars you desire. Chill to harden chocolate. When firm, cut into 1-by-2-inch bars and store in airtight container in refrigerator. *A favorite with my three sons and their friends since we got the recipe from kindergarten.* MAKES 42 BARS.

—*Dixie (Mrs. E. Leonard) Copeland, Brazos County Club*

Unbaked Cookies

½ cup (1 stick) margarine

½ cup skim milk

2 cups sugar

2 teaspoons vanilla

2 heaping tablespoons cocoa (optional)

2 cups quick-cooking oats

½ cup peanut butter

Combine margarine, milk, sugar, vanilla, and cocoa in saucepan; cook 1 minute after mixture comes to a boil. Remove from heat, and add oats and peanut butter, stirring until peanut butter is melted. Drop on waxed paper or cookie sheet by teaspoonfuls. Chill. *Good to send to school.* MAKES ABOUT 2 DOZEN COOKIES.

—*Pat McCorstin, Garland Club*

Butterscotch Noodle Candy

1 package (12 ounces) butterscotch
  morsels
1 can (3 ounces) chow mein
  noodles

1 can (6½ ounces) salted cocktail
  peanuts

Melt butterscotch morsels in double boiler, over low heat. Stir in chow mein noodles and peanuts until coated. Drop by teaspoonfuls onto waxed paper and let cool. MAKES 3–4 DOZEN PIECES.

—*Mrs. W. B. Snead, Williamson County Club*

Heavenly Taffy Bars

½ box (16 ounce box) club
  crackers
1 cup chopped pecans

½ cup (1 stick) butter
½ cup (1 stick) margarine
½ cup sugar

Use two 15-by-10-inch cookie sheets (jelly roll pan) with sides. Line bottom with single layer of crackers. Sprinkle pecans over crackers. In medium saucepan, melt butter, margarine, and sugar. Bring to a boil; cook 2 minutes, stirring constantly. Pour mixture carefully over crackers, covering completely. Bake 10–12 minutes in 350° oven. Crackers will be floating in the bubbly mixture. Cool 10 minutes, and remove crackers to rack. *Really delicious—bet you can't eat just one!* MAKES 72 BARS.

—*Mary Beth Guy, Jasper County Club*

Forgotten Cookies

2 egg whites
¾ cup sugar

½ teaspoon vanilla
1 cup semisweet chocolate morsels
  or 1 cup angel flake coconut

Beat egg whites until soft peaks form; gradually add sugar, and beat until stiff and glossy. Fold in vanilla and chocolate chips or coconut. Drop by teaspoonfuls on greased baking sheets. Place in preheated 375° oven. Immediately turn off oven, and leave overnight. MAKES ABOUT 30 COOKIES.

—*Edna M. Smith*

Potato Chip Cookies

1 cup butter, softened

½ cup sugar

1 teaspoon vanilla

½ cup crushed potato chips

½ cup chopped pecans (optional)

2 cups sifted all-purpose flour

Cream butter, sugar, and vanilla. By hand, stir in potato chips, pecans, and flour. Form into small balls; place on ungreased cookie sheet. Grease bottom of glass, dip in sugar, and use to flatten cookies. Bake at 350° for 10–15 minutes. MAKES 3½ DOZEN. —*Edna M. Smith*

Survival Made Simple

3

The Gig 'Em Gourmet

Tailgate parties are not unique to Aggieland, but there, as elsewhere, they have become a prevalent type of food service before or after football games in the fall. Tailgating takes its name from the rear of the station wagon, which can be opened down to serve as a buffet table; some have referred to the tailgate party as a "moveable feast."

Tailgaters at Texas A&M may have their food served out of coolers or out of the raised trunk of a car; some may dine on maroon linen tablecloths in the shadow of the stadium. Some visitors even do their cooking after they arrive—the brisket goes on the smoker hours before the game, and the autumn aromas are heavenly.

For LaRee and Ben Morgan of Austin, tailgating near Mt. Aggie has provided a setting for meeting old friends and former classmates and getting to know their son's friends during the football season each year. College Station's unpredictable fall weather has found them serving hurriedly off the tailgate under threatening skies; eating in the car during pouring rain; shivering in the cold as they dipped up chili; and, perhaps more often, gratefully sipping cold soup during the heat and humidity of early season games. Preparing for these reunions and the repasts served on a maroon and white quilt for a tablecloth has become a science.

"Tailgate picnics at Texas A&M have been a part of our family's tradition since our son entered as a freshman," Mrs. Morgan writes. "Over the years I have compiled sets of menus and recipes with foods that travel well and easily, do not spoil, will keep and taste good at varying temperatures, can be prepared as much as a day or two before, and can be stretched to serve extra guests who may appear. From his freshman year on, my son would bring his date (if he had one) and maybe his roommate. Each year the crowd increased, so that by the time he was a senior, we were feeding most of the seniors in his company and their dates, as well as any friends who had come to the game with us. Usually our menu includes an appetizer, a large piece of meat (such as tenderloin, brisket, or ham), various side dishes, lots of bread in case someone wants to make a sandwich, a simple, easy-to-eat dessert, and lots of drinks."

Texas A&M does not have a homecoming celebration as many universities do, but tailgating might be said to be a case of "home coming to campus."

TAILGATING TIPS

(Suggested by Mrs. Ben (LaRee) Morgan, Austin Club)

EQUIPPING THE TRAVELING KITCHEN

Paper and plastic ware for eating (with lots of extras)
Cutting board
Sharp slicing knife
Small berry baskets (or something similar) for serving chips and rolls
Serving utensils
Bottle and/or can opener
Salt and pepper in sealable containers
Bags for packing trash

PACKING COLD FOODS

—Pack cold foods in French canning jars of various sizes (the leakproof kind with rubber rings and clamp seals), or any plastic or glass containers with absolutely leakproof lids.
—Include lots of ice in the cooler or ice chest. Chunks or large cubes last longer than crushed ice and may be made at home by freezing ice in waxed milk cartons.
—Prechill all cold foods before packing.
—Wrap meats securely in heavy duty aluminum foil.
—Carry cold soups in prechilled insulated bottles.

PACKING HOT FOODS

—Use a styrofoam "cooler" to transport hot foods. If you use some other container, be sure it is leakproof.
—Take foods that are thoroughly cooked and steaming hot. Wrap them first in heavy foil, then in several thicknesses of newspaper, secured with tape.
—Preheated insulated bottles are great for hot soup or drinks.

—Pack any crushables on your menu—fruit, chips, bread, cookies—in an open basket, paper bag, or shopping bag lined with your tablecloth or blanket. This will cushion them at the same time it conserves space by using something you need to take anyway.

—Cakes baked in a covered pan and cookies are the most easily transported desserts.

—Overpack rather than underpack. Any "extra" food you take—if it's not eaten up by last-minute guests or extra-hungry Aggies—can be sent back to the dorm with the students. You can be sure it will be appreciated.

Homestyle Bread and Butter Pickles

6 quarts fresh cucumbers, sliced

12 medium onions, sliced

1 jar (4 ounces) pimientos, diced

¾ cup salt

6 cups (1½ quarts) vinegar

6 cups sugar

½ cup mustard seed

1 teaspoon turmeric powder

Combine sliced cucumbers, sliced onions, diced pimientos, and salt; let stand for 3 hours. Drain off liquid that forms. Put cucumber mixture into a large pot; add vinegar, sugar, mustard seed, and turmeric powder. Mix well and bring to a boil. While mixture is still hot, pack into sterile jars and seal. MAKES 10 PINTS OF PICKLES.

—*Mrs. Don (Jean) Kaspar, Past President (1976–77) of Federation, Victoria County Club*

My Aggie's Favorite Salsa

1 can (4½ ounces) chopped ripe olives

1 jar (8 ounces) mild or medium picante sauce

1 can (10 ounces) tomatoes and green chilies

2 tablespoons cider vinegar

1 tablespoon vegetable oil

2 ripe tomatoes, diced

6 green onions, chopped

⅛ teaspoon garlic powder

1 teaspoon salt

¼ teaspoon black pepper

Mix all ingredients. Cover and store in refrigerator for up to two weeks. Serve with tortilla chips. SERVES 15–20. —*Ruth Henry, East Bell County Club*

Layered Nacho Dip

1 can (16 ounces) refried beans

1 package (1.25 ounces) taco
  seasoning mix

1 carton (6 ounces) avocado dip

1 carton (8 ounces) sour cream

1 can (4½ ounces) chopped ripe
  olives

2 large tomatoes, diced

1 small onion, finely chopped

1 can (4 ounces) diced green chilies

1½ cups (6 ounces) shredded
  Monterey Jack cheese

corn chips

Combine refried beans and taco seasoning; spread this mixture in a
12-by-8-inch dish. Layer remaining ingredients in order listed. Serve with
corn chips. *This may be made ahead of time, covered, and refrigerated. It can
also be heated in a 350° oven for 15–20 minutes. I prefer cold to hot, but either
way, it's guaranteed to be a favorite dip.* MAKES ABOUT 8 CUPS OF DIP.

—*Billie Housman, Midland Club*

Braunschweiger Log

1 8-ounce package *sliced*
  Braunschweiger (use only sliced
  kind)

1 teaspoon prepared mustard

1 teaspoon horseradish sauce

1 teaspoon lemon juice

1 teaspoon garlic salt

1 teaspoon Worcestershire sauce

1 package (8 ounces) cream cheese,
  softened

1 cup finely chopped pecans

Chop and mash Braunschweiger. Add mustard, horseradish sauce, lemon
juice, garlic salt, and Worcestershire sauce. Mix well, roll into two logs,
and wrap in waxed paper. Refrigerate until firm. Soften cream cheese and
"frost" log. Roll in chopped pecans. Serve with party crackers or bread.
Keep very cold. SERVES 6–8 AS APPETIZER.   —*Carol Ireland, Fort Bend Club*

Norwegian Stuffed Eggs

6 hard-cooked eggs

¼ cup melted butter (no substitute)

¼ teaspoon salt

dash pepper

¼ teaspoon dry mustard

1 teaspoon (or a little more) minced onion

⅓ cup tuna, shrimp, or crabmeat

Peel eggs; slice lengthwise and remove yolks. Mash egg yolks with fork, and add melted butter which has been mixed with salt, pepper, dry mustard, and onion. Mix in tuna, shrimp, or crabmeat, and refill egg white halves. *Perfect for picnics or outdoor activities. Men, especially, really like them. Keep chilled.* MAKES 12 STUFFED EGGS. —*Kathy Hampton, Austin Club*

Drunk Wieners

½ cup catsup

½ cup bourbon

½ cup brown sugar

1 pound package of wieners, cut into ¾-inch slices

Combine catsup, bourbon, and brown sugar in sauce pan and heat. Add wiener slices. Serve with picks as hot hors d'oeuvre. MAKES ABOUT 80 BITE-SIZED PIECES. —*Clarice Bohls, Austin Club*

Pickled Wieners

2 packages (16 ounces each) wieners

1 small onion

¼ cup jalapeño peppers

vinegar (to fill jar)

Stand wieners in wide-mouthed quart jar. Add chopped onions and chopped jalapeño peppers. Fill with vinegar, and cover. Refrigerate. For full flavor, wait a week before eating. For appetizers, cut into pieces, and serve with toothpicks. *Hard-cooked eggs may be pickled the same way.* SERVES 10. —*Mary Kay Rowlett, Brown County Club*

Sausage Bread

2 loaves frozen yeast bread, thawed

1 pound pork sausage

1 green pepper, chopped

2 medium onions, chopped

½ pound cheddar cheese, grated

½ pound Monterey Jack cheese, grated

Thaw loaves of bread, according to directions on package. Crumble sausage; add green pepper and onion in skillet, and cook over low heat. With buttered fingers, press each loaf flat and pat to 15-by-8-inch size. Divide sausage mixture and cheese into two equal parts. Beginning with sausage, layer sausage and cheese on the two pressed bread doughs. Spread evenly, and roll up lengthwise as for a jelly roll. Bake on a cookie sheet at 350° until golden brown (check frozen bread directions). Remove from oven, and slice. *This is delicious for breakfast, supper, or after a football game. Serve with a salad. Bread can be made ahead of time, frozen, and then reheated.* SERVES 10–20. —*Barbara Vincent, Mid-Jefferson County Club*

Sausage and Cheese Bake

1 tube (8) crescent rolls

1 pound sausage

1 package (8 ounces) mozzarella cheese, grated

2 tablespoons chopped green pepper

¼ cup chopped onion

4 eggs, slightly beaten

¾ cup milk

½ teaspoon salt

¼ teaspoon pepper

¼ teaspoon Italian seasoning

Open canned rolls and carefully unroll. Place in bottom of 13-by-9-inch casserole dish or pan. Press perforations and edges together, pushing to cover bottom of dish. Brown sausage and drain well. Put crumbled sausage on top of dough; add grated cheese, green pepper, and onions evenly over sausage. Beat eggs slightly; add milk, salt, pepper, and Italian seasoning. Pour over layered ingredients and bake 20–25 minutes in 375° oven. Cool slightly before cutting. *This is a big hit at our tailgates. I have found that bite-sized pieces are better for tailgate picnics, because they eliminate the need for plates and forks. Be sure to take a small spatula. This dish can be stretched by adding 2 eggs, increasing milk to 1 cup, and adding more seasonings. Good both hot and cold!* MAKES 24 BITE-SIZED SERVINGS.

—*Lynda R. Wortham, Montgomery County Club*

Honey Smoked Pork Chops

2 pounds lean pork chops

1 cup chicken stock or bouillon

1 teaspoon salt

3 teaspoons sugar

2 tablespoons soy sauce

⅓ cup honey

2 cloves garlic, crushed

Arrange pork chops in oblong cake pan. Combine the rest of the ingredients and heat them slightly in microwave or on top of range. Pour sauce over chops and marinate at least 1 hour, preferably overnight, basting occasionally. Put on smoker, directly over coals, turning once or twice. Test for doneness after 30 minutes. SERVES 4–6.   —*Kathy Sayre, Waller County Club*

Oven-Barbecued Brisket

1 brisket (8–10 pounds) with bone

seasoned salt (to taste)

Worcestershire sauce (to taste)

1 bottle liquid smoke

barbecue sauce (bottled or your own recipe)

Place brisket on heavy-duty foil, and sprinkle evenly with seasoned salt, Worcestershire sauce, and liquid smoke. Pour barbecue sauce over brisket and seal in foil. Place on baking dish or pan, and roast in 250° oven for 5–6 hours. You can season the roast the night before, wrap it, and then roast it the next day. SERVES 12.   —*Amira E. Mejia, Laredo Club*

Ranch Burgers

2 packages (¼ ounce each) yeast

⅔ cup warm water

⅔ cup warm milk

¼ cup sugar

¼ cup vegetable shortening

2 teaspoons salt

2 eggs

4½–5 cups all-purpose or bread flour

Dissolve yeast in water in large mixing bowl. Add milk, sugar, shortening, salt, eggs, and 1½ cups flour. Blend together at low speed for 30 seconds. Beat 2 minutes at medium speed, scraping bowl occasionally. Stir in enough of remaining flour to make dough easy to handle. Turn dough onto lightly floured surface; knead until smooth and elastic (about 5 minutes). Place in greased bowl, turning to coat all sides. Cover and let rise in a warm place until double, about 1–1½ hours.

FILLING

2 pounds ground chuck

1 large onion, chopped

1 tablespoon chili powder

1½ teaspoons salt

½ teaspoon pepper

1 jar (8 ounces) cheese spread with jalapeño peppers

2 cans (15 ounces each) chili beans, drained

¼ cup margarine, softened

Brown ground chuck and onion in large frying pan. Pour off drippings. Add chili powder, salt, and pepper. Mix well. Stir in cheese spread and chili beans, and cook slowly 10–15 minutes. When dough has risen, divide into four portions. Roll each portion into a 10-by-14-inch rectangle ¼ inch thick. Cut each into six squares. Place about ⅓–½ cup meat filling on each square. Pull up opposite corners, and pinch together at center top. Place pinched side down on baking sheet. Bake in hot oven (400°) for 12–15 minutes, or until golden brown. Brush with softened margarine. *Burgers may be frozen and reheated.* MAKES 24 BURGERS.

—*Sandra Lehne, Austin Club*

Sweet and Sour Vegetables

1 cup sugar

2 teaspoons dry mustard

1 teaspoon salt

½ cup vinegar

1½ cups vegetable oil

1 small onion, grated

2 teaspoons poppy seed

2 cups chopped broccoli

2 cups sliced carrots

1 large green pepper, chopped

2 medium zucchini, sliced

Combine sugar, dry mustard, salt, vinegar, oil, onion, and poppy seed. Pour over raw broccoli, carrots, green pepper, and zucchini (or substitute any combination of raw vegetables you choose). Cover and refrigerate overnight. *This is a great recipe for large crowds—easy to take to picnics or meetings. It will keep in the refrigerator about 10 days.* SERVES 6–8.

—*Cathy Dietz, Fort Worth/Tarrant County Club*

Shoe Peg Salad
(Overnight Vegetable Salad)

1 can (17 ounces) tiny green peas, drained

1 can (16 ounces) French-style green beans, drained

1 can (15 ounces) shoe peg corn, drained

1 cup diced celery

½ cup diced green pepper

1 medium onion, chopped

1 jar (2 ounces) chopped pimientos, drained

DRESSING

1½ cups sugar

1 cup vinegar

½ cup vegetable oil

salt to taste

Combine dressing ingredients, and pour over mixed vegetables. Chill in refrigerator overnight. Keeps well. SERVES 10–12.

VARIATION   Add to vegetables 1 can (8 ounces) of sliced water chestnuts and ½ head of cauliflower cut into small flowerets. Onions may be green onions, and sugar may be reduced if you prefer a tart flavor.

—*Rosalie Biar, Milam County Club, and Buna Patterson, Matagorda County Club*

Picnic Pasta Salad

3 cups uncooked tortellini or spiral macaroni

¼ cup olive oil

⅓ cup white wine vinegar

½ teaspoon salt

½ teaspoon pepper

¼ teaspoon dried tarragon

½ green pepper, finely chopped

½ cup minced fresh parsley

½ cup sliced green onions

½ cup sliced ripe olives

¼ cup chopped pimiento

Cook pasta according to package directions. Drain and place in large mixing bowl. While pasta is hot, add olive oil, vinegar, salt, pepper, and tarragon, tossing lightly to blend. Refrigerate. When cool, add green pepper, parsley, green onions, ripe olives, and pimiento. Refrigerate for at least 3 hours. This salad can be served cold (transport in a cooler) or at room temperature. Refrigeration is not required after salad is made and chilled.

—*LaRee H. (Mrs. Ben) Morgan, Austin Club*

Cole Slaw

2½ cups coarsely shredded cabbage

1 cup coarsely shredded carrots

1 can (8 ounces) pineapple chunks, well-drained

⅓ cup slivered almonds, toasted

DRESSING

⅔ cup sour cream

⅔ cup salad dressing

1 teaspoon grated onion

1–3 teaspoons sugar, depending on taste

1 tablespoon lemon juice

¼ teaspoon salt

Combine first four ingredients. Mix dressing ingredients and toss with cabbage mixture. SERVES 6–8.   —*Peggy Williams, Panola County Club*

Marinated Carrots

2 cups cooked carrots, sliced

1 cup sugar

¾ cup vinegar

1 medium green pepper, chopped

1 medium onion, chopped

1 teaspoon prepared mustard

1 teaspoon Worcestershire sauce

salt and pepper to taste

½ cup vegetable oil

Combine all ingredients. Refrigerate overnight. SERVES 4.

—*Jo Frances Chastain, President (1986–87) of Federation, Rio Grande Valley Club*

Marinated Mushrooms

3 jars (4.5 ounces each) button
mushrooms

½ cup tarragon vinegar

½ cup brown sugar

¼ teaspoon salt

½ tablespoon whole black pepper

1 bay leaf

1 clove garlic, sliced

Drain mushrooms, reserving ½ cup liquid. Combine all ingredients except mushrooms, and bring to a boil in small saucepan. Pour over mushrooms. Store in a tightly sealed glass jar in the refrigerator for 24 hours. *These mushrooms are great! They will keep in the refrigerator for weeks. A small jar with a bow on top makes a nice Christmas gift.* SERVES 10.

—*Mrs. Tommy (Janet) Barre, DeWitt–Lavaca County Club*

Salad Bread (with variations)

4 cans (7.5 ounces each) buttermilk biscuits

½–¾ cup (1–1½ sticks) margarine, melted

¾ cup finely diced celery

¾ cup finely diced green pepper

½–¾ cup grated cheddar cheese

1 small jar (2 ounces) diced pimientos

Melt margarine in pan over low to medium heat; pour a small amount in a large mixing bowl. Add celery and green pepper to remaining margarine and sauté. Cook about 5 minutes, stirring occasionally. With a clean pair of small scissors, cut each biscuit into four pieces. Put into mixing bowl with melted margarine, and coat well. Add celery, green pepper, cheese, and pimientos; mix well. Spray a Bundt pan or tube pan with nonstick cooking spray. Add coated biscuit pieces. Bake in preheated 400° oven for 10 minutes; reduce heat to 350° and bake for 15–20 minutes longer, or until biscuits do not have a "gummy" appearance. Loosen around all sides with a knife as soon as bread comes out of the oven; cool in pan 5 minutes; then cool loaf upright on rack. Bread may be served immediately while hot, eaten cold, or reheated. May be reheated in a microwave oven or wrapped in foil and heated in 350° oven for 10 minutes. It is a pull-apart bread which slices nicely when cold. Can be frozen, and should be stored in refrigerator. SERVES 12 OR MORE.

VARIATIONS   Instead of celery and green pepper, use 2 or 3 of the following:

¾ cup chopped onion

¾ cup chopped chives

¾ cup chopped parsley

½ cup crumbled crisp bacon

1 small can (4 ounces) diced green chilies

1 small can (7 ounces) chopped jalapeño peppers

And for a breakfast or brunch, the sweetened version substitutes for vegetables, cheese, and pimientos, the following:

1 cup (2 sticks) margarine, melted

½ cup sugar

4 tablespoons light brown sugar

2 teaspoons cinnamon

½–1 cup chopped nuts

For the coffee cake, coat biscuit pieces thoroughly with melted margarine before adding sugar mixture. Baking instructions are the same as for salad bread. *This has been a favorite of ours for many years; it makes a nice "nonsweet" gift at Christmastime.* —*Barbara Pittard, Brown County Club*

Cheese Casserole Bread

3 tablespoons sesame seed

1 egg

1½ cups milk

3¾ cups buttermilk baking mix

1 cup shredded cheddar cheese

1 tablespoon dried parsley

¼ teaspoon pepper (optional)

Grease 2-quart round casserole; sprinkle sesame seed evenly on bottom and side. Beat egg in large mixer bowl on low speed; beat in remaining ingredients on medium speed 30 seconds. Pour into casserole. Bake at 350° for 40–45 minutes, or until wooden pick comes out clean. Invert immediately and remove casserole. MAKES 1 LOAF. —*Edna M. Smith*

Gig 'Em Gourmet

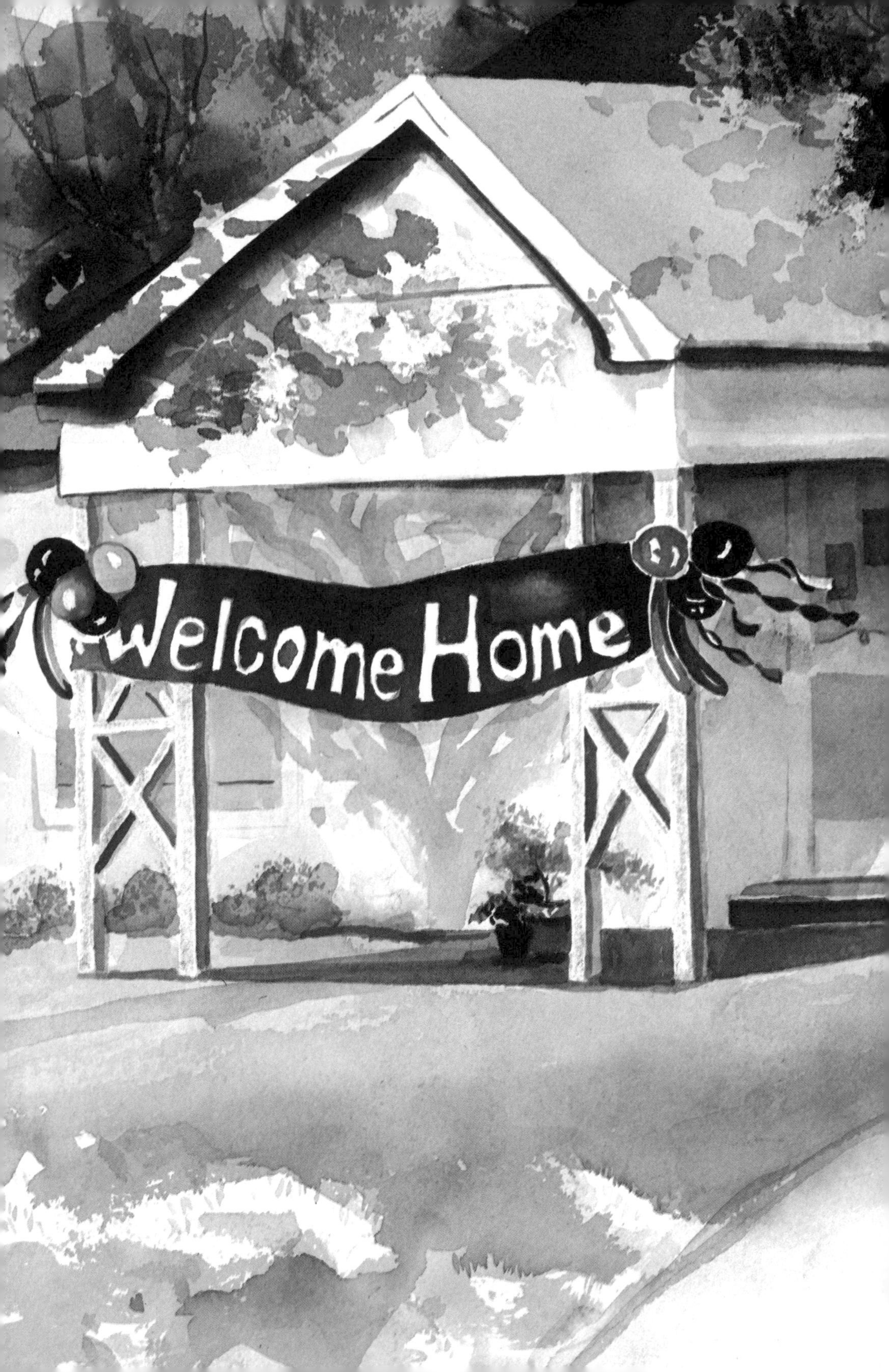
Welcome Home

Part II

Home for a Holiday

4

Party Starters

Your daughter's home, and it's time to get some of the old high school gang together again—or maybe some new college friends are visiting for the weekend or spring break. Any excuse is good for a party, and a good party frequently begins with food. Call them appetizers or hors d'oeuvre, canapés or cocktail tidbits—or even something less exotic—but call them delicious. Many of the recipes in this chapter are for finger foods, so you won't even need to get out a lot of silver and china.

Hors d'oeuvre are literally "aside from the main body of the work" or loosely, "side-dish." A canapé is a thin piece of bread or toast, pastry, or sometimes a fancy cracker combined with a topping or filling of your choice. A decorative garnish may complete the picture. Hearty or fancy, these kinds of nibbles are enjoyed by most people almost as much as a meal itself, and they certainly become a focal point for conversation.

Appetizers may precede a meal, or you may plan an entire buffet of appetizer-type foods. A typical buffet menu would include some high-protein foods such as meat, fish, eggs, or cheese, alone or as ingredients in some spread or dip. Serve your cheese at room temperature; it has more flavor that way. Vegetables, raw and crunchy, have everything: color, texture, vitamins, fiber, great taste, and best of all, few calories. Tiny toast rounds, crackers, chips, or miniature pastries provide the containers for dips and spreads. Greens such as parsley or endive may serve as a bed to hold the vegetables or pickled accompaniments.

At Christmastime you might want to try making an edible wreath. Just cover a styrofoam wreath form with plastic wrap. Using pole pins (from the florist), attach parsley sprigs to cover fully. Display a variety of vegetables on toothpicks in an artistic manner; add a bow if you wish. Your vegetables, olives, cheese cubes, and other appetizers may also be displayed and served on a styrofoam cone, making a showy, edible Christmas tree.

Miniature Meatballs à la Savage

2 pounds ground beef

1 medium onion, chopped fine

3 stalks celery, chopped fine

¼ cup tomato sauce

2 cloves garlic, pressed

salt (to taste)

black pepper (to taste)

red pepper (to taste)

Combine all ingredients; mix well. Roll into small balls and pan broil until brown, turning often. Serve with picks. Number of meatballs depends on size rolled. MAKES ABOUT 6 DOZEN 1-INCH MEATBALLS.

—*Mrs. Bert A. (Adelaide) Savage, Galveston Island Club*

Sweet-Sour Cocktail Meatballs

1½ pounds ground beef

1 cup prepared bread crumbs

½ cup sweet pickle relish

2 eggs

2 teaspoons grated onion

2 tablespoons brown sugar

½ cup milk

½–1 teaspoon salt

1–2 tablespoons vegetable oil, for browning

SWEET-SOUR SAUCE

2 cups catsup

⅓–½ cup brown sugar

1 teaspoon prepared garlic

1½ cups water

2 teaspoons steak sauce

2 teaspoons Worcestershire sauce

Combine ground beef, crumbs, pickle relish, eggs, onion, brown sugar, milk, and salt in large mixing bowl; mix with electric mixer at lowest speed. Shape meat into walnut-sized balls and brown in oil. To make sauce, combine catsup, brown sugar, garlic, water, steak sauce, and Worcestershire sauce. Pour over meatballs, and simmer 10–20 minutes. Meatballs and sauce may be transferred to chafing dish for serving. May be served with cocktail picks or as an entrée over rice. *May be prepared ahead of time and frozen. Our family has this after Christmas Eve Mass because it can be prepared ahead and will keep well.* MAKES 50 APPETIZER-SIZED SERVINGS.

—*Mrs. C. Garry Hendricks, Fort Worth/Tarrant County Club*

Rye Canapé Boat

1 package (10 ounces) of chipped
  or dried beef
1½ cups sour cream
1½ cups mayonnaise
2 tablespoons chopped onion
2 tablespoons snipped parsley

1 teaspoon chives
1 teaspoon dill weed or seed
1 teaspoon garlic powder
2 teaspoons Beau Monde seasoning
1 large unsliced loaf of rye or
  pumpernickel bread

Mix together all ingredients except the bread. Just before serving, completely hollow out loaf of rye or pumpernickel bread, leaving enough bread to make a "bowl." Tear the bread you have removed into chunks. Use these for dipping. MAKES 4–5 CUPS OF DIP.   —*Jan Fluegel, Amarillo Club*

Cheese Party Squares

1 package (2 pounds) process
  cheese spread

2 tablespoons Tabasco sauce
1 cup chopped pecans

Melt cheese over low heat with Tabasco sauce, stirring frequently. Add pecans; pour into 8-inch square buttered pan. Chill until firm; cut into small squares. SERVES 6.   —*Ruth Lindquist, Brush Country Club*

Carroll's Cheese Squares

3–4 chopped jalapeño peppers
  (seeds removed)
1 pound sharp cheddar cheese,
  shredded

6 eggs, beaten
chopped parsley, as desired

Cover 7-by-11-inch baking pan lightly with nonstick cooking spray. Layer ingredients in order given; do not mix. Sprinkle parsley on top. Bake 20–30 minutes, until set. *Great for couples' bridge club, too.* SERVES 12.
—*Carroll H. Elmer, Mainland Club*

Sausage Stroganoff

1 clove garlic

2 pounds bulk sausage

3 tablespoons all-purpose flour

2 cups milk

4 tablespoons margarine

2 large onions, chopped

1 large can (6 ounces) sliced mushrooms

2 teaspoons soy sauce

2 tablespoons Worcestershire sauce

salt, pepper, and paprika to taste

1 pint sour cream

Rub skillet with garlic; brown sausage, and drain well. Dredge sausage with flour; add milk and simmer. In another pan, sauté onions and mushrooms in margarine. Add to sausage mixture. Mix in soy sauce, Worcestershire sauce, salt, pepper, and paprika. When mixture bubbles, add sour cream. Serve hot with tiny biscuits, pastry shells, or Melba toast. SERVES 8–10.   —*Milam County Club*

Crabmeat Won Tons

3 packages (8 ounces each) cream cheese, softened

1 can (6½ ounces) crabmeat, drained

1 package small size won ton skins

small amounts water and all-purpose flour for sealing mixture

vegetable oil for deep frying

Mix cream cheese and crabmeat together ahead of time; refrigerate. Make a skin-sealing mixture of small amounts of water and flour. Lay out skins; spread sealing mixture along skin edges. Take a large teaspoon of crab mixture and place in skin; fold over, and press lightly together, trying not to leave air pockets. Press edges closed. Deep fry until skins are golden brown; remove before cream cheese mixture melts. Drain on paper towels. Serve warm. Won tons may be made ahead of time, frozen or refrigerated and then reheated before serving. *The recipe was given to me by a local restaurant.* MAKES AT LEAST 5 DOZEN.   —*Vicki Spink, Kingwood Club*

Home for a Holiday

Texas Crab Grass

½ cup (1 stick) butter

½ medium onion, finely chopped

1 package (10 ounces) frozen chopped spinach, cooked and drained

1 can (6½ ounces) crabmeat

¾ cup grated Parmesan cheese

Melba rounds

Slowly melt butter in heavy saucepan. Add onion and sauté until soft. Add spinach to onion mixture. Add crabmeat and cheese. Transfer to chafing dish and serve with Melba rounds. *This appetizer is very popular and delicious. It's a change of pace from the usual.* MAKES ABOUT 1½ CUPS.

—*Mrs. David E. (Joan) Varner, Houston Club*

Shrimp Dip I

1 package (3 ounces) cream cheese, softened

1 package (0.6 ounces) Italian salad dressing mix (dry)

1 pint sour cream

1 tablespoon chopped green pepper

2 dashes Tabasco sauce

½ cup chopped shrimp

Combine cream cheese, dressing mix, sour cream, green pepper, and Tabasco sauce; mix until well blended. Stir in shrimp. Chill, and serve with crackers. MAKES 2 CUPS OF DIP. —*Connie Clark, Garland Club*

Shrimp Dip II

3 packages (8 ounces each) cream cheese, softened

½ pint (1 cup) sour cream

¾ cup chili sauce

½ cup mayonnaise

1 clove garlic, crushed

2 pounds cooked shrimp, finely chopped

salt and pepper to taste

Mix all ingredients until well blended. Serve with chips or crackers. *Better if made early in the day and refrigerated several hours before serving.* MAKES 9 OR MORE CUPS OF DIP. —*Dolly Heintz, Montgomery County Club*

Shrimp Dip III

1 package (15 ounces) frozen tiny
   shrimp, cooked according to
   directions and drained

3 packages (3 ounces each) cream
   cheese

1 can (10¾ ounces) tomato soup

1 envelope unflavored gelatin,
   softened in ½ cup water

1 cup chopped celery

1 cup chopped onion

Cook and drain shrimp; cool. Combine cream cheese and tomato soup in saucepan. Melt over low heat, stirring frequently, until creamy. Remove from heat; add gelatin mixture. Stir well; add shrimp, celery, and onion. Spoon into oiled gelatin mold and refrigerate. Chill for several hours. Unmold on plate and serve with assorted crackers. MAKES 6 CUPS.

—*Jobey Ruffino, Brazos County Club*

Tex-Mex Layered Dip

1 can (15 ounces) refried beans

2 cups sour cream

1 package (1¼ ounces) taco
   seasoning

1 jar (8 ounces) Picante sauce

4 ripe avocados, peeled, seeded,
   and mashed

2 teaspoons lemon or lime juice

2 medium tomatoes, chopped

1 bunch green onions, with tops,
   thinly sliced

8 ounces cheddar cheese, grated

1 can (4 ounces) sliced ripe olives

toasted corn chips or tortilla chips

Spread refried beans on bottom of a 2-quart glass or decorative casserole. Mix sour cream and taco seasoning and spread on top of bean layer. Layer Picante sauce next. Mix avocados with lemon or lime juice, and add next. In order, add layers of tomatoes, green onions, cheese, and olives. Cover and refrigerate. Serve with toasted corn chips or tortilla chips. *This is good as an appetizer or to complement any Mexican food.* SERVES 12.

—*Mrs. Gene (Dottie) Garrison, Brush Country Club*

Green Chili Dip

1 can (4 ounces) diced green chilies

1 can (6 ounces) pitted black olives, chopped or sliced

2 large tomatoes, peeled and chopped

3–4 tablespoons olive oil

1–2 teaspoons white vinegar (to taste)

1 teaspoon garlic salt

Mix all ingredients. Chill at least one hour before serving. Serve with corn chips. *Recipe may also be used as a relish for pinto beans. Leftover dip (including marinade) may be frozen and added later to spaghetti sauce.* MAKES 2 CUPS.   —*Deanna (Mrs. Ben R.) Smith, Fort Worth/Tarrant County Club*

Taco Dip

2 cans (9 ounces each) bean dip

4 green onions, chopped

3 avocados, mashed, and mixed with 1 teaspoon lemon juice

1 cup shredded cheddar cheese

1 cup shredded Monterey Jack cheese

1 small can (2¼ ounces) ripe olives, sliced

4 small tomatoes, chopped

DRESSING

½ cup sour cream

½ cup mayonnaise

½ package taco seasoning mix

Mix dressing the night before assembling salad. Layer ingredients as listed in a 9-by-13-inch pan. Do not mix. Spread dressing over top. Serve with corn chips. *This is also called Pancho Villa Birthday Cake. It'll disappear fast.* SERVES 8–12.

VARIATION   (also known as Compuesta Dip): 2 cans (16 ounces each) refried beans with jalapeño (replacing bean dip)

—*Virginia Saldua, Fort Bend County Club*

Tortilla Cheese Roll-Ups

1 package (8 ounces) cream cheese, softened

1 can (4 ounces) chopped green chilies, drained

3 tablespoons sour cream

3 tablespoons picante sauce

dash seasoned salt

dash onion powder

1 package (12 ounces) flour tortillas

Mix all ingredients except tortillas. Spread mixture on tortillas, roll tightly, and wrap in plastic wrap. Chill for 3–4 hours or overnight. Slice each roll into several bite-sized pieces. *These are easy, quick appetizers, which can be prepared in advance. They add zest to a tea or shower, or they make a good snack for nibbling.* MAKES ABOUT 40 PIECES. —*Barbara Tompkins, Midland Club*

Stuffed Jalapeños

1 can (1 pound, 11 ounces) pickled jalapeños

1 package (8 ounces) cream cheese, softened

1 cup pecans, chopped

Drain jalapeños, cut them in half, and remove the seeds. Mix cream cheese and pecans, and fill jalapeño halves. MAKES ABOUT 4 DOZEN.

—*Mrs. Tommy (Janet) Barre, DeWitt–Lavaca County Club*

Bacon Appetizers

1 package (1 pound) bacon

1 package club crackers

Cut entire package of bacon slices in half. Break ¼ pound club crackers into small sections. Wrap ½ slice bacon around each small cracker section. Place on grill pan or rack so grease can drip down. Bake at 200° for 2½ hours. These appetizers may be cooked for two hours the day before and then reheated for 30 minutes before serving. *Great for parties!* MAKES 36–40. —*Sherilyn West, Lubbock Area Club*

Sausage Pinwheels

2 cups all-purpose flour

½ teaspoon baking powder

5 tablespoons vegetable shortening

⅔ cup milk

1 pound ground sausage

Mix flour and baking powder. Blend in shortening; add milk and mix. Divide dough into two parts, and roll each piece ¼ inch thick. Spread each with half of crumbled sausage, and roll as for jelly roll. Place in waxed paper and chill. (Rolls may be frozen at this time for later use.) Slice roll in ¼-inch slices and bake on ungreased cookie sheet at 400° for 20–30 minutes, or until golden brown. SERVES 24.

—*Mrs. John L. Pickering, Jr., Kingwood Club*

Sausage Swirls

4 cups all-purpose flour

¼ cup cornmeal

¼ cup sugar

2 tablespoons baking powder

1 teaspoon salt

⅔ cup vegetable oil

⅔–1 cup milk

2 pounds sausage (1 regular, 1 hot)

Sift flour, cornmeal, sugar, baking powder, and salt together. Blend in vegetable oil. Add enough milk to make a stiff dough. Roll out on a lightly floured board into an 18-by-10-inch rectangle. Spread combined sausages on the dough to cover it evenly. Roll up lengthwise, and chill well. Wrap in plastic wrap if chilling overnight. Slice about ¼ inch thick, and bake on cookie sheet. Bake in 425° oven 15–20 minutes, or until bread is golden brown and sausage well done. MAKES ABOUT 6 DOZEN SLICES.

—*Milam County Club*

Black-Eyed Pea Dip

4 cups black-eyed peas, cooked
and drained (may use canned)

5 small or 3 large jalapeños

1 tablespoon jalapeño pepper
liquid (optional)

1 can (4 ounces) chopped green
chilies

1 clove garlic, minced

½ pound Old English process
cheese, melted

1 cup (2 sticks) butter or
margarine, melted

Combine black-eyed peas, jalapeños and liquid, green chilies, and garlic in
blender or food processor. Melt cheese and butter together; stir into black-
eyed pea mixture. Serve hot or at room temperature, with nacho chips or
corn chips. *Perfect for a Cotton Bowl party!* MAKES ABOUT 6 CUPS OF DIP.

—*LaRee H. (Mrs. Ben) Morgan, Austin Club*

Guacamole

1 avocado, peeled, seeded, and
mashed

1 tablespoon chopped green chilies

1 teaspoon grated onion

1 tablespoon lemon juice

1 small tomato, chopped

½ teaspoon chili powder

dash of salt

Mix all ingredients thoroughly. *I always triple this recipe for my family of
four.* MAKES OVER A CUP.   —*Pat McCorstin, Garland Club*

Parsley Dip

1 egg

2 tablespoons tarragon vinegar

½ teaspoon prepared mustard

¼ teaspoon ground red pepper

½ teaspoon salt

1 clove garlic

1 cup parsley leaves

1 cup oil

Combine all ingredients through parsley in blender, and blend slowly. Add
the oil very slowly and continue to blend on high speed until mixture becomes thick. *This is also a good salad dressing for tossed salad, and for the
salad dressing, add 1 teaspoon curry powder.* MAKES ABOUT 1½ CUPS.

—*From* Another Hungry Aggie Cookbook, *Kingsville Club*

Artichoke Dip

1 large can (8½ ounces) artichoke
hearts, drained, squeezed dry,
and chopped

1 can (4 ounces) diced mild green
chilies

1 cup grated Parmesan cheese

1 cup mayonnaise (no substitute)

Combine all ingredients. Bake in 350° oven for approximately 20 minutes,
or until bubbly. Good with crackers or vegetables. MAKES ABOUT 3½ CUPS.

—Carol Baker, Lafayette, Louisiana, Club

Spinach Dip I (cold)

1 package (10 ounces) frozen
chopped spinach, thawed

1 small onion, finely chopped

1 can (8 ounces) water chestnuts,
finely chopped

1 cup sour cream

1 cup mayonnaise (no substitute)

1 package (1⅝ ounces) Swiss
vegetable soup mix

Squeeze moisture out of spinach by placing between paper towels. Pull
spinach apart and put into mixing bowl. Add remaining ingredients and
mix well. Chill overnight. *Good with chips or raw vegetables.* MAKES ABOUT
5 CUPS OF DIP. *—Tony Brown, Angelina County Club*

Spinach Dip II (hot)

1 package (10 ounces) frozen
chopped spinach, thawed and
well drained

1 package (8 ounces) cream cheese,
softened

½ cup mayonnaise

⅓ cup grated Parmesan cheese

2 tablespoons lemon juice

6 slices bacon, fried crisp, drained,
and crumbled

2 tablespoons green onions with
tops, chopped

Mix together all ingredients in large bowl. Heat in microwave oven 3–4
minutes at medium. Stir while warming. Serve warm with crackers. MAKES
AT LEAST 3 CUPS OF DIP. *—Maureen Thode, Fort Bend Club*

Vegetable Garden Dip (Low Calorie)

½ cup low-fat cottage cheese

1 cup plain low-fat yogurt

1 tablespoon finely grated carrot

2 teaspoons finely grated onion

1 teaspoon finely grated green
pepper

⅛ teaspoon garlic powder

Place cottage cheese in container of an electric blender; process until smooth. Transfer to bowl, and stir in remaining ingredients. Cover and chill. Serve with an assortment of raw vegetables (carrots, celery, zucchini, yellow squash, broccoli, peppers, etc.) About 12 calories per tablespoon. MAKES ABOUT 1½ CUPS.

—Rachel Gonzales, Past President (1983–84) of the Federation, San Antonio Club

Broccoli and Cheese Dip

1 package (10 ounces) frozen
chopped broccoli

1 box (1 pound) jalapeño process
cheese spread

1 can (10¾ ounces) golden
mushroom soup, undiluted

Cook broccoli according to package directions; drain. Add cheese and soup. Cook over medium heat, stirring frequently, until cheese is melted and mixture is heated throughout. Serve warm. *This may also be used as a topping for baked potatoes.* MAKES 4 CUPS.   —Betty Brashears, Lubbock Area Club

Cheese Dip

1 pound sharp cheddar cheese,
grated

16 slices crisp bacon, crumbled

12 green onions, chopped

1 cup slivered almonds, toasted

2 cups mayonnaise

Mix all ingredients in order. Almonds may be toasted in a 200° oven for 30 minutes before adding to other ingredients. Serve with crackers. MAKES ABOUT 6 CUPS OF DIP.   —Kay Thomas, Panola County Club

Chili Con Queso

1 large onion, chopped

1 large green pepper, chopped

2 tablespoons butter or margarine

2 pounds process cheese spread

1 can (10 ounces) tomatoes and diced green chilies

Sauté onion and pepper in butter or margarine until soft. Cut cheese into chunks for easier melting. Using low heat, add cheese and melt, stirring constantly. Add tomatoes and green chilies and blend thoroughly. Let mixture heat to blend flavors, but do not boil. Serve with corn chips. *Best if kept warm but also good cold.* SERVES 30 OR MORE.

—*Mrs. J. (Esther R.) Mancillas, Jr., Galveston Island Club*

Low-Cal Dip

1 8-ounce carton cottage cheese

1 small onion, chopped

2 to 3 tablespoons caraway seed

Mix together and refrigerate. Serve with chips. MAKES ABOUT 1½ CUPS.

—*Mrs. Tommy (Janet) Barre, DeWitt–Lavaca County Club*

Confetti Dip

3 egg yolks, beaten

3 tablespoons sugar

3 tablespoons white vinegar

½ teaspoon salt

2 tablespoons margarine

1 package (8 ounces) cream cheese, softened

½ cup finely chopped onions

½ cup finely chopped green pepper

1 jar (2 ounces) chopped pimientos

dash of Tabasco sauce

dash of Worcestershire sauce

Cook beaten egg yolks, sugar, vinegar, salt, and margarine in double boiler. Stir until thickened. Blend in cream cheese. Fold in remaining ingredients. Sugar may be adjusted to taste. Serve with chips or vegetable sticks. MAKES ABOUT 3 CUPS.

—*From* Hullabaloo in the Kitchen, *Dallas County Club*

Hot Dip for Cold Vegetables

1 jar (2½ ounces) sliced dried beef, snipped

1 package (8 ounces) cream cheese, softened

2 tablespoons milk

½ cup sour cream

2 tablespoons chopped onion

½ cup chopped green pepper (optional)

Mix all ingredients and put into baking dish. One-half cup chopped pecans, sautéed in butter, should be sprinkled on top. Bake at 325° for 30 minutes. Serve with raw vegetables. Dip may be prepared early, refrigerated, and then baked before serving. MAKES ABOUT 3 CUPS.

—*Jan Coggeshall, Aggie Mom and Mayor of Galveston, Galveston Island Club*

Green Onion Mousse

1 envelope unflavored gelatin

⅓ cup cold water

½ cup boiling water

1 carton (16 ounces) cottage cheese

½ cup mayonnaise

2 tablespoons lemon juice

3 green onions, chopped

5 drops green food coloring

1 teaspoon garlic salt

1 teaspoon onion flakes

1 tablespoon Worcestershire sauce

Tabasco sauce to taste (optional)

For garnishing: nuts, caviar, parsley, stuffed olives

Soften gelatin in ⅓ cup cold water; add ½ cup boiling water and stir until dissolved. Put cottage cheese and mayonnaise in blender container. Add lemon juice, onions, food coloring (you may want to substitute red at Christmas), garlic salt, onion flakes, Worcestershire sauce, and Tabasco sauce. Mix well. Add softened gelatin mixture and blend on low speed. Pour into fish-shaped mold (which has been chilled with ice water). Allow to set for several hours or overnight in refrigerator. Unmold and top with nuts and caviar. Garnish with parsley and stuffed olives. *Especially good served with party breads, smoked turkey, or smoked ham.* SERVES 8–10.

—*Harrison County Club*

Magic Spread

2 packages (3 ounces each) cream
   cheese, softened
2 tablespoons chopped celery
2 tablespoons snipped parsley
1 tablespoon chopped pimiento

⅓ cup grated raw carrot
2 teaspoons milk
1 teaspoon grated onion
dash of salt

Combine all ingredients. Cut bread into various shapes and spread with mixture. MAKES ABOUT 1½ CUPS.
        —*Milam County Club*

Artichoke Spread

2 cans (8½ ounces each) artichoke
   hearts
2 cups mayonnaise

1 package (0.07 ounces) Italian
   dressing mix

Drain and chop artichoke hearts. Mix with mayonnaise and dry dressing mix. Refrigerate and serve with crackers. MAKES ABOUT 4 CUPS.
        —*Mrs. Tommy (Janet) Barre, DeWitt–Lavaca County Club*

Jalapeño Cheese Spread

1 box (2 pounds) American cheese,
   grated
1 onion, chopped
6–8 jalapeño peppers, seeded and
   chopped

2 cups mayonnaise
garlic salt to taste

Mix all ingredients together and refrigerate in covered container. Serve with saltine crackers. This spread also makes a wonderful toasted sandwich. MAKES 7 CUPS.
        —*Mrs. Tommy (Janet) Barre, DeWitt–Lavaca County Club*

Hot Cracker Spread

1 package (8 ounces) cream cheese, softened

2 tablespoons milk

½ cup sour cream

¼ cup chopped green peppers

2 tablespoons onion flakes

1 jar (2½ ounces) dried beef, snipped

½ teaspoon garlic salt

¼ teaspoon pepper

TOPPING

½ cup nuts, chopped

2 tablespoons butter

½ teaspoon salt (optional)

Combine ingredients for the spread and spoon into dish for baking and serving. Mix the nuts, butter, and salt, and heat until crisp. Sprinkle on top of cheese mixture. Bake approximately 20 minutes at 350°. Serve warm with crackers. MAKES ABOUT 2 CUPS.   —*Carol Baker, Lafayette, Louisiana, Club*

Garlic Cheese Logs

3 packages (8 ounces each) cheddar cheese, grated

1 package (8 ounces) cream cheese, softened

1 cup chopped pecans

1 tablespoon garlic powder

paprika and chili powder for coating

Mix all ingredients well. Divide into two logs. Roll in a mixture of paprika and chili powder to taste. Cover or wrap in plastic wrap and refrigerate. Serve with round crackers. MAKES ABOUT 5 CUPS OF CHEESE.

—*Mrs. Tommy (Janet) Barre, DeWitt–Lavaca County Club*

Bacon and Almond Cheese Ball

1 pound American cheese, grated

1 package (8 ounces) cream cheese, softened

1 cup chopped toasted almonds

6 strips bacon, fried crisp and crumbled

4–5 green onions with tops, chopped

dash of salt

½ cup mayonnaise

Combine cheese, cream cheese, almonds, bacon, green onions, and salt. Mix in mayonnaise, and form into ball. If desired, roll in additional chopped almonds. Chill. (Ed. note: This makes so much you might want to form it into 2 balls and freeze one.) MAKES ABOUT 3 DOZEN SERVINGS.

—Buna Patterson, Matagorda County Club

Cheese Ball

1 package (3 ounces) cream cheese, softened

6–8 ounces process cheese spread, softened

1 cup chopped nuts

garlic salt to taste

chili powder

Combine cream cheese, process cheese spread, nuts, and garlic salt. Shape into ball; roll in chili powder. Wrap in waxed paper and chill. Serve with crackers. SERVES 8–10.

—Carol Baker, Lafayette, Louisiana, Club

Tuna Ball

1 package (8 ounces) cream cheese, softened

1 can (6½ ounces) tuna, packed in water, drained

¼ cup finely chopped onion

2 tablespoons fresh lemon juice

diced pepper to taste (may use jalapeño, green pepper, red pepper, etc.)

Mix all ingredients in bowl. Chill for 1 hour; form into ball. Serve with crackers or chips. SERVES 10–12.

—Kay Owens, Laredo Club

Party Strawberries

3 packages (3 ounces each)
   strawberry gelatin

1 can (14 ounces) sweetened
   condensed milk

2 teaspoons red food coloring

1 cup angel flake coconut

pinch of salt

½ teaspoon vanilla

1 jar (2.25 ounces) red candy
   crystals

1 jar (2.25 ounces) green candy
   crystals

Combine gelatin, milk, and food coloring; add coconut, salt, and vanilla. Stir well. Cover and refrigerate 1 hour. Remove and spoon out pieces of dough the size of walnuts onto cookie sheet. Refrigerate 1 more hour. Remove; roll and shape into strawberries. Roll each in red crystals; dip larger end into green crystals. Chill until time of serving. *Colorful and simple to prepare for parties.* MAKES 3½ DOZEN "STRAWBERRIES."

—*Sara Korczynski, Victoria County Club*

Spiced Nuts

1 cup sugar

½ teaspoon cinnamon

⅓ cup evaporated milk

1 tablespoon water

½ teaspoon vanilla

1½ cups unsalted nuts (pecans
   preferred)

Cook sugar, cinnamon, and evaporated milk in saucepan to 234° on candy thermometer (soft ball stage). Then add the other ingredients. Stir until nuts are well coated. Pour onto waxed paper. Break apart when cool. MAKES ABOUT 2 CUPS.

—*Clarice Bohls, Austin Club*

Home for a Holiday

Frozen Punch

6 cups sugar

4 cups boiling water

4 packages (3 ounces each) gelatin
  (peach recommended)

1 can (6 ounces) frozen lemonade

1 can (6 ounces) frozen orange
  juice

2 large cans (46 ounces each)
  pineapple juice

1 gallon water

1½ ounces almond extract

2 large bottles (33.8 ounces, or 1
  liter, each) ginger ale, chilled

Make a syrup of sugar and boiling water. Add any flavor gelatin to hot syrup. Stir well until dissolved. Cool syrup. Mix in lemonade, orange juice, pineapple juice, water, and almond extract. Freeze. (Freezes well in five half-gallon milk cartons.) Thaw at room temperature about 3 hours before serving. When ready to serve, add ginger ale. Punch will be slushy. *This is good for both formal and informal gatherings.* SERVES 100.

—*Mrs. Charles Patterson, West Bell County Club*

Reception Punch

2 large cans (46 ounces each)
  pineapple juice

2 cans (12 ounces each) frozen
  orange juice, thawed

1 bottle (6 ounces) lemon or lime
  juice

1 ounce vanilla

1 ounce almond extract

6 pounds granulated sugar

2 ounces citric acid (available at
  drug stores)

5 gallons water

Combine all ingredients and chill. Serve in punch bowl with cracked ice. Best if mixed several hours before serving. SERVES 80.

—*Elsie E. Krobot, Matagorda County Club*

Party Punch

2 large cans (12 ounces each) frozen lemonade, thawed

6 cans water (use lemonade cans)

½ large can (46 ounces) pineapple juice

3 bottles (33.8 ounces—1 liter each) ginger ale, chilled

ice ring with fruits added

Combine lemonade, water, and pineapple juice. Add ginger ale and ice ring just before serving. SERVES 30–40.   —*Milam County Club*

Banana Punch

1 can (46 ounces) pineapple juice

1 can (46 ounces) orange juice

5 crushed ripe bananas

juice of 1 lemon

6 cups water, heated

4 cups sugar

2–3 large bottles (33.8 ounces—1 liter each) ginger ale, chilled

Mash bananas in lemon juice and combine with pineapple juice and orange juice. Dissolve sugar in water. Cool and add to juice mixture. Freeze in containers; this makes 5½ quarts of base. Remove from freezer before serving. Add 2 or 3 bottles of chilled ginger ale over partially frozen base. SERVES 40–50.   —*Catherine Y'Barbo, Mid-Jefferson County Club*

Hot Mulled Punch

6 cups cranberry juice cocktail

8 cups apple juice

¼ cup brown sugar, packed

½ teaspoon salt

4 cinnamon sticks

1½ teaspoons whole cloves

Combine juices, sugar, and salt. Put cinnamon sticks and cloves in small cheesecloth bag. Heat for 10–15 minutes, but do not boil. Remove spice bag before serving. SERVES 20.   —*Edna M. Smith*

Slush Punch

1 large package (6 ounces) lime
  gelatin
2 cups sugar
2 cups boiling water
4 cups cold water

2 cans (46 ounces each) pineapple
  juice, or grapefruit juice or
  pineapple-orange juice
1–2 quarts lemon-lime soda

Combine gelatin and sugar; dissolve in boiling water. Add cold water and juice; mix well. Pour into three half-gallon milk cartons; freeze at least 24 hours. Remove from freezer 1½ hours before serving. Add soda. SERVES 30–40. —*Judy Hart, Brazos County Club*

Party Starters

5

Souper Suppers (And Other Fare)

Some of my favorite repasts might rightfully be called "little meals," because they don't include the standard number of courses. A Sunday night supper, an early lunch before a game, or a midnight spread all could include foods from this chapter. Your son or daughter might be driving through on the way to a football game, stopping just long enough for you to feed a hungry group of friends. These recipes will help you send them on their way full of your special brand of love.

Soups, stews, salads, and sandwiches are among those satisfying kinds of foods which can be prepared in advance (if you're warned!), or s-t-r-e-t-c-h-e-d if the number of guests is uncertain. You should select foods that can wait if necessary and can be prepared without too much wear and tear on the cook, the kitchen, or the budget.

Soup can be a great opening, or almost a meal in itself if it is the hearty kind. And almost every meal could use a salad—whether it is built of cool, crisp salad greens, the appealing colors and flavors of fresh fruits or vegetables, or a perfectly molded gelatin. A well-seasoned dressing for greens may be simple or complicated, but it should always be added sparingly and sprinkled rather than poured.

For extra heartiness, a soup and salad may be enhanced by the addition of sandwiches, muffins, or a special bread. Every nationality has its characteristic breads, which are perhaps the foods most closely connected with cultures. Breads may be the so-called quick bread variety, which are leavened with baking powder, soda, or steam. Homemade yeast breads take more time and effort to prepare, but they provide wonderful aromas and satisfying flavors and textures. For some people, they also provide cooking challenges, either real or imagined. If you are new to baking, my advice is to bake some bread with a friend. If you follow each step with an experienced bread baker, the yeast mystery, if it exists for you, will soon be solved.

Chilled Melon Soup

3 cups finely chopped ripe
 cantaloupe

3 cups finely chopped ripe
 honeydew melon

2 cups fresh orange juice, strained

⅓ cup lime juice

1 cup chilled sparkling white wine
 or champagne

½ cup plain yogurt, for garnish

½ cup sliced strawberries, for
 garnish

Set aside ½ cup each cantaloupe and honeydew melon. Puree the remaining melon in blender or processor, with orange and lime juices. Stir in reserved chopped melon. Refrigerate 3–4 hours. Just before serving, pour in the wine or champagne. Serve in chilled bowls, and garnish with a dollop of yogurt and sliced strawberries. SERVES 6–8.

—*Sandra B. Lydahl, West Bell County Club*

Mom's Bean Soup

2 cups mixed dried beans

10 cups water

ham bone or chunks of ham

smoked sausage, cut into bite-sized
 pieces

1 can (28 ounces) stewed tomatoes

1 green pepper, chopped

3–4 stalks celery, chopped

2 large onions, chopped

4–8 cloves garlic, chopped or
 pressed

1 bay leaf

Worcestershire sauce, Tabasco
 sauce, salt, and pepper to taste

juice of 1 lemon

Concoct a mixture of these or other dried beans: red beans, split peas, black beans, lentils, field peas, pinto beans, black-eyed peas, large lima beans, green lima beans, garbanzo beans, navy beans, crowder peas. Rinse beans well, cover with water, and soak overnight. Drain and add 10 cups (2½ quarts) water. Simmer beans, ham, and smoked sausage; stir occasionally, and add water if needed. Add rest of ingredients, through bay leaf, and simmer 1 more hour. Season to taste. Add lemon juice when you stop cooking. Cooking time is approximately 3½ hours. *I usually double or triple this recipe for crowds after a football game. Serve with French bread and salad. Here in Louisiana we are heavy on the Tabasco sauce so the soup is hot! Leftover soup freezes well.* SERVES 8.

—*Sally Chow, Lafayette, Louisiana, Club*

Calico Bean Soup
(or New Year's Day Bean Soup)

1 pound each of:

pinto beans

kidney beans

black-eyed peas

black beans

red beans

butter beans (limas)—3 sizes

navy, pea, and great northern
    beans

split peas

lentils

ham hock or ham bone (optional)

1 can (10 ounces) tomatoes and
    diced green chilies

1 clove crushed garlic or ⅛
    teaspoon garlic powder

juice of 1 lemon

1 large onion, finely chopped

3 ribs celery, finely chopped

½ handful of fresh parsley, snipped

salt and pepper to taste

Clean beans by removing all stones and bad beans from each package. Mix together and measure out *one pint* of mixed beans. Cover with water, add 1 tablespoon salt, and soak overnight. In the morning, pour off water and rinse beans. Cook in 3 quarts of water; add ham hock or ham bone, if desired, for more flavor. Simmer for about 3 hours, then add the other ingredients. Continue to simmer until thick. Serves a large crowd. *This is a great New Year's Day meal—serve with a spinach salad and hot bread.*

—*Betty Holmes, Amarillo Club*

Cream of Crab Soup

2 cans (10¾ ounces each) green
    pea soup

4 cans (10¾ ounces each) tomato
    soup

½ can (use soup can) dry sherry

½ can (use soup can) half and half

½ pound fresh crabmeat (or more)

Combine all ingredients in large heavy saucepan; mix well. Heat through, but do not boil. *Absolutely delicious—a family favorite.* SERVES 10.

—*Mrs. David E. (Joan) Varner, Houston Club*

Cheese Soup

¼ cup margarine

½ cup finely chopped celery

½ cup finely chopped onion

½ cup finely chopped carrots

2 cans (13½ ounces each) chicken broth

1 quart milk

¼ cup all-purpose flour

2½ tablespoons cornstarch

⅛ teaspoon baking soda

1 pound process cheese spread, grated

10 ounces longhorn cheddar cheese, grated

Melt margarine in large pot. Add celery, onion, and carrots; sauté until soft. Add broth and milk, reserving ½ cup milk. Combine flour and cornstarch in bowl; stir in reserved ½ cup milk until smooth. Add this to soup. Add soda and cheeses last. Cook at low heat until cheeses melt, stirring constantly. SERVES 6–8. *—Shirley McCutchen, Milam County Club*

E-Z Cheese Soup

1 package (24 ounces) frozen vegetables (potatoes, carrots, onion, celery)

2 cups water

2 chicken bouillon cubes

1 teaspoon parsley flakes

salt and pepper to taste

1 quart milk

3 tablespoons all-purpose flour

8 ounces process cheese spread, diced

dash of Beau Monde seasoning

Combine vegetables, water, bouillon cubes, parsley, salt, and pepper. Mix and simmer approximately 30 minutes until vegetables are tender. Mash vegetables. Add milk gradually, stirring constantly; add flour gradually, stirring constantly. Over low heat, add cheese and stir until melted. Do not boil. Add a dash of Beau Monde seasoning before serving. SERVES 6–8.

—Margie Kvinta, DeWitt–Lavaca County Club

Zucchini Bisque

1 can (10¾ ounces) condensed
   chicken broth, undiluted
½ cup water
2 medium zucchini, sliced
1 medium green pepper, sliced
1 medium onion, sliced

1 teaspoon dried basil
1 can (10¾ ounces) cream of
   potato soup, undiluted
1 cup half and half or milk
⅛–¼ teaspoon white pepper
minced fresh chives for garnish

Combine first six ingredients (through basil) in saucepan; bring to a boil. Cover, reduce heat, and simmer 20 minutes. Transfer vegetables with a slotted spoon to a blender container; add potato soup, and process until smooth. Return to saucepan; stir in half-and-half and white pepper, mixing well. Heat thoroughly and serve hot, or refrigerate and serve chilled. Sprinkle each serving with chives. MAKES 6 CUPS.

—Nell Bauer, Panola County Club

Potato Bacon Chowder

8 slices bacon
1 cup chopped onion
2 cups cubed, raw potatoes
2 cups water
1 can (10¾ ounces) cream of
   chicken soup

1 cup sour cream
1¾ cups milk
½ teaspoon salt
pepper to taste
2 tablespoons chopped parsley

Fry bacon until crisp; drain, crumble, and set aside. Sauté onion in small amount of bacon fat. Add potatoes and water. Bring to boil, cover, and simmer until tender. Stir in soup and sour cream. Gradually add milk, salt, pepper, and parsley. Add crumbled bacon. Heat to serving temperature, but don't boil. SERVES 6–8.

—From Hullabaloo in the Kitchen, *Dallas County Club*

French Dumplings for Soup

½ cup butter

1 cup water

1 cup all-purpose flour

3 eggs, well beaten

Melt butter in small saucepan; add water. When boiling, sift into the pan 1 cup flour, stirring constantly, until mixture slips from spoon. Let cool; add beaten eggs, stirring well. Shape into dumplings with small spoon; drop into boiling soup. Cover tightly and cook 3 minutes. *These are best in vegetable soup.*   —*Milam County Club*

Macaroni Salad

3 cups cooked macaroni, drained

¾ cup chopped ham

¾ cup chopped chicken

¼ cup diced celery

¼ cup minced onion

¼ cup green pepper, chopped

1 pimiento, chopped

½ cup mayonnaise

salt and pepper to taste

2 hard-cooked eggs, chopped (for garnish)

Combine all ingredients except hard-cooked eggs. Mix well. Garnish with chopped egg. MAKES 6–8 SERVINGS.   —*Inga Barrett, Titus County Club*

Yummy Rice Salad

1 tablespoon vinegar

2 tablespoons corn oil

¾ cup mayonnaise (no substitute)

1 teaspoon salt

½ teaspoon curry powder

1⅓–1½ cups uncooked rice

2 tablespoons chopped onion

1 cup chopped celery

1 package (10 ounces) frozen green peas, undercooked

Mix vinegar, oil, mayonnaise, salt, and curry powder. Following directions on package, cook rice until done but not overcooked. Add rice to curry mixture. Add onion while rice is hot. When mixture is cooled, gently mix in celery and peas. *Better the second day!* SERVES 6–8.

From Hullabaloo in the Kitchen, *Dallas County Club*

Vermicelli Salad

2 packages (10 ounces each) vermicelli

1 pint mayonnaise (no substitute)

3 tablespoons lemon juice

3 tablespoons monosodium glutamate

4 tablespoons corn oil or olive oil

1 can (4¼ ounces) chopped ripe olives

6 stalks celery with tops, chopped

1 green pepper, chopped by hand

1 small bunch green onions, chopped

1 jar (4 ounces) chopped pimientos, drained

Cook vermicelli according to package directions; drain well. Combine with all other ingredients until well mixed. Best if made ahead of time and refrigerated. —*Janice Thomas, Amarillo Club*

Frozen Avocado Grapefruit Salad

1 package (8 ounces) cream cheese, softened

1 carton (8 ounces) sour cream

¼ teaspoon salt

½ cup sugar

1 large avocado, peeled and cut into chunks

1 fresh grapefruit, peeled, trimmed, and cut into chunks

1 fresh orange, peeled and cut into chunks

2 ounces pecan pieces

Blend softened cream cheese with sour cream until smooth. Add salt and sugar; blend thoroughly. Carefully fold in avocado, grapefruit, orange, and pecans. Pour into 9-by-5-inch loaf pan and freeze until firm. Unmold by dipping into hot water until mold loosens. Slice into 1-inch slices and serve on salad greens, or serve as a loaf-shaped mold. *This recipe was a national winner in a frozen food contest.* SERVES 10–12.

—*Col. Fred W. Dollar and J. N. Maynard, TAMU Food Services Department*

Frozen Cranberry Salad I

1 pound cranberries, ground

2 cups sugar

1 cup miniature marshmallows

1 large can (20 ounces) crushed
   pineapple, well drained

1 pint whipping cream, whipped

½ cup chopped pecans

Wash berries; drain well. Grind berries in food grinder (with coarse blade) and place in large bowl. Add sugar and let stand for 2 hours. Add marshmallows and drained crushed pineapple. Whip cream and fold into mixture. Fold in chopped pecans. Pour into 9-inch-square pan or plastic container with lid and freeze overnight. SERVES 16.

—Jean Merkle, Brazos County Club

Frozen Cranberry Salad II

1 can (16 ounces) whole-berry
   cranberry sauce

1 cup sugar

4 small bananas, mashed

1 small can (8 ounces) crushed
   pineapple, drained

1 small carton (8 ounces) frozen
   whipped topping, thawed

Mix cranberry sauce and sugar together until sugar is dissolved. Add rest of ingredients and mix well. Put into freezer container and freeze until solid. SERVES 12–15.   *—From* Another Hungry Aggie Cookbook, *Kingsville Club*

Frozen Salad

1 can (14 ounces) sweetened
   condensed milk

1 small envelope whipped topping
   mix

1 can (21 ounces) cherry pie filling

1 small can (8 ounces) pineapple
   chunks, drained

1 teaspoon lemon juice

Prepare whipped topping mix according to directions on envelope. Fold in sweetened condensed milk, then cherry pie filling and drained pineapple chunks. Add lemon juice. Pour into 8-inch-square pan or dish; freeze until firm. Cut into squares and serve on lettuce leaf. (Ed. note: This makes a good, rich dessert.) SERVES 8.   *—Dorothy Lunday, Laredo Club*

Blueberry Salad

1 large package (6 ounces) black
    cherry gelatin
2 cups boiling water
1 small can (8 ounces) crushed
    pineapple and juice
1 can (15 ounces) blueberries,
    drained (reserve liquid)
water to make 1½ cups liquid with
    reserved juice

1 package (8 ounces) cream cheese,
    softened
½ cup powdered confectioners
    sugar
½ cup sour cream
¾ cup chopped nuts

Dissolve gelatin in boiling water. Add crushed pineapple and blueberries. Add cold water to blueberry juice to equal 1½ cups liquid; add to gelatin mixture. Pour into mold; refrigerate until set. Combine cream cheese, powdered sugar, and sour cream. Spread over gelatin that is firm. Sprinkle nuts on top. *Looks pretty prepared in a crystal bowl.* MAKES 6–8 SERVINGS.

—*Marilyn Anderson, Guadalupe County Club*

Quickie Fruit Salad I

1 large can (20 ounces) pineapple
    chunks (do not drain)
1 can (11 ounces) mandarin
    oranges, drained
1 can (16 ounces) fruit cocktail,
    drained

1 small bottle (6 ounces)
    maraschino cherries, drained
3 bananas, sliced
1 large package (6 ounces) instant
    French vanilla pudding mix

Combine pineapple chunks, pineapple juice, and remaining drained fruits with dry French vanilla instant pudding mix. Allow to stand for a short time; spoon onto bed of lettuce. SERVES 8.

—*Nancy Mayor, Montgomery County Club*

Quickie Fruit Salad II

1 large can (16 ounces) fruit
  cocktail (reserve juice)

1 large can (20 ounces) pineapple
  chunks (reserve juice)

1 small package (3½ ounces)
  vanilla instant pudding

2 tablespoons orange-flavored
  breakfast beverage crystals

2 bananas, sliced

Place drained canned fruit in medium mixing bowl. Save juices and add water in measuring cup to make 2 cups of liquid. Mix juices and water into pudding mix instead of milk. Add orange crystals and beat for 2 minutes. Add sliced bananas and pudding mix to fruit and mix well. Chill. SERVES 8.

—*Dorothy Lunday, Laredo Club*

Buttermilk Salad

1 large can (20 ounces) crushed
  pineapple, with juice

1 large package (6 ounces) lemon
  gelatin

2 cups buttermilk

1 large container (12 ounces)
  frozen whipped topping, thawed

1 cup chopped nuts (optional)

Combine pineapple, juice, and gelatin in saucepan; heat until boiling. Cool until mixture begins to thicken. Stir in buttermilk and thawed whipped topping. Add nuts if desired. Pour into oblong baking dish if salad is to be cut into squares for serving, or into a deep salad bowl. SERVES 12.

—*Betty Caesar, Waller County Club*

Almond Gelatin

2 envelopes unflavored gelatin

⅔ cup sugar

1½ cups evaporated milk

2½ cups water

2 tablespoons almond extract

Combine gelatin and sugar in large saucepan. Stir in evaporated milk and water. Heat, stirring constantly, until gelatin and sugar are dissolved. Let cool 20 minutes; stir in almond extract. Pour into 9-inch square pan; refrigerate until firm. Cut into diamonds. Serve plain or with mandarin oranges. *Our Aggie's favorite—an unusual recipe from several years ago.* SERVES 6.

—*Mary Lou Coleman, Austin Club*

Raspberry "Aggie Salad"

1 large package (6 ounces) raspberry gelatin (regular or sugar-free)

2 cups boiling water

1 box (10 ounces) frozen raspberries, partially thawed, with juice

1 can (16 ounces) applesauce

½ cup sour cream

1 tablespoon sugar

Add boiling water to gelatin, stirring until dissolved. Stir in raspberries; crush with spatula or potato masher. Add applesauce and mix well. Pour into 13-by-9-inch glass baking dish and chill. When firm, top with sour cream mixed with sugar. *This salad is good for any Aggie party and also wonderful at Christmas.* SERVES 8–10.   —*Joanie Abbott, Deep East Texas Club*

Strawberry Nut Salad

1 large package (6 ounces) strawberry gelatin

1 cup boiling water

2 packages (10 ounces each) frozen sliced strawberries, thawed, with juice

1 can (20 ounces) crushed pineapple, drained

3 medium bananas, mashed

1 cup coarsely chopped walnuts or pecans

1 pint (2 cups) sour cream

Combine gelatin with boiling water; stir until dissolved. Fold in strawberries with juice, drained pineapple, bananas, and nuts all at once. Pour one-half of the mixture into 12-by-8-inch dish, and refrigerate until firm. Spread sour cream over gelatin layer, and add remainder of gelatin mixture. Refrigerate until firm. Best if made a day ahead. *This has been a favorite recipe in our home for all the holidays—one of our family traditions.* SERVES 8.

VARIATION: You can increase the recipe to serve 10–12 by adding 1 small package (3½ ounces) gelatin, increasing the boiling water to 2 cups, and using 6–8 bananas.

—*Lena Grantham, Garland Club, and Paula Perkins, Orange County Club*

Pretzel Salad

2 cups crushed pretzels

¼ cup sugar

¾ cup (1½ sticks) margarine, melted

1 package (8 ounces) cream cheese, softened

1 cup sugar

1½ cups frozen whipped topping, thawed

1 large can (20 ounces) crushed pineapple, drained (reserve juice)

2 large packages (10 ounces each) frozen strawberries, drained (reserve juice)

1 large package (6 ounces) strawberry gelatin

Combine crushed pretzels, ¼ cup sugar, and the melted margarine. Press into 9-by-13-inch baking dish. Bake 10 minutes at 350°. Cool. Combine cream cheese and sugar, and fold in whipped topping. Spread over cooled pretzel mixture. Measure reserved pineapple and strawberry juices; add enough water to make 2 cups of liquid. Pour into saucepan; add gelatin and heat to boiling. Refrigerate until syrupy. Add pineapple and strawberries, and spread over cream cheese layer. Chill. *This salad may also be served as a dessert. Almost everyone who tastes it wants the recipe.* SERVES 10–12. —*Louise Johnson, Brazoria County Club*

Green Grape Salad

2 tablespoons margarine, melted

2 tablespoons all-purpose flour

1½ cups milk

24 large marshmallows

2 pounds green grapes (or tokay grapes, with seeds removed)

1 small can (8 ounces) crushed pineapple, drained

1 cup chopped pecans

Melt margarine; blend in flour. Add milk, stirring until smooth, and cook over medium heat until thick. Add marshmallows to the hot white sauce, and stir until melted. Cool. Wash grapes and remove stems. Mix grapes, pineapple, and pecans in a bowl. Pour cooled sauce over grape mixture, mix well, and chill. SERVES 6. —*From* The Hungry Aggie Cookbook, *Kingsville Club*

Broccoli Salad

2 packages (10 ounces each) frozen
  chopped broccoli

1 cup sliced green olives

½ cup chopped celery

3 hard-cooked eggs, chopped

mayonnaise to moisten, ¼–½ cup

Defrost broccoli and drain thoroughly. Combine with olives, celery, and hard-cooked eggs. Add mayonnaise to taste. Refrigerate 3–4 hours before serving. (Ed. note: sliced water chestnuts make a good, crunchy addition to this salad.) *This salad is super easy to fix; the recipe is always requested when I serve it for a luncheon.* SERVES 6–8.   —*Shirley Neal, Houston Club*

Dutch Slaw

3 pounds shredded cabbage

1 large onion, sliced thin

2 medium green peppers, sliced
  thin

1 cup sugar

DRESSING

⅓ cup vegetable oil

⅓ cup white vinegar

1 teaspoon dry mustard

1 teaspoon celery seed

1 teaspoon salt

Mix cabbage, onion, and peppers. Pour sugar over top and set aside. Cook dressing over medium heat until it comes to a boil. Pour hot dressing over mixture. Cool and store in refrigerator. Salad is better if made a day ahead and allowed to marinate; will keep 3 months. MAKES 12–14 SERVINGS.

—*Mary Ann Markey, Orange County Club*

Zucchini Salad

⅔ cup thinly sliced carrots

5 medium zucchini, thinly sliced

¼ teaspoon caraway seed (optional)

1 tablespoon chopped onion

⅛ cup white wine vinegar

¾ cup sugar

1 teaspoon salt

½ teaspoon pepper

⅓ cup salad oil

⅔ cup cider vinegar

½ cup chopped green pepper

½ cup chopped celery

Cook carrots until slightly soft; drain well. In large bowl combine all ingredients and refrigerate 6 hours or overnight. SERVES 6–8.

—From Hullabaloo in the Kitchen, *Dallas County Club*

Christmas Salad

1 head cauliflower, cut into bite-
  sized pieces

1 large can (6 ounces) ripe olives,
  drained and quartered

1 large green pepper, diced

¼ cup chopped green onion

1 small jar (2 ounces) diced
  pimiento

½ teaspoon salt

1 jar (18 ounces) Italian dressing

Combine all ingredients in large bowl; mix well after adding dressing. Cover and refrigerate for several hours. May be made a day ahead of time. SERVES 6–8.

—Vicki Spink, Kingwood Club

Home for a Holiday

Chef's Cabbage Salad

1 large head cabbage, shredded

¼ pound Kosher-style salami or Italian salami, sliced and cut into thin strips

¼ pound sliced American cheese, cut into thin strips

¼ pound sliced Swiss cheese, cut into thin strips

¼ pound sliced cooked ham, cut into thin strips

1 can (8 ounces) water chestnuts, drained and sliced

1 package (10 ounces) frozen peas, thawed, drained, but not cooked

1 bunch green onions, chopped

4 hard-cooked eggs

½ pound bacon, cooked and crumbled

DRESSING

1½ cups mayonnaise

1½ cups sour cream

2 tablespoons lemon juice

2 tablespoons sweet pickle relish

salt and pepper to taste

Place cabbage, cheeses, meats, water chestnuts, peas, and green onions in large bowl. Grate two of the hard-cooked eggs, and sprinkle over salad with the crumbled bacon. Toss with prepared dressing. Quarter the remaining two eggs, and use as a garnish on the top. *This is a meal in itself. May be served with chicken soup and French bread.* SERVES 12.

—*Dr. Barbara Flournoy, Angelina County Club*

Taco Salad

1 can (15 ounces) chili with beans, heated

2½ cups shredded lettuce

½ cup sliced ripe olives

1 medium tomato, chopped

1 cup guacamole

½ cup shredded cheddar cheese

2 cups corn chips

In two-quart salad bowl, layer hot chili, lettuce, olives, and tomato. Spoon on guacamole; top with shredded cheese and chips. SERVES 2–3.

—*Linda Nickens, Abilene Club*

Ham and Cheese Salad

5 slices (½-inch thick) of baked ham, cubed

1 package (10 ounces) cheddar cheese, cubed

2 apples, peeled and cubed

2 jars (4.5 ounces each) sliced mushrooms

1 large jar (4 ounces) diced pimientos

4 hard-cooked eggs, chopped

¼ cup diced onion

½ cup diced celery

salt and pepper to taste

mayonnaise to moisten (no substitute)

Combine all ingredients in large bowl. Add enough mayonnaise to mix well. Chill. SERVES 10–12.

—*Janet Barre, DeWitt–Lavaca County Club*

Spinach Make-Ahead Salad

1 large bunch spinach leaves, carefully washed and torn into bite-sized pieces

½ cup Swiss cheese, shredded or cubed

½ cup cheddar cheese, shredded or cubed

2 cups sliced fresh mushrooms

4 hard-cooked eggs, sliced

DRESSING

1 cup mayonnaise

½ cup sour cream

3 tablespoons milk

2 teaspoons lemon juice

2 teaspoons sugar

¼ cup finely chopped green onion

4 slices bacon, cooked and crumbled

Arrange torn clean spinach leaves in bottom of medium-sized glass bowl. Put cheeses on top. Spread mushrooms over cheese, and cover with sliced eggs. In small bowl combine thoroughly the mayonnaise, sour cream, milk, lemon juice, and sugar. Stir in onions. Spread completely over top of salad. Cover and chill overnight. To serve, remove cover, sprinkle bacon over top. *Romaine lettuce may used instead of spinach.* SERVES 6–8.

—*Delma H. (Mrs. Tim) George, Grayson County Club*

Mexican Salad

3 large tomatoes, diced

2 small cans (4 ounces each) diced
green chilies

2 small cans (2¼ ounces each)
sliced black olives

8 green onions, chopped

6 tablespoons vegetable oil

3 tablespoons vinegar

2 teaspoons garlic salt

½ teaspoon salt

½ teaspoon pepper

1 pound fresh mushrooms, thinly
sliced

Mix all ingredients together, and refrigerate in covered bowl for at least
two hours. Salad is better if made the night before. SERVES 10–15.

—Joan Richards, Panola County Club

Chicken Artichoke Salad

6–8 chicken breasts

2 boxes (8 ounces each) chicken
flavor rice and vermicelli mix

4 jars (3½ ounces each) chopped
marinated artichokes (reserve
marinade)

4 cups mayonnaise

8 green onions, chopped

1 medium-size green pepper,
chopped

2½ cups ripe olives, sliced

Cook chicken and cut meat into bite-sized pieces. Cook rice mix slightly,
using directions on box. Drain liquid from artichokes, and mix liquid with
mayonnaise. Combine all ingredients and chill overnight. SERVES 12–16.

—From Hullabaloo in the Kitchen, *Dallas County Club*

Golden Sandwiches

8 slices bread	4 slices ham
4 slices Swiss cheese	4 slices turkey
4 slices American cheese	4 slices chicken breast

BATTER

1¼ cups ice water	dash of salt
1 egg yolk, beaten	1 egg white, beaten until stiff
1½ cups self-rising flour	vegetable oil for frying

Makes 4 sandwiches using bread, cheeses, ham, turkey, and chicken. Cut into fourths, and secure with toothpicks. Set aside. To make batter, add half of water to beaten egg yolk; stir in flour, salt, and remaining water. Fold in beaten egg white. Dip sandwiches into batter. Fry in deep hot oil until golden brown. Drain on paper towels. *A pretty fruit cup would be a nice accompaniment.* MAKES 8 SERVINGS.

—*From* Hullabaloo in the Kitchen, *Dallas County Club*

Pig-a-Boos

1 large can (12 ounces) spiced ham luncheon meat	½ green pepper
	3 hard-cooked eggs
1 small package (8 ounces) process cheese spread, grated	12 finger rolls or Vienna rolls
	½–1 cup grated sharp cheese
¼ onion	

Grate the luncheon meat and cheese into a large bowl. Chop or dice the onion, pepper, and eggs; add to meat-cheese mixture and mix well. Stuff mixture into finger rolls that have been partly hollowed out; top with grated sharp cheese. Bake at 375° (or temperature suggested on roll package) until rolls are brown. Serve at once. MAKES 12.

—*Melba Spann, Titus County Club*

Maree's Open-Faced Sandwich

1 pound hot sausage

1 pound ground beef

1 pound process cheese spread

Brown meat well; drain off all fat. Melt cheese in separate pan and mix with meat. Spread on party rye, freeze, and wrap individually. When ready to serve, broil until lightly browned. A tablespoon of pizza sauce may be added on top (before broiling) for a different taste. *Great to keep on hand for a quick snack or for a party.* SERVES 16–20.

—*Mrs. Ednita W. Lane, Beaumont Club*

White Yeast Bread

2¾ cups very warm water

2 packages (¼ ounce each) dry yeast

4 tablespoons sugar

1 tablespoon salt

1 heaping cup nonfat dry milk

2 tablespoons corn oil

9 cups all-purpose or bread flour (approximately)

Measure water into a large mixing bowl; dissolve yeast and sugar. Add salt, dry milk, and corn oil. Add 4 cups of the flour, and beat until smooth. Add 3 more cups, and mix well. Keep adding flour and mixing well until dough is stiff and no longer sticks to the mixing bowl. Turn onto clean canvas-covered board (or waxed paper) that is lightly floured, and knead until smooth and elastic. Shape into ball, and place in lightly greased bowl. Grease surface of dough lightly. Cover and let rise in warm place until doubled in bulk. Punch down; let rise again until doubled. Divide dough into three equal portions. Shape each portion into a smooth ball; cover and let rest for 10 minutes. Shape into loaves, and place in greased 1-pound loaf pans. Let rise in warm place until doubled. Bake at 400° about 50 minutes. Loaves are done when they shrink from sides of pans, are golden brown, and have a hollow sound when tapped. Remove from pans, and cool top side up on racks. Do not cover while warm. *This bread keeps well frozen, and may be sliced first, for convenience. Slices may be buttered, wrapped in foil, and heated just before eating for delicious, hot, homemade bread that makes a simple meal "special."* MAKES 3 LOAVES.

—*Mrs. John F. (Becky) Schriever, Jr., San Angelo Club*

Cheese Bread

½ cup (1 stick) margarine or butter, melted

1 medium onion, finely chopped

1 teaspoon prepared mustard

poppy seed (to taste)

1 loaf French bread

1 package (8 slices) Swiss cheese

2 slices bacon

Sauté onions in margarine; add mustard and poppy seed. Cook, stirring occasionally, until onions are tender. Cut loaf into 16 slices; cut cheese slices in half. Spoon onion mixture on one side of each bread slice; place Swiss cheese on top of each slice. Assemble into loaf again; put bacon slices along top of assembled loaf. Wrap tightly in foil; do not put loaf on cookie sheet—put directly on oven rack. Bake 45 minutes at 350°. *Great as a study snack, or add a green salad for a light meal.* MAKES 16 SERVINGS.

—*Judi Woodward, Brazoria County Club*

Kraut Runzas

1 recipe of yeast roll dough

1 pound ground beef

1 medium onion, chopped

salt and pepper to taste

1 small head cabbage, chopped

Prepare roll dough according to directions. Do not let it rise. Steam ground beef and onion until done; add salt and pepper to taste. Steam cabbage separately in a very small amount of water for about 5 minutes. Mix cabbage and meat together; let cool. Roll out dough to ¼-inch thick. Cut into 4-by-6-inch rectangles. Spoon cooled mixture into center of dough, being very careful to keep edges dry of grease. Fold in corners and seal edges firmly. Place sealed side down on greased cookie sheet. Do not let rise. Bake immediately at 375° for 20–25 minutes, or until brown. *These come from the southeastern part of Nebraska. Sausage may be substituted for ground beef. They freeze well and are equally good cold or hot. Small ones may be used as appetizers.* MAKES 10–12 ROLLS. —*Gail Thompson, Brazoria County Club*

Swedish Butter Horns

1 cup butter, softened

2 cups all-purpose flour

1 egg yolk

¾ cup sour cream

¾ cup sugar

1 teaspoon cinnamon

¾ cup chopped nuts

powdered sugar icing, if desired

Mix butter and flour together until crumbly. Add egg yolk and sour cream, and chill 4 hours or overnight. Divide dough in half; roll each piece into a rectangle one-quarter-inch thick. Cut into triangles three inches at the bottom or smaller. Spread with mixture of sugar, cinnamon, and nuts (use half of mixture for each half of dough). Roll up each triangle, beginning at the larger end. Bake at 350° about 20 minutes. They may be glazed with a powdered sugar icing if desired. MAKES ABOUT 2 DOZEN.

—*Mrs. Raymond W. (Dorothy) Loan, Brazos County Club*

Extra Special Rolls

1 package (¼ ounce) dry yeast

3 tablespoons lukewarm water

½ cup vegetable shortening

1 teaspoon salt

1 cup hot water

2 eggs, beaten

½ cup sugar

4 cups all-purpose or bread flour

butter or margarine, softened

Dissolve yeast in lukewarm water and set aside. Add shortening and salt to hot water. Let stand until lukewarm. Beat eggs; mix in sugar. Add shortening and yeast mixtures. Stir in 2 cups flour and beat well with spoon. Add remaining flour gradually. Place in bowl, cover, and refrigerate overnight. Three hours before serving: With rolling pin, roll out dough in two or three rounds (depending on how large you want the rolls). Spread with soft butter or margarine. Cut pie-shaped wedges and roll up, starting at larger end. Let rise 3 hours on greased cookie sheets. Bake at 400° for 6 minutes. *These rolls are unbelievably light and will melt in your mouth.* MAKES 2–3 DOZEN ROLLS, DEPENDING UPON SIZE.

—*Barbara Boedeker, East Bell County Club*

Cottage Cheese Rolls

2 packages (¼ ounce each) dry
    yeast

½ cup very warm water

2 cups cottage cheese

¼ cup sugar

2 teaspoons salt

½ teaspoon baking soda

2 eggs, beaten

5 cups all-purpose or bread flour
    (approximately)

Dissolve yeast in very warm water. Heat cottage cheese in small saucepan over low heat until warm, but not hot. Remove from heat. In large mixing bowl, combine dissolved yeast, cottage cheese, sugar, salt, soda, eggs, and 1 cup of the flour. Beat at medium speed 2 minutes. Gradually stir in remaining flour to make a soft dough. Place dough in greased bowl. Cover and let rise in a warm place free from drafts until doubled in bulk (about 1½ hours). Turn dough onto a floured board. Divide into 24 equal balls. Place balls in two greased 9-inch round cake pans. Cover and let rise in a warm place until doubled (about 30 minutes). Bake at 350° for 20 minutes. MAKES 2 DOZEN ROLLS.
        —*Sandra Lehne, Austin Club*

Herb Breadstix

1 package (8) hot dog buns

1 cup (2 sticks) margarine, melted

½ teaspoon caraway seeds

½ teaspoon sweet basil

½ teaspoon onion powder

½ teaspoon garlic powder

¼ teaspoon leaf oregano

¼ teaspoon thyme

Cut each hot dog bun into four lengthwise pieces, making 32 sticks. Melt margarine, and add caraway seeds, basil, onion powder, garlic powder, oregano, and thyme. Brush each stick with mixture. Bake on cookie sheet in 300–325° oven 30–45 minutes, or until crisp. Sticks may need turning. *Good with salads, meals, or as snacks.* MAKES 32 STICKS.
        —*Grace B. Ffrench, Baytown Club*

Home for a Holiday

Hot Ham Sandwiches

½ cup (1 stick) margarine, softened

1 tablespoon poppy seeds

1 tablespoon onion flakes

¼ cup prepared mustard

12 or more potato rolls, split

1 pound ham slices, thinly shaved

1 pound Swiss cheese, sliced thin

Combine margarine, poppy seeds, onion flakes, and mustard. Spread split rolls with butter mixture. Add a few slices of ham and cheese. Wrap in foil, and heat in 350° oven until hot. May also be heated in microwave oven. *These may be prepared ahead of time and kept in the freezer. They are good with English pea salad, green salad, or fruit salad. I have these ready to serve after football games.* MAKES 12 SANDWICHES. —*Ruby Carpenter, Tyler Club*

Ham and Cheese Roll-Ups with Aggie Slaw

2½ pounds red cabbage, shredded

2½ pounds green cabbage, shredded

2 cups golden raisins

2 cans (20 ounces each) crushed pineapple, well drained

½ teaspoon salt

⅓ cup sugar

4 cups mayonnaise (no substitute)

68 slices ham (approximately 4 inches by 6 inches)

68 slices muenster cheese (approximately 4 inches by 6 inches)

Coarsely shred trimmed cabbages. Plump raisins in boiling water 5 minutes; drain and set aside. Completely drain pineapple in colander, pressing with back of spoon to remove juice. Combine salt, sugar, and mayonnaise; blend with raisins and pineapple. Stir into combined shredded cabbages. Layer one slice of cheese on one slice of ham. Place ¼ cup of slaw on ham and cheese. Roll up and secure with toothpicks. Repeat to make 68 Roll-Ups. For appetizer-sized servings, cut into smaller pieces and place on a bed of red cabbage leaves. Half of slaw mixture may be placed in a bowl in the center of the platter. Two Roll-Ups combined with fruit salad, crackers, or rolls are a good luncheon combination. *This recipe was prepared for an Aggie Moms' luncheon.* MAKES 68 ROLL-UPS OR 34 ½-CUP SERVINGS OF SLAW. —*Mrs. Frank W. (Juanita) Spillers, Brazoria County Club*

Roll-Ups

1 pound bologna

1 pound ham

1 jar (10 ounces) pickle relish

½ cup salad dressing

salt to taste

1 loaf sandwich bread (as fresh as possible)

½ cup (1 stick) margarine, melted

Grind meats together in food grinder or processor. Add relish, dressing, and salt. Cut crusts off sandwich bread. Spread meat mixture on bread and roll up. Place on cookie sheet. Using a brush, spread melted margarine on top of rolls. Bake at 250° until light brown. Serve warm. *Sandwich rolls may be spread and frozen until ready to use.* MAKES ABOUT 2 DOZEN ROLL-UPS.

—*Charlotte Foreman, Orange County Club*

Muffins (with variations)

2 cups sifted all-purpose flour

3 teaspoons baking powder

½ teaspoon salt

2 tablespoons sugar

1 egg, beaten until frothy

1 cup milk

¼ cup melted butter

Mix flour, baking powder, salt, and sugar. Beat egg until frothy; stir in milk and melted butter. Add liquid to flour mixture all at once; stir quickly until just mixed but still lumpy. Fill greased muffin cups two-thirds full. Bake at 425° about 25 minutes. MAKES ABOUT 14.

VARIATIONS: (1) Sprinkle tops of unbaked muffins with ½ cup finely chopped apple. Combine ¼ cup sugar and ½ teaspoon cinnamon; shake over apple. (2) Combine ½ cup raisins and ½ cup chopped walnuts; add to sifted dry ingredients. (3) Add ¾ cup raw cranberries, chopped, and ¼ cup sugar to sifted dry ingredients. (4) Add ½ cup crisp chopped bacon to sifted dry ingredients. (5) Fill muffin cup one-third full; put 1 teaspoon jelly, jam, or marmalade in each cup; add remaining batter. (6) Add ¾ cup grated sharp cheddar cheese to sifted dry ingredients.

—*Mrs. W. Wade (Cora Lee) Darsey, San Angelo Club*

Sausage on Rye

1 pound hot sausage, crumbled

1 pound ground beef, crumbled

¼ cup onions, chopped

1 tablespoon oregano

1 teaspoon Worcestershire sauce

1 teaspoon garlic salt

1 pound process cheese spread, cut in cubes

2 loaves party rye bread

Brown meats and onions together and drain fat. Add the oregano, Worcestershire sauce, garlic salt, and cheese to the meat and onion mixture and heat until the cheese is melted. Spread the meat-cheese mixture on the party bread. Freeze in single layers on a cookie sheet; transfer to zippered bag. Do not thaw before baking at 400° for 10 minutes. Serve hot. *These are great for parties—men love them!* MAKES 48 INDIVIDUAL SERVINGS.

—*Carolyn Hartman, West Bell County Club*

Summer Sausage

5 pounds ground beef

½ teaspoon garlic powder

½ teaspoon onion powder

1 tablespoon mustard seed

6 tablespoons quick-curing salt (not table salt)

2 tablespoons liquid smoke

2 tablespoons cracked pepper

2 cups water

Put ground beef in one bowl. Combine all other ingredients in another bowl and mix well. Pour over ground beef, and mix well. With *wet* hands, form mixture into four 2½-inch-diameter rolls. Wrap rolls separately in foil. Refrigerate 24 hours. Poke holes in bottom of each foil roll in three places. Place on broiler rack, filling broiler pan about one-third full of water. Bake 90 minutes at 325°. Turn off oven, but keep sausage rolls in for another 30 minutes. Unwrap and place on paper towels to blot grease. Rewrap in plastic wrap and foil. Refrigerate or freeze. To use immediately, slice and serve with crackers or bread, cheese, and mustard. *Great while watching football on TV.* SERVES 24–30. —*Janet Schroeder, Kingwood Club*

Yummy Pizza Loaves

1 large loaf French bread, split
  lengthwise

butter or margarine, softened, to
  spread on both halves

1 pound ground chuck

garlic powder, seasoned salt, and
  red pepper to taste

1 small carton (8 ounces) sour
  cream

1 jar (14 ounces) pizza sauce

½ cup chopped onion (green
  onions preferred)

1 large green pepper, chopped

1 small can (2¼ ounces) sliced ripe
  olives, drained

1 small can (4 ounces) sliced
  mushrooms, drained

chopped jalapeño pepper
  (optional)

⅔ cup grated sharp cheddar cheese

⅔ cup grated (or equivalent slices)
  mozzarella cheese

Slice French bread lengthwise; spread with butter or margarine on each half. Brown chuck; add garlic powder, seasoned salt, and red pepper. Drain off fat, and mix in sour cream. Spread a layer of pizza sauce on one side of bread; add meat mixture. Drizzle with more pizza sauce. Add onion, green pepper, olives, mushrooms, and jalapeño (if desired). Top with cheddar and mozzarella cheeses. Add a layer of pizza sauce on other half, and put loaf together on large piece of foil. Cover loosely for baking at 350° until cheese melts—20–30 minutes. For a crisper loaf, uncover during last 5 minutes of baking. Cut into slices. *As the mother of two Aggie football players, I know better than to pretend that this would feed 6–8 hungry athletes! But it's delicious, filling, and much cheaper than buying pizza. Add a large salad, and get out your electric knife for easy slicing. Also good cold, so these loaves could go tailgating.* SERVES 6–8.   —*Wanda Walker, Port Arthur Club*

Double-Decker Pizza

DOUGH

1 package (¼ ounce) dry yeast
1 cup warm water (105–110°)
3½ cups all-purpose flour

2½ teaspoons sugar
½ cup dry onion flakes
2 tablespoons olive oil

TOMATO SAUCE

1 cup chopped onion
1½ tablespoons olive oil
2 cans (14½ ounces each)
tomatoes, drained
2 cloves garlic, minced

½ teaspoon salt
½ teaspoon pepper
1 bay leaf
1 cinnamon stick
½ teaspoon oregano

FILLING

¾ pound sweet Italian sausage
¾ pound mozzarella cheese, grated
2 cups sliced mushrooms

2 medium green peppers, sliced
⅔ cup grated Parmesan and
Romano cheeses

To make dough: Dissolve yeast in warm water; set aside. Combine flour, sugar, onion flakes, and olive oil. Mix well; let rise 45 minutes. To make sauce: Sauté onion in olive oil. Add tomatoes, garlic, salt, pepper, bay leaf, cinnamon stick, and oregano. Let simmer until thick. Remove bay leaf and cinnamon stick. Divide dough in half. Roll dough to fit 8- or 9-inch iron skillet, extending up sides. Spoon on sausage, mozzarella cheese, mushrooms, and half of the green peppers. Roll out second half of dough, putting on top of first layer of ingredients; seal edges. On top of second crust layer, add tomato sauce, Parmesan and Romano cheeses, and remaining green pepper. Bake 45 minutes at 450°. SERVES 3–4.

—*Anne Cassens, Orange County Club*

"Not Ever Enough" Cinnamon Rolls

2 cakes yeast or 2 packages dry
    yeast (not rapid rise type)

¼ cup lukewarm water

1 cup milk, scalded

¼ cup butter

½ cup sugar

1 teaspoon salt

2 eggs, well beaten

5 cups all-purpose flour

melted butter

brown sugar

cinnamon

chopped pecans (optional)

Soften yeast in lukewarm water; stir until dissolved. Combine milk, butter, sugar, and salt, and cool to lukewarm. Add beaten eggs and dissolved yeast. Add flour, and turn out on floured board. Knead in rest of flour to make soft dough. Do not add any flour after dough has risen. Put in greased bowl, cover, and let rise until doubled in bulk. Turn dough out on floured board. Roll into a rectangle about ¼ inch thick. (You may want to divide dough before rolling.) Spread dough with melted butter; sprinkle with cinnamon, brown sugar, and pecans if desired. Roll up tightly from the long side. Cut slices ½ inch thick. Place in greased pan ½ inch apart. Bake at 350° on top rack until light brown (about 15 minutes). *I usually double this recipe so there are some to take back to school. This is my grandmother's recipe.* MAKES ABOUT 2 DOZEN ROLLS.

—*Dee Brents, Fort Worth/Tarrant County Club*

Swedish Nut Ring

1 package (¼ ounce) dry yeast

¼ cup warm water

¾ cup milk, scalded

¼ cup shortening or margarine

¼ cup sugar

½ teaspoon salt

1 egg, beaten

3½–4 cups all-purpose flour

2 tablespoons butter or margarine,
    softened

½ cup finely chopped nuts

¼ cup brown sugar

chopped nuts and maraschino
    cherries for garnish

Dissolve yeast in warm water; set aside. Scald milk; add shortening, sugar, and salt. Cool to room temperature. In large mixing bowl, combine yeast,

1 beaten egg, milk mixture, and flour. Beat well. When dough leaves sides of bowl, turn out onto floured surface. Knead 5 minutes. Place in greased bowl, and allow to rise in warm place until doubled in bulk (at least 1 hour). Punch down; roll into rectangle 18-by-7 inches and ½ inch thick. Spread with butter; sprinkle with nuts and brown sugar. Roll (jelly-roll style) from long side, sealing edges. Shape into ring on baking sheet, with the seal on the bottom. Tuck ends inside each other. Make 6 slashes partly through on top. Cover and put in a warm place to double again. Bake at 350° for 20–25 minutes, or until golden brown. Glaze with powdered confectioners sugar and water glaze while warm, if desired. Sprinkle with chopped nuts and cherries. SERVES 12. —*Anne Cassens, Orange County Club*

Bran Bread

1½ packages yeast

1 cup warm water

1 cup high-fiber bran cereal

1 cup *hot* water

½ cup sugar

1 cup (2 sticks) margarine,
   softened

1 teaspoon salt

2 eggs

6–7 cups all-purpose or bread
   flour

Add yeast to warm water and set aside. Add bran to hot water and set aside. In large mixing bowl, cream together the sugar, margarine, and salt. Add eggs and mix well. Add the yeast and bran mixtures, and mix all thoroughly. Add 4 cups of the flour, stirring well. Add remaining flour gradually, and mix well. Cover and let rise until doubled—about 1½ hours. Place on floured board, and knead well. Make into rolls or loaves, and place in greased baking pans. Cover and let rise again (30–60 minutes). Bake loaves for 35 minutes at 350° (longer if you like it browner), and rolls at 400° for 15 minutes. *This is a favorite of friends and family. Our Aggie expects bran bread to be waiting at home and also to travel back to school. Freezes and mails well.* MAKES 3 LOAVES. —*Mary Wyly, Amarillo Club*

Pão Doce (Holiday Sweet Bread)

3 tablespoons sugar

2 packages (¼ ounce each) active
   dry yeast

½ cup lukewarm potato water

1 cup mashed potatoes

⅛ teaspoon ginger

½ cup milk, scalded

2 teaspoons salt

6 eggs

1¾ cups sugar

½ cup melted butter or margarine

8 cups all-purpose flour

1 egg, beaten (for topping)

Add sugar and yeast to warm potato water; stir until dissolved. Blend in mashed potatoes and ginger. Set aside to rise until doubled in bulk. Scald milk, add salt, and cool to lukewarm. Beat eggs; add sugar gradually while continuing to beat; stir in cooled butter. Combine yeast and egg mixtures; blend thoroughly. Add scalded milk; stir in 2 cups of the flour. Beat 5 minutes. Add remaining flour gradually, kneading when dough becomes too stiff to beat. Turn out on floured board, and knead 10 minutes, adding only enough extra flour to prevent sticking. Place dough in large oiled bowl, cover, and let rise in warm place until doubled in bulk. Divide dough into 4 portions; shape into round loaves on oiled cookie sheets or place in oiled loaf pans. Allow to rise until doubled in bulk. Brush loaves with beaten egg. Bake at 350° for 30–50 minutes or until brown. MAKES 4 LOAVES. —*Naomi Turpin, Amarillo Club*

Kolache

2 cups milk
½ cup sugar
½ cup vegetable shortening
2 teaspoons salt
1 or 2 yeast cakes (0.6 ounces
   each)

3 egg yolks
5–6 cups all-purpose flour
fruit fillings of your choice
melted butter for brushing tops

In small saucepan, heat milk just until bubbles form around edge of pan; remove from heat. Add sugar, shortening, and salt, stirring until shortening is melted. Let cool to lukewarm. Pour lukewarm milk mixture into large mixing bowl; sprinkle yeast cake(s) over, stirring until yeast is dissolved. Add egg yolks, and 1½ cups of the flour, beating until smooth. Add remainder of flour gradually, beating until dough is smooth and leaves sides of bowl. Turn out onto lightly floured pastry board. Knead until dough is satiny and elastic. Place in lightly greased large bowl; cover with towel. Let rise in warm place until doubled in bulk (about 1 hour). Punch down dough. Turn out onto lightly floured pastry board; knead 10–15 times. Shape dough into balls, and place on greased cookie sheet. Flatten by placing thumb into balls. Add a spoonful of your favorite filling in the indentation. Let rise until double in size. Brush tops with melted butter. Bake at 350° for 15–20 minutes. When done, sprinkle tops with Kolache Crumble.

KOLACHE CRUMBLE

½ cup sugar
½ cup all-purpose flour

4 tablespoons butter, slightly
   softened
½ teaspoon vanilla

Mix sugar and flour together. Cut in the butter, and add the vanilla. Crumble between your fingers until well mixed. Sprinkle on kolache rolls. *This is an old family recipe which has been handed down through the generations.* MAKES ABOUT 2 DOZEN KOLACHES.   —*Jo Ann Kolar, Victoria County Club*

Old-Fashioned Sticky Buns

5½–6½ cups all-purpose flour

2 packages (¼ ounce each) active
  dry yeast

½ cup sugar

1½ teaspoon salt

½ cup butter or margarine,
  softened

1½ cups very warm (120°) tap
  water

2 eggs

2 teaspoons cinnamon mixed with
  ⅓ cup sugar

6 tablespoons butter or margarine,
  softened (additional)

vegetable oil

These old-fashioned buns feature an easier, new-fashioned preparation. Combine 2 cups flour, *undissolved* yeast, sugar, and salt in large mixing bowl. Stir well to blend. Add butter and hot tap water. Beat with electric mixer at medium speed for 2 minutes, scraping bowl occasionally. Add eggs and 1 more cup of flour. Beat at high speed for 1 minute or until thick and elastic. Gradually stir in just enough of remaining flour (2½–3½ cups) with wooden spoon to make a soft dough which leaves sides of bowl. Turn out onto floured board and knead 5–10 minutes, or until dough is smooth and elastic. Cover with plastic wrap and a towel. Let rest 20 minutes on board. Punch down. Divide dough in half. Roll each half into a rectangle 18 by 12 inches. Spread with 3 tablespoons of the additional softened butter, and sprinkle with half of cinnamon mixture. Beginning at long side, roll dough and seal edges. Cut each roll into 18 slices. Place cut side down in pans which have been well greased and have the following caramel sauce in the bottom of each.

CARAMEL SAUCE

1 cup light brown sugar

1 cup light corn syrup

¼ cup butter or margarine

Mix brown sugar, corn syrup, and butter together in saucepan; bring to a boil. Reduce heat. Simmer for 1 minute. Pour equal amounts in baking pans (three 8-inch-square pans work well), which have been greased. Cool sauce before adding rolls. Brush dough lightly with oil. Cover pans loosely with plastic wrap. Refrigerate 2–24 hours. When ready to bake, remove from refrigerator. Uncover. Let stand 10 minutes while preheating oven to

375°. Bake for 20–25 minutes on a lower oven rack. Turn out of pan immediately so that sticky caramel sauce runs over the buns. May be prepared the night before and then popped into the oven in the morning for fresh rolls for breakfast. MAKES 3 DOZEN STICKY BUNS.

—*Carol Cupples, Kingwood Club*

Cherry-Go-Round Coffee Cake

1 cup milk, scalded

½ cup sugar

1 teaspoon salt

½ cup (1 stick) margarine

1 envelope (¼ ounce) dry yeast

¼ cup warm water

1 egg

4 cups all-purpose flour, divided

FILLING

½ cup brown sugar

½ cup all-purpose flour

1 can (16 ounces) sour pie
  cherries, drained

½ cup chopped pecans

½ cup (1 stick) margarine, melted

Scald milk in saucepan; stir in ½ cup sugar, salt, and 1 stick margarine. Let mixture stand until lukewarm. Dissolve yeast in water, and add to milk mixture. In large mixing bowl combine milk mixture, egg, and half the flour. Beat until smooth. Add 2 more cups flour and mix well. Cover tightly with plastic wrap or foil, and put in refrigerator. Dough may be filled and baked anytime after 2 hours but within the next 2 days. To make filling, combine brown sugar, flour, drained cherries, and pecans. Cut dough in half; roll each half into oblong 14 by 7 inches. Spread with melted margarine; spread with cherry mixture. Roll up from long side and seal edges. Form two rings on greased baking sheet, with sealed edges down. Cut two-thirds of the way through rings at 1-inch intervals. Twist each section sideways. Cover with towel, and let rise in warm place until doubled (1 hour or more). Bake at 375° about 25 minutes. Top with drizzled powdered sugar icing while warm. Second ring may be frozen until needed. *These have gone to the Fightin' Texas Aggie Band, home football games, and final reviews.* SERVES 24 (OR 12–15 AGGIES).

—*Jackie Jenson, Baytown Club*

Bran Refrigerator Rolls

1 cup vegetable shortening

1 cup boiling water

¾ cup sugar

1 cup high-fiber bran cereal

1½ teaspoons salt

2 cakes yeast

1 cup lukewarm water

6 cups (or more) all-purpose flour

2 eggs, beaten

melted butter or margarine (for topping)

Combine shortening, boiling water, sugar, bran cereal, and salt; let cool. Dissolve yeast in lukewarm water; add to cooled bran mixture. Stir in flour (gradually) and add beaten eggs; mix thoroughly. Roll out in circle on floured surface, ½ inch thick. Cut into triangles; brush with melted butter or margarine. Roll up, starting at large end of triangles. Place on greased baking sheets. Let rise for about 1½ hours. Bake in 450° oven until golden brown. Unused dough may be stored, covered, in refrigerator. *In our home, no holiday meal would be complete without these rolls.* MAKES 36 ROLLS.

—*Marilyn Anderson, Guadalupe County Club*

Aggie Cinnamon Rolls

2 packages (¼ ounce each) yeast (or use 1 rapid rise package)

½ cup warm water

1 teaspoon sugar

1 cup milk, heated

⅓ cup margarine or butter

⅓ cup sugar

1 teaspoon salt

1 cup cold water

2 eggs

7–8 cups all-purpose flour

Combine yeast, warm water, and 1 teaspoon sugar; set aside to rise. Heat milk; add margarine, sugar, and salt, stirring until dissolved. Add cold water. In large mixing bowl, beat eggs; add yeast mixture, mixing well. Add cooled liquid. Gradually add flour to make a stiff dough. Divide dough in half, and knead in mixer or by hand. Grease a large bowl, put dough in, cover, and set in a warm place to rise until double in size—45 minutes to 1 hour. In the meantime, prepare filling.

FILLING

½ cup (1 stick) margarine

1½ cups sugar

2 teaspoons cinnamon

½ cup chopped pecans and raisins (optional)

Melt margarine, and set aside to cool. Combine sugar, cinnamon, pecans, and raisins. When dough has doubled, cut in half. Place half on floured surface and roll into rectangle. Cover surface with half of melted margarine. Sprinkle with half of filling mixture, and spread evenly. Roll from long side (as for jelly roll); seal and slice in 1-inch slices. Place in well-greased baking pan, with sides nearly touching. Repeat with second half of dough and filling. Place in warm place to rise until double (about 30 minutes). Bake at 350° for 25–30 minutes, or until light brown. While still hot, pour the glaze over it.

GLAZE

1 box (16 ounces) powdered confectioners sugar

½ cup water or milk, heated

2 tablespoons butter or margarine

Combine powdered sugar, hot water or milk, and butter or margarine; mix well, and pour over rolls. Best eaten hot, but can be frozen. MAKES ABOUT 4 DOZEN ROLLS.   —*Jo Nell Carter, Deep East Texas Club*

Buttermilk Rolls

1 cup buttermilk

1 teaspoon salt

¼ teaspoon baking soda

¼ cup sugar

1 package (¼ ounce) yeast

¼ cup warm water

2 tablespoons vegetable oil

3 cups all-purpose flour

Heat buttermilk to boiling point. Mix in salt, soda, and sugar. Cool somewhat. Dissolve yeast in warm water. Mix with buttermilk, oil, and flour. Cover and let rise on board for 15 minutes. Roll out and cut with biscuit cutter. Put rolls in greased pan, cover, and let rise for 1½ hours. Bake in 375° oven about 30 minutes or until golden brown. MAKES 15 ROLLS.

—*Jo Ann Stoner, Amarillo Club*

THE 12ᵀᴴ MOM. ᴀTᴍ

6

The Twelfth Mom

Leave it to the Twelfth Mom. She stands ready, too, in her kitchen instead of at the stadium. Since 1922 the Texas A&M student body has stood during football games, indicating their readiness to serve as part of the team if needed. The support has become more symbolic than real, but traditions are—well, traditional at A&M, and spirit-building is a most important ingredient in the nurturing of a Texas Aggie.

This chapter could be subtitled "Feeding a Small Army," since most of the recipes included will serve ten or more (although several moms caution in their recipes that the servings are not necessarily Aggie-sized). Mom is usually ready to serve whatever is called for—a reception, a buffet supper, or the main dishes at a church supper. Planning is the secret to serving more than your usual number of family members; don't laugh at list-making. Using some make-aheads are musts, too, since entertaining needs to be fun for the host and hostess as well as the guests.

Barbecues have always been a favored way to feed the hungry. The outdoor meal may be served from a picnic table beneath a shade-giving tree, or on a deck, or beside a swimming pool. Many men enjoy cooking outside and develop their own "specialties of the house" (or patio, or backyard, or boat).

Serving in a casual way is not governed by the time of day or the location. Breakfasts, luncheons, and brunches are popular meals for entertaining guests. Buffets may be casual or not, but are most definitely an easy way to serve a large group. The word buffet has turned into an adjective meaning "serve yourself." Maybe it's just another way of showing your willingness to be a part of the team.

Marinated Green Beans

3 cans (16 ounces each) French cut green beans, drained

1 medium onion, sliced into thin rings

8 strips bacon, fried crisp and crumbled

½ cup slivered almonds

⅓ cup sugar

⅓ cup vinegar

3 tablespoons bacon grease

Drain beans and put into casserole dish. Top with onion rings, crumbled bacon, and almonds. In separate bowl, mix together the sugar, vinegar, and bacon grease. Pour over casserole, and marinate for several hours or overnight in refrigerator. Bake at 350° for 45 minutes. *This is a great recipe to prepare ahead of time. I use it often.* SERVES 10 OR MORE.

—*Ruby Carpenter, Tyler Club*

Baked Beans

8 slices of bacon

1 cup brown sugar

1 teaspoon dry mustard

½ teaspoon garlic powder

½ teaspoon salt

½ cup vinegar

4 large onions, chopped

1 can (15 ounces) butter beans, drained

1 can (15 ounces) green beans, drained

1 can (15 ounces) lima beans, drained

1 can (15 ounces) dark red kidney beans, drained

1 can (11 ounces) baked beans and juice

Fry bacon; drain, crumble, and set aside. Add to bacon grease: brown sugar, dry mustard, garlic powder, salt, and vinegar. Stir and blend. Add onions; cover and cook 20 minutes on low. Combine onion mixture with all beans, and bake in a 13-by-9-inch pan for 1 hour at 350°. Beans may also cook all day in a slow cooker on low. Sprinkle on bacon at serving time. SERVES 12.

—*Elsie (Mrs. Glenn) Dressen, Brazoria County Club*

Rice and Broccoli Casserole

1 package (10 ounces) frozen broccoli (or equivalent fresh)

margarine for sautéeing

½ cup chopped onions

½ cup chopped celery

1 can (10¾ ounces) cream of mushroom soup, undiluted

1½ cups cooked rice

salt and pepper to taste

1 cup grated cheese

Cook broccoli according to package directions; drain. Sauté onions and celery in margarine until slightly limp but not brown. Combine broccoli, onions, celery, soup, rice, salt, and pepper in greased casserole. Sprinkle with cheese. Bake at 350° for 30 minutes. Freezes well. SERVES 8–10.

—*From* Hungry Aggie Cookbook, *Kingsville Club*

Baked Corn

2 cans (17 ounces each) whole kernel corn, drained

1 can (17 ounces) cream style corn

1 egg, beaten

1 tablespoon margarine

1 tablespoon all-purpose flour

salt, pepper, and paprika to taste

Combine corn, egg, margarine, flour, salt, and pepper in greased 13-by-9-inch baking dish. Sprinkle with paprika. Bake at 350° approximately 45 minutes. SERVES 12. —*Ollie Pickering, Orange County Club*

Hominy Casserole

4 cans (15½ ounces each) yellow hominy, drained

½ cup (1 stick) margarine

1 medium onion, chopped

2 cans (10¾ ounces each) cream of mushroom soup

1 small jar (8 ounces) pasteurized process cheese spread (jalapeño is good)

crushed corn chips for topping

Butter large baking dish. Brown onion in margarine; combine with hominy, soup, and cheese spread; mix well. Sprinkle crushed corn chips on top, and bake at 350° until bubbly, approximately 30 minutes. *I ate this for the first time at a church supper. It has been a winner ever since.* SERVES 8–10.

—*Johnnie Young, Fort Worth/Tarrant County Club*

Sweet Potato Soufflé

3 cups mashed sweet potatoes
  (fresh or canned)
1 cup sugar
½–1 cup evaporated milk or
  homogenized milk
1 teaspoon vanilla (optional)

½ cup melted butter
2 eggs, beaten
spices (optional): ¼ teaspoon
  ground cloves, ½ teaspoon
  cinnamon, ½ teaspoon nutmeg

Combine all ingredients in mixer. Mix until lumps are gone, and mixture is creamy. Pour into 14-by-9-inch buttered baking dish. Bake at 350° for 30–35 minutes. Remove from oven, and add one of the following toppings.

TOPPING I

1 cup brown sugar, packed
⅓ cup all-purpose flour

⅓ stick butter, melted
1 cup chopped nuts

TOPPING II

¾ cup crushed cornflakes
½ cup light brown sugar

½ cup chopped pecans
¼ cup (½ stick) butter, melted

For either topping, combine ingredients and crumble over the hot casserole. Return to oven and bake 10 minutes more. *Great for buffets and for holidays. Many friends said they were not sweet potato eaters until they tasted this excellent fluffy casserole. Almost as good as dessert.* SERVES 8–10.

—*Melba Fussell, Mid-Jefferson County Club, Esther Matera, San Antonio Club, and Mrs. Fred L. (Mildred) May, Past President of Federation (1975–76), San Antonio Club*

Cranberry Salad

1 large box (6 ounces) raspberry
  gelatin
2 cups sugar
3 cups boiling water
1 package (16 ounces) fresh
  cranberries

1 can (8 ounces) crushed pineapple
1 cup diced celery
1 cup chopped pecans

Mix dry gelatin with sugar; add boiling water, and stir until dissolved. Set in refrigerator to chill. Grind fresh cranberries. Add cranberries, crushed pineapple, celery, and pecans to gelatin mixture. Chill until firm. *Can be made ahead of time; will keep up to a week in the refrigerator.* SERVES AT LEAST 14. —*Pat Payne, Orange County Club*

Apricot Delight Salad

1 large can (28 ounces) apricots, drained and chopped (reserve liquid)

1 large can (20 ounces) crushed pineapple, drained (reserve liquid)

1 cup reserved fruit juice

1 large package (6 ounces) orange gelatin

2 cups boiling water

¾ cup miniature marshmallows

TOPPING

½ cup sugar

3 tablespoons all-purpose flour

1 egg, slightly beaten

1 cup juice (reserved from above)

2 tablespoons butter

½ pint whipping cream, whipped

6 ounces sharp cheddar cheese, grated

Drain and chill fruit. Dissolve gelatin in boiling water, and add 1 cup of fruit juice. Pour into 9-by-13-inch pan. Chill until partially set. Fold in fruit and marshmallows; spread with topping. To prepare topping, combine sugar, flour, and egg. Stir in remaining 1 cup of fruit juice and cook over low heat, stirring constantly until thickened. Add butter and cool thoroughly. Fold in whipped cream. Spread on top of congealed salad and sprinkle with grated cheese. Cut into squares. *This has been a family favorite for years. It goes well with any meat entrée and is especially nice to serve around the holidays.* SERVES 12. —*Mrs. William G. (Judy) Jolly, Jr., Houston Club*

Twelfth Mom

Pineapple-Cranberry Salad

1 pound fresh cranberries

1¾ cups sugar

1 can (20 ounces) crushed
   pineapple, with juice

1 cup chopped pecans

1 pound miniature marshmallows

1 large container (12 ounces)
   frozen whipped topping, thawed

Grind cranberries; combine with sugar, and let set in refrigerator overnight. Combine crushed pineapple, pecans, marshmallows, and whipped topping. Fold in sweetened cranberry mixture. This stores well and may be frozen. *My younger son loved this recipe when I prepared it for the family one Christmas. He called it "Pink Stuff," and it became a tradition in our home every holiday menu thereafter.* MAKES 10–12 SERVINGS.

—*Mary Beth Guy, Jasper County Club*

Ukrainian Borsch

2 pounds soup meat, cubed

½ pound lean smoked pork
   (optional)

2½ quarts water

1 bay leaf

6 peppercorns

1 clove garlic

1 cup carrots, chopped

1 cup celery greens, chopped

½ cup onion greens, chopped

¼ cup parsley, chopped

8 medium beets

1 cup shredded cabbage

3 large potatoes, peeled and
   chopped

6 tomatoes, peeled and chopped

1 cup cooked navy beans (optional)

1 tablespoon vinegar

1 teaspoon sugar

1 tablespoon all-purpose flour

1 tablespoon butter

sour cream for garnish

Put soup meat in deep kettle; cover with 2½ quarts water. Bring to a boil; cover for 15 minutes. Skim; add bay leaf, peppercorns, garlic, carrots, celery, onion, and parsley. Simmer, covered, for 2 hours. Cook 7 of the beets, unpeeled, in soup or separately. Peel remaining beet and grate. Mix with 3 tablespoons water and set aside (this is for coloring, to be added at the last moment). When beets are tender, peel and dice. Add beets to soup, along with cabbage, potatoes, tomatoes, and beans (if desired). Add vinegar and sugar. Cook for another hour. Skim off excess fat. Thicken soup with flour, browned separately in butter; bring to a boil. Add beet juice drained from raw beet for color. Serve hot in large soup plates or bowls. Garnish with dollop of sour cream. *A complete meal in itself—a cross between American stew and American boiled dinners. I combined several old and new cook book recipes to make the one my family likes best.* MAKES 3 QUARTS.

—Vicki Spink, Kingwood Club

Super Potato Casserole

8 potatoes

½ cup butter, melted

½ cup milk, heated

salt, pepper, and garlic powder to
   taste

grated Parmesan cheese

1 bunch green onions with tops,
   chopped

1 pint sour cream

3 eggs

bread crumbs

cheddar cheese, grated

paprika

Peel potatoes; boil until tender; drain. In large mixer bowl, place potatoes, melted butter, and hot milk. Mix until mashed and smooth. Add salt, pepper, garlic powder, Parmesan cheese, and green onions. Stir in sour cream and eggs. Place in large greased casserole; sprinkle with bread crumbs, cheddar cheese, and paprika. Bake at 300° for 30–40 minutes, or until set. SERVES 10–12.

—Maggie Jahn, Past President of Federation (1985–86), DeWitt–Lavaca County Club

Company Chicken Salad

6 cups diced cooked chicken

4 cups diced celery

6 tablespoons lemon juice

2 cups chopped pecans

4 cups halved seedless white
   grapes

1½ cups mayonnaise

olives and sweet pickles to taste
   (chopped)

2 cups sour cream

½ cup diced pimientos

Combine chicken, celery, lemon juice, pecans, grapes, mayonnaise, olives, and sweet pickles (if desired); mix well. Fold in sour cream and pimientos. Chill well. SERVES 16–20.

—Ruth Walters, Orange County Club

Chicken Spinach Casserole

1 hen or 2 large frying chickens, cooked and boned (reserve stock)

¼ cup butter

¼ cup all-purpose flour

1 cup milk

½ package (10 ounces) of small, flat egg noodles

1 pint sour cream

⅓ cup lemon juice

2 teaspoons seasoned salt

1 teaspoon monosodium glutamate (optional)

½ teaspoon cayenne

1 teaspoon paprika

1 teaspoon salt

1 teaspoon pepper

1 can (6 ounces) mushroom stems and pieces, with juices

1 can (8 ounces) diced water chestnuts

1 small jar (2 ounces) diced pimientos

½ cup chopped onion

½ cup chopped celery

1 package chopped frozen spinach, cooked and drained

1½ cups grated Monterey Jack cheese

Cook chicken in seasoned water until tender; remove and cut into large bite-sized pieces (at least 4 cups). Reserve stock. Melt butter in large saucepan; stir in flour. Add milk and 1 cup reserved chicken stock. Cook over low heat, stirring constantly, until sauce thickens. Cook noodles; drain well. To thickened cream sauce add sour cream, lemon juice, seasoned salt, monosodium glutamate, cayenne, paprika, salt, and pepper; mix well. Fold in noodles, spinach, mushrooms, water chestnuts, pimientos, onion, and celery. Butter a 3-quart casserole; put in a layer of cream sauce–noodle mixture, then a layer of chicken. Repeat layers of sauce and chicken until used up. Top with grated cheese. Bake in 350° oven until bubbly, about 25 minutes. SERVES 8–10.

—*Wanda (Mrs. E. A.) Pauler, Past President of Federation (1979–80), Beaumont Club*

Home for a Holiday

Chicken Gourmet

1 can (10¾ ounces) cream of mushroom soup

1 can (10¾ ounces) cream of celery soup

1 can (10¾ ounces) cream of chicken soup

1 medium green pepper, chopped

5 green onions (with tops), chopped

1¼ cups uncooked long grain rice

½ cup (1 stick) margarine, melted

6 chicken breasts, split

1 teaspoon salt

1 teaspoon pepper

2 teaspoons paprika

Combine soups, green pepper, onions, and rice in large bowl. Add ¼ cup of the melted margarine. Pour mixture into a 9-by-13-inch baking pan sprayed with nonstick cooking spray. Lightly season chicken breasts with salt and pepper, and place them on top of the soup mixture. Drizzle the remaining margarine over the chicken, and sprinkle with paprika. Cover with foil, and bake in a 250° oven for 2½ hours. *This is a very versatile dish. It may be assembled the night before, refrigerated, and baked the next day. You need to add only a salad and crusty hot rolls for a complete meal. Try lemon bisque for dessert.* SERVES 10–12.　　　　　—*Mary Beth Guy, Jasper County Club*

Chicken Spectacular

3 cups cooked chicken

1 package (6 ounces) long-grain and wild rice, prepared according to package directions

1 can (10¾ ounces) cream of celery soup

1 medium jar (4 ounces) chopped pimientos

1 medium onion, chopped

2 cups French-style green beans, drained

1 cup mayonnaise (no substitute)

1 can (8 ounces) diced water chestnuts

salt and pepper to taste

Combine all ingredients, and pour into 2- or 3-quart casserole. Bake 25–30 minutes at 350°. *To make ahead and freeze, do not bake prior to freezing. If you precook the onions, you need only to heat.* SERVES 8–10.

—*Milam County Club*

Twelfth Mom

Chicken Tetrazzini

6 pounds boned, cooked chicken, cut into bite-sized pieces (reserve stock)

¼ cup (½ stick) margarine

1 green pepper, chopped

1 large onion, chopped

1 cup (2 sticks) margarine

⅔ cup all-purpose flour

2 cups milk

salt and pepper, to taste

½ pound Old English cheese, sliced or diced

½ pound American cheese, sliced or diced

1 can (6 ounces) mushrooms

1 pound spaghetti or vermicelli, cooked in chicken stock

Prepare chicken, reserving 2 cups stock. Sauté green pepper and onion in ¼ cup margarine. Set aside. Make a white sauce with 2 sticks margarine, flour, milk, salt, pepper, and chicken stock. Cook until mixture begins to thicken, stirring constantly. Add Old English and American cheeses, and stir until melted. In large bowl, combine peppers, onions, cheese sauce, mushrooms, chicken, and spaghetti; mix well. Pour into large casserole, and bake at 350° until heated through and bubbly—at least 30 minutes. SERVES 12–14. —*Mrs. Delores Rothmann, Mid-Jefferson County Club*

Chicken and Rice Casserole

1 large frying chicken

½ cup chopped onion

½ cup chopped celery

seasoned salt and pepper to taste

1 package (6 ounces) wild and long grain rice mix (discard seasoning packet)

3 cups water

1 tablespoon butter

1 can (10¾ ounces) cream of mushroom soup, undiluted

1 can (10¾ ounces) cream of chicken soup, undiluted

½ can (6 ounces) water chestnuts, sliced

1½ cups chicken broth (reserved from cooking chicken or canned broth)

2½ cups crushed corn flakes

½ cup melted butter

Stew chicken with onion, celery, and seasonings in small amount of water until tender. Reserve broth. Remove chicken from bones while still warm, then dice. Combine rice mix (without seasoning packet), water, and butter in saucepan with tight-fitting lid; simmer for 15 minutes. Combine diced chicken, cooked onion and celery, rice, soups, water chestnuts, and broth in 13-by-9-inch baking dish. Top with crushed corn flakes and melted butter. Bake at 350° about 50 minutes, or until lightly browned on bottom. *This casserole may be put together and frozen to be baked later.* SERVES 10–12.

—*Mrs. James M. Edwards, Brazos County Club*

Spaghetti Delight

4 large onions, chopped

3 cloves garlic, minced

1 large green pepper, chopped

1 cup vegetable oil

2 cans (10¾ ounces each) tomato soup

1 can (15 ounces) tomato sauce

1 can (12 ounces) whole kernel corn

2 cans (6 ounces each) sliced broiled mushrooms (reserve liquid)

1½ pounds lean ground beef

1 package (16 ounces) spaghetti, cooked according to package directions

salt, pepper, and red pepper to taste

1 pound grated American cheese

Sauté onions, garlic, and green pepper in oil. Add soup, tomato sauce, and corn. Simmer ground beef in liquid from mushrooms. Add with mushrooms to tomato mixture. Prepare spaghetti according to directions, drain, and combine with tomato mixture. Season to taste. Add half of the grated cheese. This is a thick mixture. Divide into two buttered 3-quart casseroles. Sprinkle remaining cheese on top of each casserole. Cover; bake 35–45 minutes at 350°. Freezes nicely before baking. *This is a great dish following a football game. I like to use an extra pound of meat and additional cheese.* EACH CASSEROLE SERVES 8. —*Merlene Bravenec, East Bell County Club*

Fiesta Spaghetti

½ cup vegetable oil

2 large onions, chopped

2 ribs celery, chopped

2 cloves garlic, crushed

1 pound lean ground beef

1 can (4 ounces) mushroom stems and pieces, with juice

3 cans (6 ounces each) tomato paste

2½ tablespoons chili powder

2 teaspoons salt

1 cup water

1 pound thin Italian spaghetti, cooked according to package directions

½ pound cheddar cheese, grated

¾ cup evaporated milk

Saute onions, celery, and garlic in oil. Add ground beef, and cook until gray and crumbly. Add mushrooms, tomato paste, chili powder, salt, and water. Simmer over low heat 15 minutes. In a separate kettle, boil spaghetti according to package directions (until semi-tender). Drain well. In greased 2½-quart casserole, layer spaghetti, meat mixture, and half of grated cheese. Pour evaporated milk over the layers, and top with remaining cheese. Bake 20–30 minutes at 350°. *The evaporated milk may sound a bit unusual, but don't omit it, because the dish is delicious. I got this recipe from an early TV cooking show and have served it to hungry crowds ever since. It is very economical; just add a tossed salad and garlic bread, and your meal is complete.* SERVES 12.   —*Diane S. Thompson, Mainland Club*

Mama Renée's Spaghetti Sauce

2 pounds ground top round (ground twice)

6 medium onions, chopped

½ cup (1 stick) butter

1 small bunch parsley, chopped

2 large cans (28 ounces each) tomatoes

3 cans (6 ounces each) Italian tomato paste

3 paste cans of water

2 green peppers, chopped

4 garlic cloves, finely chopped

1 or 2 cans mushrooms (any size)

1 pound sharp cheese, grated

1 tablespoon Worcestershire sauce

1 teaspoon mustard

peel of 1 lemon, grated

salt, black pepper, red pepper and/ or Tabasco sauce, to taste

Brown meat and onions in butter. Add chopped parsley, tomatoes, tomato paste, water, green pepper, and garlic. Cook 1 hour, making a thick sauce. During the last 15 minutes, add mushrooms, cheese, Worcestershire sauce, mustard, lemon peel, salt, pepper, red pepper and/or Tabasco sauce. A good "meatless" sauce may be made by omitting the ground beef, adding a half-pound or more of grated cheese, 1 more green pepper, and doubling the mushrooms. Serve with pasta of your choice, prepared according to package directions. *This can also be cooked slowly for 3 hours or so before cheese is added. Freezes very well.* SERVES 12.

—*Mrs. Frank E. (Renée) Vandiver, Honorary President of Federation*

Hungarian Goulash

3 tablespoons vegetable shortening

3 medium onions, chopped

2 cloves garlic, chopped

1½ pounds ground beef

1 package (8 ounces) wide noodles

1 can (8 ounces) tomato sauce

1 pound cheddar cheese, diced

1 can (4 ounces) sliced mushrooms, with liquid

1 small can (2¼ ounces) sliced ripe olives

¾ cup water

2 teaspoons Worcestershire sauce

dash of Tabasco sauce

In a large skillet, melt shortening; add onions and garlic, and cook very slowly. Add ground beef, and cook until slightly brown. Cook wide noodles in separate pan according to package directions; drain. Add the tomato sauce, cheese, mushrooms, olives, water, Worcestershire sauce, and Tabasco sauce. Add to meat mixture; mix well. Pour into buttered casserole—one large or two medium—and sprinkle with cheese. Bake at 350° until bubbly and slightly browned, 30–45 minutes. *This casserole may be put together a day ahead and refrigerated or frozen. Serve with hot garlic bread and a tossed salad.* SERVES 12. —*Mrs. Ralph (Evelyn) Streckfuss, Waller County Club*

Company Lasagna

1 pound Italian sausage (or pork sausage)

1 clove garlic, minced

1 tablespoon whole basil

1½ teaspoons salt

1 large can (28 ounces) tomatoes

2 cans (6 ounces each) tomato paste

10 ounces lasagna

3 cups cottage cheese

1 cup grated Parmesan cheese

2 tablespoons parsley flakes

2 beaten eggs

1 teaspoon salt

½ teaspoon pepper

1 pound sliced mozzarella cheese

Brown meat slowly; spoon off excess fat. Add garlic, basil, salt, tomatoes, and tomato paste. Simmer uncovered, 30 minutes, stirring occasionally. Cook lasagna in large amount of boiling salted water until tender; drain and rinse. Combine cottage cheese, Parmesan cheese, parsley, eggs, salt, and pepper. Place half the lasagna in 13-by-9-inch baking dish; spread with half of the cottage cheese filling; add half of the mozzarella cheese and half of the meat sauce. Repeat layers. Bake at 375° about 30 minutes. Let stand 10 minutes before cutting into squares. *May assemble early and refrigerate; allow 15 minutes longer in oven.* MAKES 12 SERVINGS.

—*Inga Barrett, Titus County Club*

Easy Lasagna

1 pound ground beef

1 large jar (32 ounces) thick spaghetti sauce

1½ cups water

2 cups small-curd cottage cheese

3 cups (12 ounces) shredded mozzarella cheese

2 eggs

¼ cup chopped parsley

1 teaspoon salt

½ teaspoon pepper

8 ounces lasagna noodles, uncooked

grated Parmesan cheese for topping

Brown ground beef; drain fat. Add spaghetti sauce and water; simmer about 10 minutes. Combine cottage cheese, mozzarella cheese, eggs, parsley, salt, and pepper in large bowl; mix well. Pour 1 cup meat sauce in bottom of 13-by-9-inch baking pan. Layer 3 pieces of uncooked lasagna over sauce; cover with 1½ cups meat sauce. Spread half of cheese filling over sauce. Repeat with layers of lasagna noodles, sauce, and cheese filling. Top with remaining sauce and grated Parmesan cheese. Cover with foil and bake at 350° for 55–60 minutes. Remove foil, and bake 10 minutes longer. Allow to stand about 10 minutes before cutting. *No need to cook lasagna noodles separately—this works!* SERVES 8–10. —*Pat Bielamowicz, Garland Club*

Lasagna

1 large yellow onion, chopped

4 cloves garlic, chopped

½ cup parsley, chopped

½ cup celery leaves, chopped

¼ cup olive oil

2 pounds ground chuck

3 cans (15 ounces each) tomato sauce

3 cans (6 ounces each) tomato paste

2–3 sauce cans water

¼ teaspoon ground cloves

salt and pepper to taste

canned mushrooms (amount may vary), or fresh mushrooms, sliced

1 tablespoon sugar

1 box (16 ounces) lasagna noodles, prepared according to package directions

3 packages (8 ounces each) shredded mozzarella cheese

1 package (8 ounces) Romano cheese, grated

2 packages (8 ounces each) cream cheese, sliced, *or* mix together in blender 2 cups cottage cheese and 2 eggs

salt and pepper to taste

Put onion, garlic, parsley, and celery leaves in food processor and chop until fine. Brown vegetables in ¼ cup olive oil. Add ground chuck to browned vegetables and brown, stirring often. Pour off any excess fat. Add tomato sauce, tomato paste, and 2 or 3 sauce cans (30–45 ounces) of water to meat mixture. Add cloves, salt, and pepper to taste. Drain mushrooms; add to sauce. Bring to a boil; cover and simmer for 2–3 hours. During the last ½ hour, add 1 tablespoon sugar. After cooking noodles, lay on paper towels and pat dry. Layer lasagna as follows: Cover bottom of two 14-by-11-inch baking pans with sauce. Lay noodles on top of sauce. Cover

noodles with sauce; add sliced cream cheese or cottage cheese mixture, mozzarella cheese, and Romano cheese. Repeat until you have three layers. Bake at 350° for 1 hour, or until completely baked through and bubbly. *Lasagna may be made ahead of time and refrigerated or may be frozen.* MAKES 20 SERVINGS.
—*Mary Louise Giamfortone, Mainland Club*

Joan Varner's 6-Hour Roast

6-pound rump roast (lean, boneless, and rolled)

salt, pepper, and garlic salt to taste

½ bottle (10 ounces) steak sauce

suet (4-by-6-inch piece)

Rub roast with salt, pepper, and garlic salt; spread with steak sauce. Put suet on top and wrap in freezer paper. Freeze completely seasoned. To cook, remove from freezer, remove paper. Cook frozen at 225° for 6 hours. During last hour of cooking baste with the following.

SAUCE

⅓ cup water

1 teaspoon garlic salt

½ cup steak sauce

Mix together, and baste every 20 minutes during last hour of cooking. *Great for a buffet; serve with Parker House rolls.* SERVES 18.
—*Mrs. David E. (Joan) Varner, Houston Club*

Aggie Stew

1½ –2 pounds ground chuck

2 tablespoons margarine

1 large onion, diced

4 green onions, diced

3 stalks of celery, diced

1 small green pepper, diced

2 tablespoons chili powder

1 tablespoon sugar

1 can (16 ounces) tomatoes, with juice

1 can (15 ounces) chili-flavored red beans

1 can (17 ounces) whole kernel corn

6 medium potatoes, diced

approximately 4 cups of water

Brown ground beef in margarine. Add other ingredients in order listed above. Bring to a boil. At this point, stew may be put into a slow cooker and left to simmer on low all day. Simmer until potatoes are done. *This has always been a favorite for after-the-game or for feeding a houseful of boys.* SERVES 8–10.

—*Mary Ann Murphy, Brazoria County Club*

Bevo-Beater Beef Stew

25 pounds stew meat

salt and pepper, to taste

6 gallons water

1 teaspoon garlic powder

1 jar beef base

10 pounds onions, cut into large chunks

10 pounds potatoes, cut into chunks

12 pounds carrots, cut into chunks

1½ pounds all-purpose flour

4 ounces salt (by weight)

1 tablespoon ground pepper

2 tablespoons chili powder

Sprinkle meat with small amount of salt and pepper. Brown meat. Add 5½ gallons of the water, beef base (a commercial product which comes in a 1-pound jar; condensed beef bouillon could be substituted with a reduction in water), and garlic powder. Simmer for 1 hour, 15 minutes. Add carrots, potatoes, and onions. Cook for 45 minutes, or until tender. Combine flour, salt, pepper, and chili powder with remaining ½ gallon water. Mix with a wire whip. Add slowly to the stew, stirring constantly to prevent lumping. Serve with corn muffins or biscuits. *Beef stew is one of the most requested entrées at Cain Hall; it is prepared in an enormous cooking pot, as you might imagine.* YIELDS APPROXIMATELY 100 SERVINGS (BUT NOT NECESSARILY 100 AGGIE ATHLETES).

—*Myrt Davidson, Manager, Cain Hall*

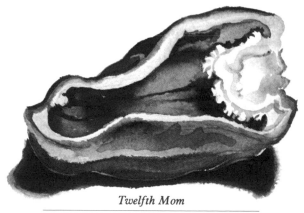

Twelfth Mom

7

Ready When You Are

There seems to be precious little time for mom and dad to visit with a son or daughter who has gone off to college. Even when the student comes home for a visit, there are friends to see, places to go, maybe even laundry to wash. When the family finally sits down to relax together, mom will not want to miss the latest campus news because she has to run off to the kitchen to fix dinner. And she will not have to if she plans well and, especially, if she knows how to take advantage of that marvelous invention, the microwave oven.

Microwave cooking is no longer the wave of the future—it is the wave of the present. It has been estimated that half of all American homes would include a microwave oven by the end of 1986. Some of these oven owners are students, who may even have learned their first cooking by this miraculous method; some dormitories even offer microwave privileges to residents. Many more users are the busy moms who are enjoying them for their convenience. With the help of a microwave oven many parts of meal preparation can be completed very quickly and easily.

Although microwave ovens generally do not replace conventional cooking appliances entirely, automatic microwave cooking is tasty, easy, efficient, and cool. The thawing that might need to be done at a moment's notice is not only possible but fast. Melting, sautéeing, softening, heating, and reheating are frequently accomplished in seconds. Leftovers take on renewed glamour when reheated in a microwave.

Notwithstanding all of these pluses, microwaving cooking is different and requires the new oven owner to spend some time reading the manual, studying a good microwave cookbook, and then doing some experimenting. Microwaves are waves of energy, not heat. There is no hot air involved; food is cooked by microwaves traveling directly to the food itself. Microwaves are either reflected, passed through, or absorbed, depending upon the material contacted, and foods are materials that absorb the waves. Because timing is critical *and* different, instructions should be carefully followed for best results. Most foods, for instance, require stirring or turning a quarter-turn at least once—usually halfway through—for even cooking. The recipes in this chapter should all be prepared that way.

And who knows—maybe microwave cooking will prompt a role reversal, with son or daughter giving cooking instructions to mom.

MICROWAVE TIPS (Adapted from the bulletin of the Microwave Oven and Appliance Center, Houston)

1. If you use a wooden spoon to stir items for a short time, you do not need to remove the spoon each time you stir.
2. When seasoning with salt, you can add it to the water in cooking vegetables, but should add it only at the end in cooking meats. Salt draws out the moisture in cooking meats.
3. Use your microwave oven to soften rapidly foods which should be "spreadable"—cold icings, frostings, cheese spreads from a jar (remove metal cover), honey, butter, cream cheese (remove foil wrap), or other spreads, etc.
4. Dry herbs from your garden by placing between paper towels and heating 1 or 2 minutes until they can be crumbled.
5. Warm baby's bottle 30–40 seconds for 4-ounce bottle or 1 minute for 8-ounce bottle.
6. Having difficulty shelling nuts? Try this: Place about 2 cups of nuts with 1 cup water in 1-quart casserole. Cook 4–5 minutes. Nut meats slip out whole after cracking.
7. Use olive oil on meats to keep juices inside.
8. To get more juice out of a fresh lemon, microwave 45 seconds.
9. For pie à la mode, scoop ice cream onto pie. Microwave 35 seconds. Pie will be warm, but ice cream will not be melted.
10. To ripen avocados, microwave 30–45 seconds. Skins will come off very easily.
11. To brown ground meat for your favorite dish, place meat in a hard plastic collander. Shape meat in a doughnut shape. The center of the collander should be free. Set collander in another dish. Microwave meat 5–7 minutes per pound. After cooking, shake the collander, and you have greaseless browned meat.
12. Want a perfect pie? Make sure you cook the pie crust first. A 9-inch crust cooks 5–6 minutes on high. Then add your filling and finish cooking.

Bacon Sticks

10 *thin* breadsticks (any flavor)

5 slices bacon, halved lengthwise

½ cup grated Parmesan cheese

Dredge one side of halved bacon strip in Parmesan cheese; roll against breadstick diagonally. Repeat with each breadstick. Place on microwave-safe dish or paper plate lined with paper towels. Microwave on high 4½–6 minutes. Roll breadsticks in remaining Parmesan cheese. *Delicious and quick.* MAKES 10 WHOLE STICKS OR 20 HALVES.

—*Mrs. John L. (Patty) Pickering, Kingwood Club*

Smoked Wieners

1 package (16 ounces) wieners

1 jar (8 ounces) smoked mustard

1 tablespoon liquid smoke

1 jar (10 ounces) currant jelly or grape jelly

Cut wieners into 1-inch pieces. Heat mustard, liquid smoke, and jelly in microwave-safe dish for 3 minutes. Add cut-up wieners, and cook 4 minutes on medium. Serve hot on toothpicks. *These may also be made in a saucepan or fondue pot.* MAKES ABOUT 50 BITE-SIZED PIECES.

—*Sherilyn West, Lubbock Area Club*

One-Dish Macaroni Beef Casserole

½ pound ground beef

1 small onion, finely chopped

1 cup uncooked macaroni

1 can (8 ounces) tomato sauce

1½ cups water

⅓ cup catsup

1 can (7 ounces) whole kernel corn, undrained

1 tablespoon brown sugar, packed

½ teaspoon salt

¼ teaspoon pepper

¼ teaspoon chili powder

Crumble ground beef into 2-quart glass casserole. Stir in chopped onion. Cover with glass lid or plastic wrap, and microwave on high for 3 minutes. Drain fat, and stir in remaining ingredients. Re-cover. Microwave on defrost for 30–35 minutes, or until macaroni is tender. Let stand, covered, 5 minutes before serving. SERVES 4–6.

—*Joyce Boyles, Baytown Club*

Swedish Meatballs

¾ cup dry bread crumbs

1 pound ground beef

½ pound ground pork

1½ teaspoons salt

⅛ teaspoon pepper

1 teaspoon Worcestershire sauce

½ cup milk

1 egg

To prepare dry bread crumbs, place several slices of bread in a low oven to dry them out. This will take 2–3 minutes. Place the bread, broken into pieces, into a blender, and crumb. Combine all ingredients. Mix well. Roll into small meatballs not over 1 inch in diameter. Place meatballs on a paper plate, arranging with space around each one. Cook on high for 5½–7 minutes, or until brown. Serve with colored toothpicks. *These meatballs are also good in spaghetti sauce.* MAKES 1 DOZEN MEATBALLS.

—*Millie Bartlett, Bee County Club*

Meatballs and Veggies

4 medium carrots, thinly sliced

1 large potato, peeled and cut into ½-inch cubes

1 medium onion, thinly sliced

2 tablespoons water

1 tablespoon instant beef bouillon granules

2 teaspoons parsley flakes

MEATBALLS

1 pound lean ground beef

¼ cup dry bread crumbs

1 egg

1 teaspoon bouquet or Worcestershire sauce

1 teaspoon salt

¼ teaspoon garlic powder

⅛ teaspoon pepper

¼ teaspoon dry mustard

In 12-by-8 inch baking dish, combine vegetables, water, bouillon granules, and parsley flakes. Cover with plastic wrap. Microwave on high 3 minutes. In the meantime, mix ground beef, crumbs, egg, bouquet or Worcestershire sauce, salt, garlic powder, pepper, and dry mustard until well blended. Shape into 14 to 16 meatballs. Arrange meatballs on top of vegetables. Replace plastic wrap. Microwave on high 11–15 minutes, or until vegetables are tender, stirring after half the cooking time. *Who says dinner parties are hard? This recipe give you your main dish in one-half hour!* SERVES 4–6.

—*Aletha Kirkwood, Port Arthur Club*

Stuffed Green Peppers

4 large green peppers

1 pound lean ground beef or
  ground turkey

1 medium onion, finely chopped

¼ teaspoon pepper

1½ cups cooked rice

1 can (8 ounces) tomato sauce

1 teaspoon salt

Wash peppers; cut in half lengthwise. Remove seeds and white membranes. Microwave on high 5 minutes. Crumble beef or turkey into a 1½-quart microwave-safe casserole; add onion. Cook uncovered on high for about 5 minutes, stirring once during cooking period. Cook until meat loses its red color. Drain fat, if any. Combine cooked meat with pepper, cooked rice, ½ cup of tomato sauce, and salt. Fill green pepper halves with mixture, mounding mixture on top. Place in microwave-safe baking dish; top peppers with remaining tomato sauce. Cover with waxed paper; cook on high approximately 5 minutes, or just until peppers are tender. *Ground turkey may be found in the frozen food section of the grocery store. It can be used in any dish as a substitute for ground beef and is less expensive.* SERVES 4.

—*June Swenson, Austin Club*

Microwave Lasagna

1 pound ground beef

1 jar (32 ounces) spicy spaghetti
  sauce

½ cup water

1 teaspoon salt

1 package (8 ounces) lasagna
  noodles

2 cups ricotta or small-curd cottage
  cheese

3 cups shredded mozzarella cheese

½ cup grated Parmesan cheese

In 2-quart casserole, microwave crumbled ground beef 5–6 minutes on high, or until no longer pink. Drain off excess fat. Add spaghetti sauce, water, and salt. Microwave covered 5–6 minutes on high, or until hot. In a 13-by-9-inch glass baking dish, layer ⅓ of sauce, ½ of the *uncooked* lasagna noodles, 1 cup of ricotta or cottage cheese, and ⅓ of the mozzarella cheese. Repeat layers, ending with sauce. Sprinkle with Parmesan cheese. Cover with plastic wrap or waxed paper, and microwave for 30 minutes on high. Let stand 5 minutes. SERVES 6.

—*Carol Ireland, Fort Bend Club*

Super Chicken Enchiladas

1 dozen corn tortillas

1 diced onion (optional)

2 cans (6 ounces each) white meat chicken, diced

2 packages (10 ounces each) Monterey Jack cheese, grated

2 small cans (4 ounces each) green chilies, drained, seeded, chopped (reserve two whole for garnish)

1 can (10¾ ounces) cream of chicken soup

½ pint (1 cup) sour cream

In microwave oven, heat tortillas wrapped in waxed paper, six at a time, for 20 seconds on high to soften; or, in conventional oven, wrap in foil and heat 5 minutes at 400°. Place in center of each softened tortilla: ½ teaspoon onion, ½ tablespoon chicken, and ½ tablespoon grated cheese. Roll each tortilla, and place seam side down in 13-by-9-inch coated glass baking dish. Mix chopped chilies, chicken soup, and sour cream until smooth. Add any remaining diced chicken. Spread over enchiladas, carefully covering all exposed edges of tortillas. To cook in microwave: use high power for 6 minutes, or until heated through. Add remainder of cheese, and cook 3 minutes until cheese bubbles. Garnish with whole chilies. For conventional cooking: sprinkle remainder of cheese on top; garnish with whole chilies. Heat 25 minutes in 350° oven, or until heated through and cheese bubbles. *Delicious with refried beans and green salad, this entire festive Mexican meal can be prepared and served within 30–45 minutes. It's ideal for any busy Aggie, former Aggie, or even an Aggie mom who's really an ex–Baylor Bear.* SERVES 6. —*Jerrie Sue Cleaver, West Bell County Club*

Easy Chicken Bake

1 package (2–3 ounces) seasoned coating mix for chicken

2 tablespoons grated Parmesan cheese

2 teaspoons parsley flakes

4 medium chicken breasts

¼ cup milk

Place coating mix, cheese, and parsley flakes in plastic bag. Dip chicken breasts in milk; then shake in bag to coat. Place skin-side up in 12-by-8-inch baking dish. Cook on high for 20–25 minutes, or until done.

—*Jeri Kelley, Grayson County Club*

Chicken Divine

1 chicken, cooked and deboned

1 package (10 ounces) frozen broccoli spears

1 can (10¾ ounces) cream of chicken soup, undiluted

½ teaspoon curry powder

½ cup mayonnaise

¼ cup lemon juice

¾ cup grated cheese

½ cup bread crumbs

slivered almonds (optional)

Microwave chicken in 4-quart simmer pot (not metal) 15–18 minutes on high. Cook broccoli in package 12–14 minutes on high. Mix soup, curry powder, mayonnaise, and lemon juice. Layer cooked broccoli, chicken, and soup mixture. Sprinkle with cheese, bread crumbs, and almonds. Microwave on roast setting (medium) 12–14 minutes. SERVES 4–6.

—*Carol Ireland, Fort Bend Club*

Rice Casserole

½ cup (1 stick) margarine, melted

1 small onion, chopped

½–1 green pepper, chopped

1 cup uncooked rice

1 small can (4 ounces) mushrooms

1 can (14½ ounces) chicken broth

1 teaspoon salt

Sauté onions and green peppers in melted margarine in large skillet. Add rice and cook until it begins to brown. Add mushrooms and cook about 5 minutes longer, stirring frequently. Heat chicken broth in microwave or in saucepan. Pour rice mixture into 2½–3-quart casserole; add heated broth and salt. (Use small amount of broth to get all of rice mixture from skillet.) Cover casserole, and bake until liquid is absorbed. I bake this in the microwave at bake power (medium) for about 20 minutes. May also be baked in a conventional oven at 350° for 40 minutes. SERVES 4.

—*Dorothy Pollock, San Antonio Club*

Microwave Rice Pilaf

3 tablespoons butter or margarine

⅓ cup chopped onion

⅓ cup chopped green pepper

⅓ cup shredded carrot

1 cup water

dash pepper

1½ teaspoons instant chicken bouillon

¼ teaspoon salt

1 cup quick-cooking rice

Combine butter or margarine, onion, green pepper, carrot, water, pepper, bouillon, and salt in 2-quart casserole. Cover with glass lid. Microwave for 5–8 minutes on high, or until boiling. Stir in rice; re-cover. Let dish sit, covered, 5 minutes, or until all liquid is absorbed. Stir and serve. SERVES 4.

—*Frances Pesek, DeWitt–Lavaca County Club*

Eggplant Salad (Camponata)

1 large or 2 small eggplants, sliced

salt

4 onions, sliced

3–4 green peppers, sliced

6 celery stalks, sliced

vegetable oil for coating

1 large (6 ounces) or 2 small cans (4 ounces each) sliced mushrooms

green salad olives

ripe olives, sliced

1 large can (12 ounces) tomato paste

2 tablespoons sugar

hot pepper sauce, to taste

Slice and salt eggplant on both sides and let bubble at room temperature. Slice onions, green peppers, and celery in food processor. Coat lightly with oil, cover, and microwave on high 10 minutes, or until done. When eggplant is bubbly, rinse lightly, and cut into cubes. Cover and cook in microwave on high 5 minutes (or in saucepan on conventional range). Combine mushrooms, green olives, and ripe olives with vegetables. Put into large saucepan, and heat until boiling (about 5 minutes on high), but not sticking. Add tomato paste, sugar, and hot pepper sauce to taste. Chill, and serve with crackers or Melba toast rounds. *Any leftover camponata is a delicious addition to your favorite spaghetti sauce.* —*Mary Riggs, Houston Club*

Quick Potatoes

4 potatoes

¼ cup chopped onions

¼ cup chopped green pepper

salt and pepper to taste

small amount of margarine (optional)

Place peeled, sliced potatoes in microwave dish. Mix in onions and green pepper; season to taste with salt and pepper. If desired, dot with margarine. Cover. Cook in microwave on high for 5–7 minutes. SERVES 4–6.

—*Anne Cassens, Orange County Club*

Mexicali Corn Casserole

1 small green pepper, chopped

1 small onion, chopped

1 can (12 ounces) whole kernel corn with red and green sweet peppers

2 cans (14 ounces each) chili without beans

6 cups cooked rice, prepared according to package directions

In a 3-quart casserole dish, combine green pepper, onion, corn, and chili. Cover and heat on high 5–6 minutes. Serve over rice. SERVES 6–8.

—*Carol Ireland, Fort Bend Club*

Bread Pudding I

2 cups milk

7 slices day-old (or older) bread

1 tablespoon margarine

2 eggs, slightly beaten

1¼ cups sugar

¼ teaspoon salt

¾ teaspoon cinnamon

1 teaspoon vanilla

¼ teaspoon pecan extract (optional)

½ cup raisins

Heat milk in 4-cup glass measuring cup for 3 minutes on high. Tear bread into small pieces; spread pieces of bread into a 2-quart microwave-safe baking dish. Stir margarine, eggs, sugar, salt, cinnamon, vanilla, pecan extract, and raisins into the hot milk. Pour mixture over bread. Microwave on high for 8 minutes, rotating bowl every 2 minutes. Allow to stand 30 minutes before serving. Serve with whipped cream if desired. Good cold, just as it is. *Bread pudding has such a bland sound, but this recipe will change your idea of that! So easy, and tastes great for days.* SERVES 6.

—*Mrs. Carolyn Greer, Mid-Jefferson County Club*

Bread Pudding II

4 slices brown bread	¾ cup pecans
2 cups milk	1 teaspoon vanilla
3 eggs, beaten	¾ cup raisins
1 cup sugar	3 tablespoons butter, melted
1 teaspoon cinnamon	

Break bread into small pieces; pour milk on top and let soak. Beat eggs and add sugar. Add to bread mixture. Combine cinnamon, pecans, vanilla, raisins, and butter and add. Pour into microwave-safe baking dish, and microwave 3 minutes on high. Stir. Microwave another 3 minutes on high. Let set 5–10 minutes. SERVES 6–8. —*Carol Ireland, Fort Bend Club*

Microwave Fruit Pizza

CRUST

½ cup powdered confectioners sugar	2 cups all-purpose flour
1 cup (2 sticks) margarine, softened	

FILLING

1 package (8 ounces) cream cheese, softened	1 can (14 ounces) sweetened condensed milk
⅓ cup lemon juice	1 teaspoon vanilla

TOPPING

4 cups fruit, sweetened to taste	4 tablespoons cornstarch

For crusts, cream powdered sugar and margarine. Stir in flour. Roll out or press into two pizza pans. Prick bottoms with fork and bake at 350° for 20 minutes or until golden brown. Cool.

For first layer, mix cream cheese, lemon juice, sweetened condensed milk, and vanilla until well blended. Spread over cooled crust; chill.

For topping: Boil apricots, strawberries, mandarin oranges or any fruit desired, with sugar and cornstarch until thick. A quick way to do it is in the microwave oven. Put fruit with juice in an 8-cup glass measuring pitcher; stir in sugar and cornstarch. Microwave on high for 5–6 minutes, or until thickened, stirring every minute or so. This way the fruit will not scorch as easily as it does on top of a stove. Spread cooled mixture over cream cheese mixture and chill. Slice in wedges. MAKES 2 PIZZAS; EACH SERVES 6–8.   —*Joycelynn Arnold, DeWitt-Lavaca County Club*

Almond Bark Cookies

1¾ cup almond bark

1 cup crunchy peanut butter

2 cups dry roasted peanuts, whole
  or chopped

3 cups crisp rice cereal

2 cups miniature marshmallows

Melt almond bark and peanut butter in microwave on high, for 2 minutes, or in 200° oven. Stir in peanuts, cereal, and marshmallows. Drop by teaspoonfuls onto waxed paper. Store in a cool place. *These are great for those who want something good without much work.* MAKES ABOUT 5 DOZEN COOKIES.   —*Delores Rydell, Bee County Club*

Microwave Chocolate Chip Bars

1 cup butter or margarine

1 cup brown sugar, packed

2 eggs

1 teaspoon vanilla

1 cup all-purpose flour

1 cup quick-cooking oats

1 teaspoon baking powder

1 cup semisweet chocolate morsels

¼ cup chopped nuts

Put butter in glass microwave-proof bowl; cook on high for 45 seconds to soften. Beat in brown sugar, eggs, vanilla, flour, oats, baking powder, chocolate morsels, and nuts. Spread batter in buttered 12-by-8-inch microwave-safe dish. Cook on 50 percent power (simmer) for 16 minutes, or until no longer doughy; rotate once. Cool. Cut into bars. MAKES 24.   —*Abilene Club*

Caramel Corn I

1 batch popped popcorn

5 tablespoons butter

½ cup brown sugar

3 tablespoons light corn syrup

¼ teaspoon salt

¼ teaspoon vanilla

⅛ teaspoon baking soda

Make a batch of popcorn. In a large plastic or glass mixing bowl, combine butter, brown sugar, corn syrup, salt, and vanilla. Microwave for 2–3 minutes. Mixture should be bubbly hot. Add baking soda; the syrup will turn foamy. Mix in popped corn; stir well. Pour out onto aluminum foil and cool. Break into crunchy chunks.　　　　—*Lucy Vogel, West Bell County Club*

Microwave Peanut Brittle

1 cup raw peanuts

1 cup sugar

½ cup light corn syrup

⅛ teaspoon salt

1 teaspoon vanilla

1 teaspoon butter

1 teaspoon baking soda

In a 1½-quart casserole, stir together peanuts, sugar, corn syrup, and salt. Cook 8 minutes on high, stirring well after 4 minutes. Stir in vanilla and butter and cook 2 minutes longer on high. Remove; add baking soda, and quickly stir until light and foamy. Immediately pour onto lightly greased baking sheet. Spread out thin. When cool, break into pieces. Store in tightly covered container. MAKES ABOUT 1 POUND.

　　　　—*Nelda Newman, Victoria County Club*

Microwave Peanut Butter Fudge

2 cups creamy peanut butter

1 package (6 ounces) semisweet
　chocolate morsels

1 package (6 ounces) butterscotch
morsels

2 cups pecan pieces

Place peanut butter, chocolate morsels, and butterscotch morsels in microwave in glass dish. Microwave until soft, but not runny. Cream together and add pecans. Drop onto waxed paper, or pour into 8-inch square buttered pan. Refrigerate until firm. Cut into squares if cooled in pan. MAKES 50–60 PIECES.　　　　—*Lois Carraway, Liberty County Club*

Caramel Corn II

½ cup butter or margarine

¼ cup light corn syrup

1 cup brown sugar

½ teaspoon salt

½ teaspoon baking soda

4–6 quarts popped corn

Combine butter, syrup, brown sugar, and salt in an 8-cup glass measuring cup or a 3-quart mixing bowl. Bring to a boil in the microwave on high, then cook 2½ minutes. Stir in baking soda (syrup will foam). Pour over popped corn in a large grocery bag that has been sprayed with a non-stick cooking spray. Stir lightly to combine. Put the bag in the microwave and cook on high 2½ minutes, stirring after 1 minute. Remove from microwave, and spread caramel corn on a cookie sheet to cool. Break apart. Pecans or peanuts can be mixed with the popcorn if desired. Syrup can be increased if you want more "sweetness." Store in air-tight containers. *A favorite dorm snack; mails well.*   —*Marilyn Anderson, Guadalupe County Club*

Leche Pogada

2 cups pecan pieces or small
   pecans

1 can (14 ounces) sweetened
   condensed milk

½ cup (1 stick) margarine, melted

⅔ cup brown sugar

1 teaspoon vanilla

Toast pecans in glass dish for 8 minutes on high; turn and stir every 2 minutes. Add sweetened condensed milk and brown sugar to melted margarine in 4-cup mixing bowl. Microwave on high for 7 minutes, stirring and turning every 2 minutes. Beat with electric mixer until stiff. Stir in pecans and vanilla, and mix well. Pour into greased 8-inch square dish. Chill. Cut into small pieces, and refrigerate. MAKES 3–4 DOZEN PIECES.

—*Mrs. C. O. (Martha) Smith, Austin Club*

Dough Ornaments

½ cup salt

2 cups all-purpose flour

¾ cup warm water

Mix salt, flour, and warm water together; knead until pliable. Work into shapes, or roll out and cut into shapes. Place on cardboard sprinkled with salt. Microwave on high 1 minute per ornament plus 2 more minutes.

—*Carol Ireland, Fort Bend Club*

8

My Favorite's Favorites

Aggie parents look forward to the periodic return of their college students. The young men and women who show up on the doorsteps may have made a special trip for a birthday or other occasion. These are true homecomings—the times for family feasts, for traditional holidays, or the weekends of R and R (rest and recreation) which come during the year.

Most Aggie moms have in their recipe files (or in their heads—or even in their computers) certain recipes that they know are special favorites of their families. "Why don't you make————?" might be filled in with anything from apple pie (in our family) to enchiladas in someone else's. It's probably *not* a food from the typical dining hall menu. Or if it is, Mom's version will probably have very different seasonings.

Many of the recipes in this chapter include comments from Aggie moms such as, "This has become a family tradition at our Thanksgiving dinner," or "This is what ———— requests instead of a birthday cake." There may even be a special bowl or plate that is customarily used to serve the favorite food, and sometimes even whole menus are repeatedly requested.

This chapter includes several recipes with origins in the family's ethnic roots and traditions. It is important that such offerings be passed on from generation to generation, and it is a well-known fact that many of the methods are best taught by one person working side-by-side with another. Learning to make some Norwegian specialties is one of my fond memories of family, and I think this is a common kind of heritage-enhancer. Did you ever consider jotting down some background facts along with that special recipe in the file? This information might be interesting and important to future generations. Many families are even preparing their own cookbooks—what an inheritance this would be!

Crabby Cheese

2 tablespoons butter

½ pound fresh mushrooms, sliced

2 tablespoons all-purpose flour

1 can (10¾ ounces) chicken broth

1 can (10¾ ounces) cream of
mushroom soup

1 package (8 ounces) Old English
cheese slices

1 package (6 ounces) frozen
crabmeat, thawed

2 ounces dry sherry

English muffins or pastry shells

Sauté mushrooms in butter. Remove mushrooms, and add flour to butter and juice to make a thick roux. Slowly add chicken broth, and allow to thicken. Add cream of mushroom soup and bring to very slow boil. Reduce heat and add cheese slices. Allow cheese to melt, and add crabmeat and mushrooms. Just before serving, stir in sherry. Serve over toasted English muffins or in pastry shells. *Good for brunch or luncheon. Aggies prefer muffins, and love this with eggs and hash browns.* SERVES 4–6.

—*From* Hullabaloo in the Kitchen, *Dallas County Club*

Curried Beef Cubes

2 pounds beef chuck, cut in ¾-
inch cubes

⅓ cup all-purpose flour

⅓ cup vegetable oil

1 large onion, chopped (about
1 cup)

1 clove garlic, minced (or
equivalent garlic powder)

1 teaspoon salt

¼ teaspoon pepper

2 cans (8 ounces each) seasoned
tomato sauce

1½ cups water

2–3 teaspoons curry powder

1 package (10 ounces) frozen
French-style green beans

hot cooked rice or buttered
noodles

Roll beef cubes in flour, and brown in hot oil in skillet. Combine onion, garlic, salt, pepper, tomato sauce, and water; pour over meat. Cover and cook slowly over low heat until meat is fork-tender, about 1½ hours. Stir in the curry powder. Add green beans and cook until beans are tender, about 15 minutes. Separate beans with fork as they cook. Serve over hot rice or buttered noodles. MAKES 6 SERVINGS. —*Alice Guelker, Austin Club*

Osso Buco (Italian Braised Veal Shanks)

4 tablespoons butter

1½ cups finely chopped onions

½ cup finely chopped carrots

½ cup finely chopped celery

1 teaspoon finely chopped garlic

6–7 pounds veal shank or shin
    sawed (not chopped) into pieces
    2 inches long

salt and pepper to taste

all-purpose flour (for coating)

½ cup olive oil

1 cup dry white wine

½ teaspoon dried or fresh basil

½ teaspoon dried thyme

¾ cup chicken stock (fresh or
    canned)

6 parsley sprigs

2 bay leaves

3 cups canned tomatoes, drained,
    and coarsely chopped

GREMOLATA (TOPPING)

1 tablespoon grated lemon peel

1 teaspoon finely chopped garlic

3 tablespoons finely chopped
parsley

Melt butter in heavy Dutch oven (which has a tightly fitting lid). Sauté onions, carrots, celery, and garlic for 10–15 minutes. Remove from heat. Season veal with salt and pepper; coat with flour. Brown in skillet in heated olive oil. Place veal pieces standing upright on vegetables; tie with string around circumference. Discard almost all of the fat from skillet; add wine and boil, reducing to about ½ cup liquid. Stir in basil, thyme, chicken stock, parsley, bay leaves, and tomatoes. Bring to a boil, and pour over veal. Place in preheated 350° oven for 1 hour, 15 minutes, or until veal is tender. To serve, arrange veal on large platter; spoon sauce and vegetables over the top. Sprinkle the top with gremolata, the piquant garni. Osso buco may be served with buttered pasta or saffron rice. *This meal can be cooking while you're enjoying your guests.* SERVES 6 TO 8.

—*Barbara Ferreri, Brazos County Club*

Chinese Pepper Steak

1 pound round steak, cut into very thin strips

2½ tablespoons vegetable shortening

salt and pepper to taste

1 can (10¾ ounces) condensed onion soup

½ soup can of water

½ cup chopped tomatoes

2 teaspoons soy sauce

1 large green pepper, cut into very thin strips

1 tablespoon cornstarch

2 tablespoons water

rice, prepared according to package directions

Brown steak in shortening. Pour off fat; add salt and pepper. Add soup, water, tomatoes, soy sauce, and green pepper strips. Cover and cook over low heat until tender, about 30 minutes. Combine cornstarch and water; mix until smooth. Gradually stir into meat mixture. Cook until thickened. Serve over rice. SERVES 4.   —*Shirley McCutchen, Milam County Club*

Beef Stroganoff

1 pound round steak, cut into small cubes

2 tablespoons butter

1 cup thinly sliced mushrooms

½ cup onions, chopped

1 clove garlic, minced

2 tablespoons additional butter

3 tablespoons all-purpose flour

1 tablespoon tomato paste

1¼ cups beef stock or 1 can (10¾ ounces) condensed beef broth

1 cup sour cream

rice or noodles, cooked according to package directions

Brown steak in butter quickly, turning to brown all sides. Add mushrooms, onions, and garlic; cook 3–4 minutes, or until onion is barely tender. Remove meat and mushrooms from skillet. Add 2 tablespoons butter to pan drippings. When melted, blend in flour. Stir in tomato paste. Slowly pour in cold beef stock or broth, stirring constantly, until mixture thickens. Return meat and mushrooms to skillet. Stir in sour cream; heat briefly. Serve with rice or noodles. *This has become a family favorite for winter suppers.* MAKES 4 OR 5 SERVINGS.   —*Vicki Spink, Kingwood Club*

Burgundy Beef Stew

2 pounds round steak, cut into
   1-inch strips
1 cup celery, cut into 1-inch pieces
2 cups sliced carrots
1 can (14½ ounces) tomatoes
1 can (4 ounces) mushrooms

2 medium onions, sliced
1 cup burgundy wine
3 teaspoons all-purpose flour
1 teaspoon sugar
1 teaspoon salt

Combine all ingredients in large greased baking dish. Bake 4 hours at 350°.
SERVES 6.   —*Mary Lou Perry, Orange County Club*

Julee's Meat Loaf

2 pounds ground beef
dash of ground cumin
dash of garlic salt
dash of pepper
½ teaspoon chili powder (or more
   to taste)
1 egg
1 can (8 ounces) tomato sauce

1 can (5⅓ ounces) evaporated milk
10 saltine crackers, crumbled
1 medium onion, chopped
4 ounces process cheese spread,
   cubed
1 envelope onion-mushroom soup
   mix

Combine all ingredients in order. Mix until well blended, and place in baking dish. Bake at 350° for 55 minutes. Remove from oven, add topping, and return to oven for 5 minutes.

TOPPING

¼ cup catsup
¼ teaspoon nutmeg

dash of dry mustard
3 tablespoons brown sugar

Mix together and spread evenly over top of meat loaf. SERVES 6–8.
                —*From* Hullabaloo in the Kitchen, *Dallas County Club*

Meat Loaf

2 pounds lean ground beef

1 cup oats

2 eggs

½ cup catsup

1 small onion, chopped

1 teaspoon salt

½ teaspoon black pepper

¼ cup catsup (for topping)

Combine all ingredients except catsup for topping. Press into loaf pan. Top with ¼ cup catsup, and bake at 350° for about 1 hour, 15 minutes. SERVES 6–8.   —*Sylvia Kocian, Victoria County Club*

Meat Surprise

1½–2 pounds round steak or beef skirts (fajitas)

2 tablespoons vegetable oil

salt, pepper, and garlic powder to taste

1 can (10¾ ounces) cream of mushroom soup

1 soup can water

2 tablespoons margarine

6 green onions, chopped

8 ounces fresh mushrooms, sliced

1 package (10 ounces) broccoli spears, thawed

Cut steak into small pieces; sprinkle with salt, pepper, and garlic powder. Brown in heated oil over medium heat, stirring frequently. Add soup and water; lower temperature to low, cover, and simmer for half an hour. In a small skillet, melt margarine. Sauté green onions and mushrooms. Add broccoli spears; simmer about 5 minutes. Add all to meat mixture and simmer, covered, 5–10 minutes. Serve with rice or wild rice and garlic bread. SERVES 8.   —*Rosa M. Silva, Laredo Club*

Tex-Mex Cornbread Casserole I

1 pound ground beef

1 onion, chopped

1 small can (14½ ounces) tomatoes

1 small can (7 ounces) jalapeño
  peppers, chopped

garlic salt, salt, and pepper to taste

1½ cups cornmeal

¼ teaspoon salt

1 can (17 ounces) cream-style corn

¼ cup bacon drippings or
  vegetable oil

½ teaspoon baking soda

1 teaspoon sugar

2 eggs, beaten

2 cups grated sharp cheddar cheese

Brown ground beef in large skillet. Add onion, tomatoes, jalapeño peppers, and seasonings to taste. Cook until well done. Drain liquid. In a large bowl, combine cornmeal, ¼ teaspoon salt, cream-style corn, bacon drippings or vegetable oil, soda, sugar, and eggs. Mix well. In large greased baking dish, spread half of batter on bottom of pan. Top with meat mixture. Sprinkle half of cheese over meat. Spread remaining batter over all, and top with remaining cheese. Bake for 30 minutes at 350°. Cool 5 minutes before serving. *I use green chilies instead of jalapeño peppers, which are a little warm for my family. You might try half of each. Also, this is wonderful reheated.* SERVES 6–8.   *—Juanelle King, Lubbock Area Club*

Tex-Mex Cornbread Casserole II

1 pound ground beef

½ large onion, chopped

salt and pepper to taste

1 package (6 ounces) cornbread
  mix

1 can (17 ounces) cream-style corn

1 egg

1 can (7 ounces) chopped green
  chilies

8 ounces grated cheddar cheese

Brown ground beef and onions; drain fat. Season with salt and pepper. In medium bowl, combine cornbread mix, cream-style corn, and slightly beaten egg. Spread half of batter in greased 10-inch pie plate (a thin layer). Spoon on ground beef-onion mixture. Add chilies and cheese, and top with remaining cornbread batter. Bake uncovered at 350° for 40–50 minutes, or until golden brown and sizzling. *Be careful not to use cornbread muffin mix by mistake; it's too sweet. This casserole is good for crowds!* SERVES 4–6.

—Helen Sartain, Amarillo Club

Tex-Mex Mexican Cornbread Casserole III

1 pound ground beef	2 eggs, beaten
¼ cup chopped onion	⅔ cup buttermilk
2 tablespoons chopped jalapeño peppers	1 package (6½ ounces) cornbread mix
1 can (17 ounces) cream-style corn	4 slices cheese

Preheat oven to 425°. Brown beef until crumbly; drain. Add onions and jalapeño peppers; continue cooking until onions are clear. In a bowl, combine eggs, corn, and buttermilk. Add cornbread mix, and stir until well moistened. Pour half of cornbread batter into greased 9-inch square pan. Top with beef mixture, cheese slices, and the remaining cornbread batter. Bake for 25 minutes at 425°. SERVES 4.   —*Linda Kinard, Abilene Club*

Meatball-Garden Skillet

¼ cup chopped onion	1 can (10¾ ounces) beef consommé
1 tablespoon butter or margarine	6–10 small potatoes or 6 medium potatoes, quartered
½ pound ground beef	
½ pound ground veal	12 small carrots or 6 medium carrots, halved
2 tablespoons all-purpose flour	
1½ teaspoons salt	2 cups fresh green peas or 1 package (10 ounces) frozen peas
½ teaspoon pepper	
1 egg	1 bunch green onions, cut into 1-inch lengths
¼ cup milk	
additional butter or margarine for skillet	1 teaspoon salt
	¼ teaspoon pepper
2 additional tablespoons all-purpose flour	

Cook chopped onion in butter until tender but not brown. Add to ground beef, ground veal, flour, salt, pepper, egg, and milk. Beat thoroughly, and form into 1″ balls. In large skillet, brown balls lightly in a little additional butter or margarine. Shake skillet to turn the meatballs as they brown.

Push the balls aside. Blend 2 tablespoons flour into fat in skillet; add the consommé. Cook, stirring constantly, until mixture thickens. To complete the dish, add the "garden": potatoes, carrots, peas, and onions, arranged attractively. Sprinkle with salt and pepper. Cover skillet and simmer until vegetables are tender, about 30 minutes. Garnish with snippets of parsley just before serving. *If you use frozen instead of fresh peas, separate them and add during the last 5 minutes of cooking time. Our son thinks this dish is worth driving home for!* MAKES 6 SERVINGS. —*Waldean Richter, Brush Country Club*

Pie à la Hamburger

1 9-inch prepared pastry shell	¼ teaspoon pepper
Parmesan cheese	1 teaspoon sweet basil
1 pound lean ground beef	¼ cup catsup
2 tablespoons butter or margarine	6 slices American cheese
1 teaspoon salt	6 thin slices fresh tomato

Prepare pastry (the one below or your own recipe) and roll to fit into a 9-inch pie plate. Sprinkle with Parmesan cheese. Lightly brown meat in butter, keeping it crumbly. Sprinkle meat with salt, pepper, and sweet basil; top with catsup. Dice 3 slices of cheese and add to meat. Drain off fat; spoon mixture into prepared pie shell. Arrange slices of tomato over meat. Bake in preheated oven for 15 minutes at 450°. Cut remaining slices of cheese into 6 wedges; arrange on top of pie. Place under broiler for 2–3 minutes, until cheese is melted.

PASTRY SHELL

3 cups all-purpose flour	1 egg
1 teaspoon salt	6 tablespoons warm water
1¼ cups vegetable shortening	1 teaspoon vinegar

Sift together flour and salt. Add shortening, and mix with a fork until crumbly. Add egg, water, and vinegar. Form dough into five balls, and chill in refrigerator. Each ball makes one crust. Remaining dough may be frozen for future use. *This pie is a favorite of my three Aggies—one they always request when they come home.* SERVES 6. —*Shirley L. Neal, Houston Club*

Barbecued Hamburger

1 pound ground beef

1 onion, diced

salt and pepper to taste

SAUCE

½ cup catsup

1 teaspoon prepared mustard

1 tablespoon brown sugar

1 tablespoon all-purpose flour

1 teaspoon vinegar

Brown ground beef. Add diced onion, and sauté until onions are tender. Pour off grease. Season with salt and pepper. Combine catsup, mustard, brown sugar, flour, and vinegar. Pour over browned meat, and simmer about 15 minutes. Serve on hamburger buns. *This is an all-time favorite! Can be frozen to be served later.* SERVES 4. —*Madonna Keyser, Pasadena Area Club*

Hamburger Pie

2 pounds ground beef

1 onion, chopped

salt and pepper to taste

small amount all-purpose flour to thicken

water to prepare gravy

1 package (10 ounces) frozen mixed vegetables

dash of browning and seasoning sauce

5 medium cooked potatoes, mashed

½ cup warm milk

1 egg, beaten

salt and pepper to taste

1 cup shredded American cheese

Brown ground beef and onion; drain off excess fat. Add salt, pepper, and a small amount of flour to thicken. Add frozen vegetables and enough water to make a gravy. Add a dash of browning sauce for color. Cook together until thickened. Pour into a casserole that has been sprayed with nonstick cooking spray. Cook potatoes; mash while hot. Add warm milk and beaten egg; season with salt and pepper. Drop in mounds over casserole. Sprinkle potatoes with shredded cheese. Bake at 350° for 25 minutes. SERVES 6–8.

—*Karen Hermes, DeWitt–Lavaca County Club*

Double Burgers

1 package (4 ounces) saltine
   crackers, finely rolled

2 pounds ground beef

½ cup catsup

2 eggs

1 small onion, chopped

½ teaspoon garlic salt

¼ teaspoon pepper

6 slices processed American cheese

Combine cracker crumbs, ground beef, catsup, eggs, onion, garlic salt, and pepper. Mix well; shape into 12 thin patties. Top 6 patties with slice of cheese; put remaining meat patties on top, sealing well. Broil about 5 minutes on each side. MAKES 6 DOUBLE BURGERS.   —*Carol Ireland, Fort Bend Club*

Spaghetti and Meatballs

16 ounces spaghetti

1 medium onion, chopped

3 tablespoons vegetable shortening

1 can (10¾ ounces) tomato soup,
   undiluted

2 cans (6 ounces each) tomato
   paste

2 cups water

1 tablespoon sugar

1 teaspoon salt

pepper to taste

Prepare spaghetti according to directions on package. For sauce, cook onion in shortening until golden. Add remaining ingredients; simmer for 45 minutes. Add browned meatballs.

MEATBALLS

1–1½ pounds ground beef

1 cup bread crumbs

½ cup Parmesan cheese

dash of garlic powder

½ cup milk

2 eggs

salt and pepper to taste

Combine ground beef, crumbs, cheese, garlic powder, milk, eggs, salt, and pepper. Shape into small balls; brown on all sides. Add to prepared sauce; keep hot. Serve over cooked spaghetti. *An Aggie favorite.* SERVES 6–8.

—*Aileen Batte, Hays County Club*

Spaghetti Pie

6 ounces dry spaghetti

2 tablespoons butter or margarine

⅓ cup grated Parmesan cheese

2 well-beaten eggs

1 cup (8 ounces) cottage cheese

1 pound ground beef

½ cup chopped onion

¼ cup chopped green pepper

1 cup canned tomatoes, cut up, with juice

1 can (6 ounces) tomato paste

1 teaspoon sugar

1 teaspoon dried oregano, crushed

½ teaspoon garlic salt

½ cup (about 2 ounces) shredded mozzarella cheese

Cook spaghetti according to package directions; drain. (You should have about 3 cups of cooked spaghetti.) Stir in butter or margarine, Parmesan cheese, and beaten eggs. Form spaghetti mixture into a "crust" in a buttered 13-by-9-inch baking dish. Spread cottage cheese over bottom of spaghetti crust. In skillet, cook ground beef, onion, and green pepper until vegetables are tender and meat is browned. Drain, and stir in undrained tomatoes, tomato paste, sugar, oregano, and garlic salt. Heat through. Turn meat mixture into crust. Bake, uncovered, in 350° oven for 20 minutes. Sprinkle mozzarella cheese on top. Bake 5 minutes longer, or until cheese melts. SERVES 6–8.   —*Carol Ireland, Fort Bend Club*

Spaghetti Pancake

8 ounces spaghetti

2 eggs, beaten

4 ounces cheese, grated

4 ounces luncheon meat, corned beef, or ham, diced

salt and pepper to taste

2 tablespoons vegetable oil

tomato and parsley for garnish

Cook spaghetti according to package directions. Combine with eggs, cheese, diced meat, salt, and pepper in large bowl; mix well. Heat oil in large skillet; pour in mixture. Cook until both sides are golden brown. Garnish with tomatoes and parsley. SERVES 4.

—*Gladys McMahon (Montgomery), San Antonio Club*

Chicken and Dressing

1 package (16 ounces) corn bread stuffing

1 can (10¾ ounces) cream of mushroom soup, undiluted

2 eggs, well beaten

2 cups chicken broth

2½ cups diced chicken

½ cup milk

2 tablespoons chopped canned pimiento

Toss stuffing mix with half of the can of soup, chicken broth, and beaten eggs. Spread mixture in 11-by-7-inch baking pan. Top with cooked chicken. Combine remaining half can of soup with milk and pimiento; pour over all. Cover with foil. Bake in 350° oven for 45 minutes, or until set. SERVES 6–8.

—*From* Another Hungry Aggie Cookbook, *Kingsville Club*

Chicken Spaghetti

1 stewing hen, boiled, boned, and cut into pieces (reserve broth)

2 packages (10 ounces each) spaghetti

1 medium onion, chopped

3 tablespoons bacon grease or vegetable oil

½ cup (1 stick) margarine

2 cloves garlic, chopped

1 green pepper, chopped

1 stalk celery, chopped

1 can (4 ounces) sliced mushrooms

1 can (20 ounces) tomatoes

1 tablespoon chili powder

salt and pepper to taste

½ cup reserved chicken broth

¼ pound cheese, grated

Boil hen; remove from bones and cut up. Prepare spaghetti according to package directions. Brown chopped onion in bacon grease. Add margarine, garlic, green pepper, celery, mushrooms, tomatoes, chili powder, salt, and pepper. Cook down. Add spaghetti and ½ cup chicken broth. Cook a few minutes. Add chicken, and place grated cheese on top. Put in oven for a few minutes to melt cheese. If spaghetti seems dry, add a little more chicken broth. *This is one of our Aggie's favorites.* SERVES 8–10.

—*Waldean Richter, Brush Country Club*

Teriyaki Chicken

6 chicken breast halves, boned and skinned

½ cup soy sauce

½ cup vegetable oil

2 teaspoons sugar

½ cup orange juice

2 teaspoons freshly grated ginger root or 1 teaspoon ground ginger

1 pressed garlic clove

Place chicken breasts in glass baking dish. Combine remaining ingredients, and pour over chicken breasts. Marinate chicken in refrigerator for 1 hour. Remove chicken breasts from marinade; place on broiler pan. Broil on each side until golden brown, basting occasionally with reserved marinade. SERVES 6.   —*Carol Cupples, Kingwood Club*

Chicken Breasts Wellington

2 tablespoons butter

1 bunch green onions, chopped

½ cup sliced fresh mushrooms

2 tablespoons butter

4 chicken breasts, halved, skinned, and boned

salt and pepper to taste

1 package (17¼ ounces) frozen puff pastry, thawed according to directions

1 egg, beaten with 1 teaspoon water

WINE SAUCE

3 tablespoons butter

3 tablespoons all-purpose flour

¼ teaspoon salt

⅛ teaspoon pepper

¾ cup canned chicken broth

½ cup water

¼ cup sherry wine

Sauté green onions and mushrooms in butter until soft. Remove and set aside. Add butter, and sauté chicken breasts, cooking 3 minutes on each side. Sprinkle lightly with salt and pepper. Divide sautéed onions and mushrooms in center of each chicken breast. Fold sides of each breast over the ends, making sure they overlap. Take one section of thawed puff pastry, and roll into circle ⅛-inch thick on lightly floured board. Put one chicken breast with folds down on round, and fold over sides, then ends, making sure dough is tight over breast. Repeat for each breast. Put fold-side down on cookie sheet. Cut a small X or daisy out of extra dough for each breast. Beat egg with water and brush tops of each one. Prick each several times with a fork. Bake at 425° for 15–18 minutes, or until golden. Serve with wine sauce. For sauce: melt butter in heavy skillet; add flour, stirring until smooth and lightly browned. Add salt, pepper, broth, water, and wine. Cook over medium heat, stirring constantly, until mixture is thickened. *Very elegant but simple—I like to serve it with Aunt Betty's Rice, which follows.* SERVES 4.

AUNT BETTY'S RICE

¼ cup butter

1 cup long grain white rice

2 tablespoons chopped onion

¼ teaspoon fines herbes

¼ teaspoon Beau Monde seasoning

½ teaspoon Worcestershire sauce

1 can (14½ ounces) beef broth

1 can water

½ can sherry wine

Brown rice in butter; add onions, but do not brown. Add fines herbes, Beau Monde, Worcestershire sauce, beef broth, water, and sherry. Cover and cook until tender. It may be necessary to add additional water.

—*Dee Brents, Fort Worth/Tarrant County Club*

Baked Chicken with Rice

2 cups uncooked white rice

1 package (1⅜ ounces) onion soup mix

1 frying chicken (2–3 pounds), cut up

pepper to taste

1 can (10¾ ounces) chicken gumbo soup

1 can (10¾ ounces) cream of mushroom soup

3 cups water

butter

Spread rice evenly in bottom of well greased 13-by-9-inch baking pan; sprinkle with one-fourth of the onion soup mix. Place chicken on rice; sprinkle with remaining onion soup mix and pepper. Combine soups and water in separate bowl; blend well and pour over chicken. Dot with butter. Cover with foil, and bake at 325° for 1½-2 hours. SERVES 6–8.

—*Bernice Cariker, Panola County Club*

Golden Chicken Nuggets and Honey Dressing

3 whole chicken breasts, skinned
  and boned
½ cup all-purpose flour
¾ teaspoon salt

3 teaspoons sesame seeds
1 egg, slightly beaten
½ cup water
hot vegetable oil for deep frying

HONEY DRESSING

¾ cup mayonnaise (no substitute)
⅓ cup honey
1 tablespoon grated lemon rind

¾ teaspoon lemon juice
¼ teaspoon ground ginger

Cut chicken into pieces 1 inch by 1½ inches and set aside. Combine flour, salt, sesame seeds, beaten eggs, and water in a shallow bowl. Heat vegetable oil for deep-fat frying. Dip chicken nuggets into flour mixture, and fry in hot oil until golden brown. Serve with honey dressing. To make dressing, combine mayonnaise, honey, lemon rind, lemon juice, and ginger; mix well and chill for at least 1 hour. Use as a dip for nuggets. *Young people love this.* SERVES 4.　　　—*Dr. Barbara Flournoy, Angelina County Club*

Chicken Supreme

1 frying chicken, (3–3½ pounds),
  cut into serving pieces
2 tablespoons melted butter or
  margarine
1 teaspoon salt
¼ teaspoon pepper
1 can (4 ounces) mushroom stems
  and pieces, with liquid and
  additional water to make ¾ cup

¾ cup powdered non-dairy
  creamer
1 tablespoon all-purpose flour
1 teaspoon paprika
1 teaspoon Worcestershire
  sauce

Place chicken in shallow baking dish, 13 by 9 inches. Brush with melted butter; sprinkle with salt and pepper. Bake at 400° for 45 minutes. Drain mushroom liquid, and add water to make ¾ cup. In mixing bowl, using wire whip, blend non-dairy creamer, flour, mushroom liquid and water, paprika, and Worcestershire sauce. Add mushroom pieces. Spoon over chicken, and continue baking 10–15 minutes longer at 400°. *Cook macaroni or noodles, and serve with sauce.* SERVES 4. —*Maureen Thode, Fort Bend Club*

Deep Dish Chicken Pot Pie

6 tablespoons butter or margarine

½ cup chopped celery

⅓ cup all-purpose flour

7 teaspoons instant chicken-flavored bouillon or 7 chicken-flavored bouillon cubes

⅛–¼ teaspoon pepper

4½ cups milk

3 cups cubed cooked chicken

1 cup sliced cooked carrots or 1 small can (8¼ ounces)

1 cup sliced cooked potatoes or 1 small can (15 ounces)

1 cup frozen green peas, thawed

3 cups buttermilk baking mix

1 cup milk

1 egg yolk plus 1 tablespoon water (optional)

Preheat oven to 375°. In large saucepan, cook celery in butter or margarine until tender. Stir in flour, bouillon, and pepper; add 4½ cups milk. Cook and stir until thickened and bubbly. Stir in chicken, carrots, potatoes, and peas; remove from heat. In medium bowl, combine baking mix and milk; mix well. Turn two-thirds of dough into well-greased 13-by-9-inch baking dish; sprinkle with flour. With floured hands, pat evenly over bottom and up sides of dish. Pour chicken mixture into prepared dish. Turn remaining one-third of dough onto a well-floured surface; knead until smooth. Roll out to ⅛-inch thickness. Cut into eight 3-inch rounds; arrange on top of casserole. If desired, beat egg yolk with water and brush on rounds. Bake 25–30 minutes, or until crust is golden. Refrigerate leftovers. *Instead of the frozen peas and cooked carrots, I often use one-half package of frozen peas and carrots. This recipe is good when you have leftover potatoes, carrots, or peas. It is a good dish to take to a pot-luck dinner—it serves many and goes fast.* SERVES 8. —*Shirley E. Priest, Liberty County Club*

Chicken Casserole

1 frying chicken (2–3 pounds)
1 box (6 ounces) wild rice with
  seasonings
1 can (10¾ ounces) cream of celery
  soup
1 can (8 ounces) water chestnuts,
  drained and sliced thin
1 can (16 ounces) French-style
  green beans
1 small jar (2 ounces) diced
  pimientos
½ cup mayonnaise
salt and pepper to taste

Cook chicken, debone, and cut into bite-sized pieces. Cook rice as directed on package. Mix chicken, rice, soup, water chestnuts, green beans, pimientos, mayonnaise, salt, and pepper in a large casserole dish. Cover with foil. Bake at 350° for 45 minutes. SERVES 8–10.

—*From* Hungry Aggie Cookbook, *Kingsville Club*

Chicken Casserole for Company

1 frying chicken (2½–3 pounds),
  cooked and deboned (reserve
  broth)
1 package (10 ounces) vermicelli
1 rib celery
salt and pepper to taste
1 package (10 ounces) frozen
  broccoli
1 can (10¾ ounces) cream of
  mushroom soup
½ can (12 ounces) evaporated milk
¾ pound process cheese spread,
  cubed or sliced
bread crumbs for topping
  (optional)

Cook and debone chicken; cut into small pieces. Cook vermicelli in chicken broth, adding celery rib. Drain; combine vermicelli and chicken. Cook broccoli until tender; drain, and spread on bottom of baking dish. Add part of chicken-vermicelli mixture; salt and pepper to taste. Combine soup, evaporated milk, and process cheese spread in saucepan; cook, stirring, until cheese is melted. Add part of cheese sauce to casserole. Layer chicken-vermicelli and cheese sauce until all mixtures are used up. Bread crumbs may be sprinkled on top if desired. Bake for 30 minutes at 350°. SERVES 6.

—*Avis Morris, Orange County Club*

Wild Rice Chicken

2 cups cooked, diced chicken

1 package (6 ounces) wild rice with seasonings, cooked according to package directions

1 can (10¾ ounces) cream of celery soup

1 medium onion, chopped (or cook chicken with onion and celery leaves)

1 can (10 ounces) French-style green beans, drained

1 cup mayonnaise

1 can (8 ounces) sliced water chestnuts, drained

1 medium jar (4 ounces) diced pimientos

1½ cups grated process cheese spread

Combine all ingredients except grated cheese in large bowl; mix well. Put in 2-quart baking dish (13-by-9-inches), and top with grated cheese. Bake at 350° for 25 minutes, or until cheese melts and casserole is bubbly hot. *To serve a few more, add more chicken and 1½ cups cooked white rice.* SERVES 6–8.

—*Charlene Ogg, DeWitt–Lavaca County Club*

Baked Chicken Salad

2 tablespoons corn oil margarine

1 cup thinly sliced celery

½ cup chopped onion

½ cup mayonnaise

½ cup dairy sour cream

1 tablespoon lemon juice

½ teaspoon salt

⅛ teaspoon pepper

2 cups cubed cooked chicken

½ cup slivered almonds, toasted

1 can (6 ounces) sliced mushrooms, drained

¼ cup crushed potato chips

Melt margarine in large skillet over medium heat. Add celery and onion; cook about 4 minutes, or until tender. Remove from heat. Stir in mayonnaise, sour cream, lemon juice, salt, and pepper until well blended. Add chicken, almonds, and mushrooms; toss to coat well. Spoon into 1½-quart casserole. Sprinkle with crushed potato chips. Bake at 325° for 25–30 minutes or until bubbly. SERVES 4–6.

—*Susie Spaniel, Brush Country Club*

Chicken Curry

3 pounds skinned and boned
  chicken breasts
½ cup vegetable oil
3–4 garlic cloves, crushed
4 onions, chopped
1 bay leaf, crushed
1 teaspoon cinnamon
5–6 whole cloves

1 tablespoon salt
1 tablespoon curry powder
2 teaspoons paprika
1 teaspoon pepper
½ teaspoon cumin
½ teaspoon coriander
2 ripe tomatoes, peeled and
  chopped
1–1½ cups water

Trim and cut meat into strips; set aside. Sauté garlic and onions in oil until golden brown. Add bay leaf, cinnamon, and cloves; cook, covered, for 5 minutes. Add strips of chicken and cook, uncovered, until tender. Stir in remaining ingredients. Cover and cook about 1 hour. Serve with rice, prepared according to package directions. Serve with condiments such as chutney, green onions, minced hard-cooked eggs, almonds, peanuts, coconut, and crumbled bacon. *Spices may be increased to taste. Beef round steak may be substituted for chicken.* SERVES 8.

—*Dr. Barbara Flournoy, Angelina County Club*

Eleanor's Chicken Breasts

5–6 chicken breasts
salt and pepper to taste
flour for dredging
vegetable oil
1 clove garlic, chopped

1 teaspoon basil
1 can (10¾ ounces) consommé or
  bouillon, undiluted
1 cup sauterne wine
1 jar (4.5 ounces) button
  mushrooms

Dredge chicken breasts in salt, pepper, and flour; brown in vegetable oil. Place flat side down in casserole; sprinkle on chopped garlic and basil. Pour on consommé, and bake in 350° oven for 30 minutes. Add sauterne, and cook until liquid has cooked down, about 20 minutes. Add mushrooms and continue cooking about 10 minutes. Serve over long grain and wild rice, prepared according to directions. SERVES 5–6.

—*Betty Funk, Mid-Jefferson County Club*

Chicken Divan

1 package (10 ounces) frozen
  broccoli spears
3–4 servings sliced cooked chicken
1 can (10¾ ounces) cream of
  chicken soup

⅓ cup milk
½ cup shredded cheddar cheese

Cook broccoli according to package directions and drain; arrange in shallow baking dish. Top with chicken slices. Blend soup and milk, and pour over chicken. Top with shredded cheese. Bake at 450° for 15 minutes, or until light brown and bubbly. MAKES 3–4 SERVINGS.

—Pat Payne, Orange County Club

Hot Chicken Salad

2 chickens (3½–4 pounds each),
  cooked (reserve broth)
1 medium onion
2 cups chopped celery
2 cans (8 ounces each) water
  chestnuts
10 hard-cooked eggs
1½–2 cups chicken broth

2 cans (10¾ ounces each) cream of
  mushroom soup
¾ cup mayonnaise
1 tablespoon lemon juice
dash Tabasco sauce
salt and pepper to taste
1 package (12 ounces) potato chips

Boil or pressure-cook chicken; debone and cut into small pieces. Set aside. Finely chop onion, celery, and water chestnuts; set aside. Chop hard-cooked eggs. Combine broth, soup, mayonnaise, lemon juice, Tabasco sauce, salt, and pepper, and beat until well blended. Crush potato chips. Spray large casserole with nonstick cooking spray. Add a layer of half the chicken; a layer of vegetables; a layer of eggs; a layer of chips. Pour half of soup mixture evenly over the top. Repeat with other half of ingredients in the same order. Cover. Bake at 350° for 35 minutes. SERVES 8.

—Carney R. Nolan, Lafayette, Lousiana Club

King Ranch Casserole

1 hen or frying chicken, or
  4 chicken breasts, cooked and
  boned (reserve stock)
onion and celery to taste
¼ cup (½ stick) margarine, melted
8–10 soft corn tortillas
1 small onion, chopped (optional)
⅓–1 can (10 ounces) tomatoes and
  green chilies, depending on taste

1 can (10¾ ounces) cream of
  mushroom soup
1 can (10¾ ounces) cream of
  chicken soup
1 soup can chicken broth
½–¾ pound cheddar cheese,
  grated

Simmer chicken or chicken pieces, onion, and celery in water to cover, until meat is fork-tender (depending on chicken, usually 45 minutes–2 hours). Debone in large pieces while still warm. Melt margarine in 3-quart casserole. Line bottom and sides with tortillas, cutting to fit if necessary. Add a layer of chicken pieces. Combine onion, tomatoes and green chilies, soups, and chicken broth; pour half over chicken. Layer more tortilla pieces, chicken, and sauce. Bake at 375° for 30–40 minutes. Sprinkle with grated cheese; return to oven long enough to melt cheese. (Ed. note: This casserole may be put together and refrigerated ahead of time; increase baking by 10–15 minutes.) SERVES 6–8.

—*From* The Hungry Aggie Cookbook, *Kingsville Club, and Mrs. J. (Esther R.) Mancillas, Jr., Galveston Island Club*

Chicken Crunch Casserole

3 cups chicken, cooked, boned,
  and cut up in small pieces
1 can (10¾ ounces) cream of
  chicken soup
1 can (8 ounces) water chestnuts,
  drained and sliced
1 can (4 ounces) sliced mushrooms,
  with juice
½ cup chopped onions (white or
  green onions)

½ cup sour cream
1 can (8 ounces) crescent dinner
  rolls
⅔ cup grated cheese (American,
  cheddar, or Swiss)
2–4 tablespoons margarine,
  melted
½ cup slivered almonds
⅔ cup mayonnaise

In large saucepan, combine chicken, soup, water chestnuts, mushrooms, mayonnaise, onions, and sour cream. Heat until quite warm but do not boil. Pour into ungreased 13-by-9-inch casserole. Separate crescent roll dough into two rectangles. Place over hot mixture. Top with grated cheese and melted margarine; sprinkle almonds over all. Bake for 20–25 minutes at 350°. (Ed. note: This would also be a good recipe for leftover turkey.) SERVES 8–10.   —*Mrs. Ed Moroney, Mainland Club*

Oven-Fried Chicken with Honey Butter Sauce

6 leg-thigh chicken quarters	¼ teaspoon pepper
1 cup all-purpose flour	2 teaspoons paprika
2 teaspoons salt	½ cup (1 stick) margarine, melted

SAUCE

¼ cup melted butter	¼ cup lemon juice
¼ cup honey	

Dip chicken pieces into mixtures of flour, salt, pepper, and paprika. Melt margarine in a shallow baking pan in a hot oven. Remove pan from oven; as pieces of floured chicken are placed in pan, turn and coat with margarine. Bake, skin side down, in a single layer. Bake at 400° for 30 minutes. Turn chicken, and coat with sauce made of melted butter, honey, and lemon juice. Bake 30 more minutes, or until tender. Spoon honey-butter sauce over chicken again. SERVES 6.   —*Inga Barrett, Titus County Club*

Apple-Stuffed Spareribs

2 racks spareribs

½ cup chopped celery and leaves

1 onion, chopped

1 tablespoon chopped parsley

¼ cup butter or margarine

4 cups diced, peeled tart apples

¼ cup brown sugar, packed

¾ teaspoon salt

¼ teaspoon each: sage, thyme, marjoram, pepper

4 cups toasted coarse bread crumbs

about 1 cup water

Cook celery, onion, and parsley in butter 5 minutes. Add apples, brown sugar, salt, sage, thyme, marjoram, and pepper, and simmer 5–10 minutes. Add bread crumbs and water, and mix. Place one rack of ribs in large roasting pan; spread with stuffing; cover with other rack. Tie firmly with string. Roast at 350° in covered pan about 3 hours, or until done. Remove cover during last hour of roasting. *This is our daughter's favorite dinner— often requested for her birthday.* SERVES 5. —*Mary Lou Coleman, Austin Club*

Peach-Glazed Spareribs

1 can (16 ounces) sliced peaches, drained

½ cup brown sugar

¼ cup catsup

¼ cup vinegar

2 tablespoons soy sauce

½ teaspoon garlic powder

1 teaspoon salt

1 teaspoon ground ginger

dash pepper

4–6 pounds country-style backbone or spareribs

Puree peaches in blender or food processor. Combine with brown sugar, catsup, vinegar, soy sauce, garlic powder, salt, ginger, and pepper; blend well. Allow one pound of ribs per person; grill until almost done (these can be oven-baked if outdoor grill is not available). Baste with sauce until well done. SERVES 4–6. —*Diane Hoelscher, Golden Spread Club*

Home for a Holiday

Pork Roast

1 pork loin roast (3–5 pounds)

1 can (10¾ ounces) tomato soup

⅓ cup onion, chopped

⅓ cup celery, chopped

1 clove garlic, minced

2 tablespoons brown sugar

2 teaspoons prepared mustard

4 drops Tabasco sauce

2 tablespoons Worcestershire sauce

2 tablespoons lemon juice

Place pork loin roast in roasting pan in oven heated to 325°. Do not cover. Figure 35–45 minutes per pound of meat. One hour before cooking time is up, pour drippings off. Combine remaining ingredients and pour over roast. Continue roasting; baste frequently. SERVES 6–8.

—*Mrs. James Lamp, Austin County Club*

Ham and Spaghetti Casserole

⅓ cup margarine

3 green peppers, diced

2 large onions, chopped

2 cups diced ham

3½ cups canned tomatoes

1 large can (8 ounces) mushrooms

½ teaspoon paprika

1 teaspoon pepper

½ pound uncooked spaghetti

¾ cup grated American cheese

In large sauté pan, lightly brown peppers and onions in melted margarine. Add ham, tomatoes, mushrooms, paprika, and pepper. Heat just to simmer, and add spaghetti broken up into 6-inch pieces. Remove from heat, and pour into 13-by-9-inch baking dish. Sprinkle cheese on top. Bake 25 minutes at 350°. *This was a blue ribbon-winning entry in a newspaper contest.* SERVES 6.

—*Mrs. Bud (Eve) Chalmers, Lafayette, Lousiana Club*

Ham and Broccoli Casserole

2 packages (10 ounces each) frozen chopped broccoli

2 cups diced ham

1½ cups (6 ounces) shredded cheddar cheese

1 cup buttermilk baking mix

3 cups milk

4 eggs

Cook broccoli according to directions on package; drain. Spread cooked broccoli in ungreased 13-by-9-inch pan. Layer ham and cheese over broccoli. Beat together the baking mix, milk, and eggs; slowly pour over cheese. Bake uncovered at 350° for 1 hour. SERVES 8.   *—Kathy Miller, Garland Club*

Sausage and Rice Casserole

2 tablespoons margarine

1 large onion, chopped

1 cup uncooked rice

1–1½ pounds bulk pork sausage

8 ounces (1 cup) sour cream

8 ounces cheddar cheese, grated

1 can (4 ounces) diced green chilies

paprika

margarine

Sauté onions in margarine. Cook rice in salted water, according to package directions. Brown sausage, crumble, and mix with cooked rice, onion, and sour cream. Place half of this mixture in a greased 2-quart casserole. Top with half of grated cheese and all of green chilies. Add rest of rice mixture, and top with remaining cheese. Dot with margarine, and sprinkle with paprika. Bake 30 minutes at 350°. *The original recipe was for a rice side dish to accompany meat. I added the pork sausage to make it a main dish, and we love it this way.* SERVES 4–6.   *—Maureen Thode, Fort Bend Club*

Buttermilk Fried Rabbit

1 fryer rabbit, cut up

salt and pepper to taste

1 teaspoon garlic salt (optional)

1 cup buttermilk

1 cup all-purpose flour

1 cup vegetable shortening

parsley for garnish

Wash rabbit pieces; dry on paper towel. Sprinkle with salt, pepper, and garlic salt. Dip in buttermilk. Put flour in paper or plastic bag; add rabbit pieces and shake to coat well. When shortening is hot, add rabbit. Cook until golden brown and tender, turning once. Drain on paper towel. Arrange on platter, and garnish with parsley. *Domestic rabbit can be used in chicken recipes. Cook at lower heat and longer, so rabbit will become tender. Common herbs used in rabbit cookery include: sage, fines herbes, oregano, sweet basil, thyme, rosemary, bay, and cumin.* SERVES 6.

—*Mrs. Robert W. Berry, Lubbock Area Club*

Cranberry Sauce

1 bag (16 ounces) fresh cranberries

1 cup sugar

1 cup water

1 cup sherry wine

1 teaspoon cinnamon

2 tablespoons water

1 teaspoon cornstarch

In a saucepan, combine cranberries, sugar, 1 cup water, and sherry. Simmer until cranberries dissolve. Stir in cinnamon. Combine 2 tablespoons water with cornstarch; stir into cranberry mixture. Simmer for 15 minutes, or until thickened. Cool and refrigerate. MAKES ABOUT 6 CUPS.

—*Diana M. de Gonzales, Eagle Pass Club*

Cranberry Currant Walnut Sauce

1 pound fresh cranberries

1¼ cups sugar

1 cup red currant preserves (jelly may be used)

1 cup water

1 cup coarsely chopped walnuts

2 tablespoons orange zest, minced

Wash and check cranberries, discarding any that are not good. Combine cranberries, sugar, preserves, and water in large saucepan; heat to boiling and reduce heat. Simmer uncovered for 20 minutes; skim foam. Remove from heat, and stir in walnuts and orange zest. Refrigerate overnight. *This will keep in the refrigerator several weeks. It is a nice change from traditional cranberry sauce and is very good with game.* MAKES 6 CUPS OF SAUCE.

—*Marilyn Putz, Rio Grande Valley Club*

Lamb Shanks in Wine

4 lamb shanks, browned in
vegetable oil

1 teaspoon dill seed

½ teaspoon oregano

1 teaspoon rosemary

¼ teaspoon garlic powder

½ cup brown sugar

1 cup white wine or cooking
sherry

1 large onion, sliced

Wash and pat dry the shanks. Brown quickly in minimal amount of oil.
Place in baking container in single layer, not overlapping. Combine dill
seed, oregano, rosemary, garlic powder, brown sugar, and wine or sherry.
Distribute evenly over shanks. Arrange onion slices evenly over meat. Bake,
covered, for 2½ hours at 300°. Uncover and bake for 30 minutes longer.
Remove meat, and boil liquid down to half. Pour over meat, which has
been placed on a platter or serving dish. Serve with rice, plain or pilaf.
SERVES 4.   —*Melba W. Cox, San Angelo Club*

Tomato-Zucchini Bake

4 medium zucchini (or yellow
squash, or both), sliced

2 stalks celery, sliced diagonally

1 medium onion, chopped

½–1 can (10 ounce can) tomatoes
and diced green chilies

1 package (8 ounces) process
cheese spread, shredded

salt and pepper to taste

1 cup bread crumbs

6 tablespoons margarine, melted

Cook squash, celery, and onion in small amount of water until barely
tender; drain. Add tomatoes and green chilies and cheese; mix well. Salt
and pepper to taste. Melt margarine; combine with bread crumbs. Sprinkle on top of casserole, and bake at 350° until bubbly hot, about 30 minutes. *If you want a very tangy casserole, use the whole can (10 ounces) of
tomatoes and green chilies.* SERVES 4.   —*Tillie Mudd, DeWitt–Lavaca County Club*

Mammy's Yellow Velvet

1 cup yellow squash, fresh or
frozen, sliced

1 cup cream-style corn

2 tablespoons butter or margarine

½ teaspoon salt

⅛ teaspoon pepper

¼ cup half and half or heavy cream

Cook squash using as little water as possible. Combine cooked squash and corn; add butter, salt, pepper, and half and half. Simmer 2–3 minutes. Serve hot. SERVES 4.

—Claire Buenz, Baytown Club

Mom's Yummy Potatoes

½ cup (1 stick) butter

2 cups half and half

1 tablespoon salt

½ pound grated American cheese

1 package (32 ounces) frozen hash brown potatoes

8 ounces sour cream

Grease a 13-by-9-inch glass casserole. Heat butter, salt, half and half, and cheese until melted. Mix well with potatoes. Pour in baking dish, and bake, uncovered, at 350° for 1 hour. Add sour cream, mix slightly, and cook for another 15 minutes. *Delicious, and perfect with any meat.* SERVES 8.

—Mrs. Jeanette Jackson, Austin County Club

Sweet Potato Bake

1 can (16 ounces) whole sweet
  potatoes, drained

salt to taste

½ cup brown sugar, firmly packed

1 tablespoon cornstarch

¼ teaspoon salt

1 cup orange juice

2 tablespoons sherry or rum

½ cup walnut halves, broken into
  large pieces

½ teaspoon grated orange peel

Arrange sweet potatoes in a shallow 1-quart baking dish. Sprinkle lightly with salt. Combine brown sugar, cornstarch, salt, and orange juice in a saucepan. Blend well. Cook over high heat, stirring constantly, until mixture boils. Add sherry or rum, and blend well. Pour over sweet potatoes, and sprinkle with walnuts and orange peel. Bake, uncovered, at 350° for 25 minutes. *These are also known as "drunk potatoes." They are a real hit at Thanksgiving and Christmas. You may want to use additional sherry or rum.* SERVES 4.

—Patsy Hudson, Fort Bend Club

Texas Squash

2 yellow squash, sliced

1 medium green pepper, chopped

1 rib celery, chopped

2 fresh medium tomatoes, chopped

1 small onion, chopped

2 tablespoons raw rice

½ teaspoon pepper

2 teaspoons salt

1 tablespoon brown sugar

2 tablespoons margarine

Combine squash, green pepper, celery, tomatoes, onion, rice, pepper, and salt. Put in greased casserole. Sprinkle with brown sugar, and dot with margarine. Cover and bake 40–50 minutes at 350°. SERVES 4.

—*Jo Frances Chastain, President of Federation (1986–87), Rio Grande Valley Club*

Squaw Squash

4–6 cups sliced yellow squash or zucchini (or a mixture)

1 cup chopped onions

¼ cup (½ stick) margarine

1½–2 cups grated cheese (almost any kind)

½ cup cracker crumbs

1 egg

1 can (10¾ ounces) cream of mushroom soup

1 teaspoon salt

½ teaspoon garlic powder

1 can (4 ounces) diced green chilies

Wash and slice squash; chop onions. Sauté in margarine about 20 minutes (not too well done). Butter 13-by-9-inch casserole dish. Combine cheese (reserving ½ cup for topping) and remaining ingredients in separate bowl. Add squash and onions. Pour into baking dish, and top with reserved cheese. Bake 30 minutes at 375°. *If your family likes squash, better double this one. My family likes it served with garlic toast.* (Ed. note: If you like your vegetables on the crunchy side, don't sauté the squash, but bake it uncooked. If you like the squash to be softer, sauté first.) SERVES 8.

—*Carole S. Jones, Fort Worth/Tarrant County Club*

Hominy

½ cup (1 stick) margarine

½ onion, chopped

½ green pepper, chopped

1 stalk celery, chopped

1 large can (30 ounces) hominy, drained

1 can (10¾ ounces) cream of mushroom soup, undiluted

1 can (10 ounces) tomatoes and green chilies

1½ cups grated cheddar cheese

Sauté onion, green pepper, and celery in margarine about 10 minutes. Add drained hominy, soup, tomatoes and green chilies, and cheese; mix well. Pour into a buttered 1½-quart casserole dish. Bake in 350° oven for 30–40 minutes. SERVES 6. —*Carolyn Granz, Victoria County Club*

Fresh Vegetable Casserole

⅓ cup uncooked rice

½ pound fresh green beans

3 or 4 tomatoes, quartered

1 green pepper, sliced

4 yellow squash, sliced

6 green onions, tops included, chopped

salt to taste

½ cup (1 stick) margarine

Combine rice, beans, tomatoes, green pepper, squash, green onions, and salt. Spoon into large casserole, and dot with slices of butter. Cover and bake at 350° for 1½ hours. *A great way to use fresh garden vegetables.* SERVES 4–6. —*Barbara Scott, Amarillo Club*

Broccoli Casserole

4 tablespoons butter

1 medium onion, chopped

1 heaping tablespoon all-purpose
   flour

½ cup water

1 package (10 ounces) frozen
   broccoli, cooked

1 jar (8 ounces) pasteurized
   process cheese spread or 8
   ounces grated cheese

1 egg, beaten

Sauté onion in butter. Stir in flour and water; cook until thick. Add broccoli and cheese. Beat egg, and add to mixture. Bake in greased casserole for 25–35 minutes at 350°. *Delicious even after it gets cold.* SERVES 6.

—*Mrs. J. (Esther R.) Mancillas, Jr., Galveston Island Club*

Corn Casserole

1 can (17 ounces) cream-style corn

1 cup raw spaghetti, broken into
   2–3-inch pieces

1 cup grated cheddar cheese

1 teaspoon grated onion

1 tablespoon chopped green
   pepper

1 tablespoon diced pimientos (or
   red bell pepper)

¼ cup (½ stick) butter, melted

crumb topping

additional melted butter, as desired

Combine corn, spaghetti, cheese, onion, green pepper, pimientos, and melted butter in casserole several hours before baking. If too thick, add a small amount of milk. Bake at 350° for 30–45 minutes. During the last 10 minutes, add crumb topping (herb-seasoned stuffing mix works well) and more melted butter. *This recipe is very easy to double if your family is larger, if you want it for a party, or to take to a covered dish supper.* SERVES 3 OR 4.

—*Mrs. L. W. (Nan) Forney, Liberty County Club*

Green Bean–Corn Casserole

1 can (12 ounces) white corn, drained

1 can (16 ounces) French-style green beans, drained

½ cup sour cream

½–1 cup grated American cheese

1 can (10¾ ounces) cream of celery soup

½ cup chopped onions

2 tablespoons margarine or butter

buttered cracker crumbs for topping

Combine corn, beans, sour cream, cheese, and soup. Sauté onions in margarine; add to mixture. Pour into baking dish; top with buttered cracker crumbs. Bake at 350° for approximately 30 minutes, or until bubbly around edges. SERVES 6. —*Gayle Minear, DeWitt–Lavaca County Club*

Green Beans Oregano

2 cans (16 ounces each) French-cut green beans

2 tablespoons dried onions

1 can (10¾ ounces) cream of mushroom soup

1 can (3 or 4 ounces) sliced mushrooms

4 slices crisp bacon, crumbled

¼ teaspoon oregano

toasted almonds for garnish (optional)

Drain and rinse green beans. Combine onions, soup, mushrooms, 2 slices of the crumbled bacon, and oregano. Gently fold in beans. Place in 1½-quart casserole, and bake at 350° for 20 to 25 minutes. Garnish top with remaining bacon and toasted almonds, if desired. *This dish goes well with beef, pork, or fish. The original recipe recommended mixing it ahead of time, covering, and storing overnight in the refrigerator. This brings out the oregano taste.* SERVES 6. —*Mrs. M. S. (Lydia) Norman, Liberty County Club*

California Baked Rice

4 or 5 slices bacon

½ cup chopped celery

½ cup chopped onion

green onion and green pepper
    (optional)

2 cups water

1 cup cream of chicken or cream of
    mushroom soup

1 cup grated cheese

2 cups instant rice

1 small can (4 ounces) mushrooms

salt and pepper to taste

Fry bacon until crisp; remove from pan. In drippings, sauté celery, onion, and optional green onion and green pepper (chopped), if desired. Combine water, soup, cheese, rice, mushrooms, salt, and pepper in a 1½-quart casserole. Top with crumbled bacon. Cover and bake at 375° for 30 minutes. SERVES 4–6. —*Paula Perkins, Orange County Club*

Egg Rice

4 tablespoons margarine

½ cup chopped onion

¼ cup chopped green pepper

2 cups long grain white rice,
    cooked according to package
    directions (or use leftover rice)

2 eggs

salt and pepper to taste

2 slices cheddar cheese (optional)

bread crumbs (optional)

In medium-sized skillet over medium heat, melt margarine and sauté onions and green pepper. Add cooked rice, eggs, salt, and pepper, and stir until eggs coat rice. Cook over medium heat, stirring constantly, about 5 minutes. Place slices of cheese over mixture. Sprinkle with bread crumbs, and remove from heat. *This is a great way to use your leftover rice.* MAKES 6–8 SERVINGS. —*Diane Nugent, Victoria County Club*

Potato Supreme

6 medium potatoes

½ cup grated cheddar cheese

⅓ cup chopped green onion

1 pint (2 cups) sour cream or plain yogurt

salt and pepper to taste

Boil unpeeled potatoes. Drain and chill. Peel and grate potatoes, and add cheese, green onion, sour cream, salt, and pepper. Bake in 1½-quart casserole at 350° for 35 minutes. SERVES 6–8.

—Johnine Leininger, DeWitt–Lavaca County Club

Easy Potato Casserole

½ cup (1 stick) margarine, melted

1 onion, chopped, or 2 tablespoons dried onions

1 package (32 ounces) frozen hash brown potatoes, separated

1 can (10¾ ounces) cream of chicken, cream of mushroom, or cream of celery soup

2 cups grated cheddar cheese

1 cup sour cream

2 cups crushed cornflakes or ½ cup herb seasoned stuffing mix for topping

Sauté onion in margarine if using fresh onion. Cool slightly, and combine with potatoes, soup, cheese, and sour cream, in 13-by-9-inch casserole. If using cornflake topping, combine with an additional ½ cup (1 stick) melted margarine. Bake 45 minutes at 350°. *May be mixed and frozen ahead of time.* SERVES 8–10.

VARIATION: To serve 12 people, add an additional can of soup (a second flavor would be good), 1 more cup grated cheese, and 1 more cup sour cream. *—Judy LeBlanc, Mid-Jefferson County Club, and Avis Morris, Orange County Club*

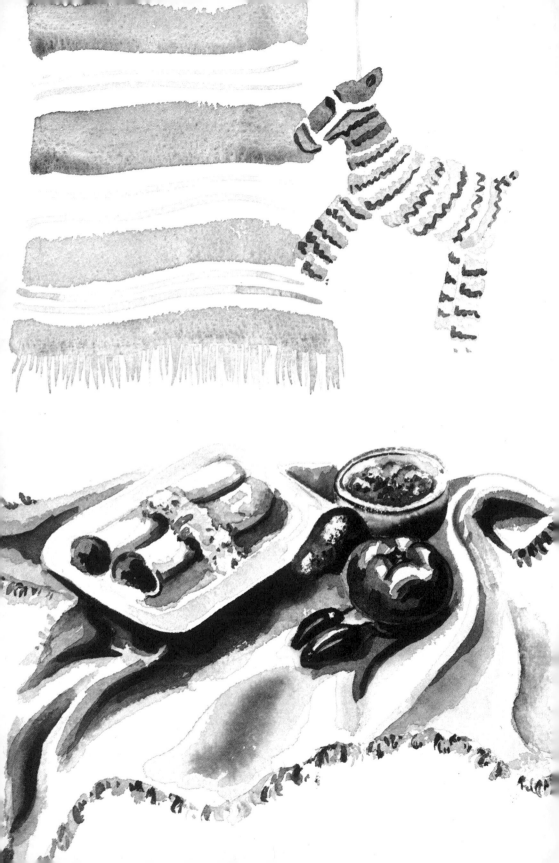

9

My Roommate's from New Jersey

"Mom, I'm coming home next weekend, and I'd like to bring my roommate. He's from New Jersey, you know, and he needs to taste some real Texas-style cooking. Can you handle it?"

If you're an Aggie mom, you probably can.

This is an opportune time for Aggie moms to show off some of the specialties of their particular regions. Because Texas and Louisiana are both Gulf Coast states, seafood is usually plentiful and delicious. If you have access to fresh shrimp or crawfish, you should try using these recipes. There are also combinations of seafood and pasta, for instance, which are not only delicious but economical to serve.

One popular cuisine in this area is known as Tex-Mex, a form that starts with Mexican ingredients and adds special touches of the Southwest. Tex-Mex is a flourishing type of cookery throughout the United States at present, with commercial taco and fajita eateries springing up in some rather surprising places. Tex-Mex seasonings vary, from mild to quite hot, but frequently rely on chili, red pepper, jalapeño pepper, and cumin for the "fire." (But did you know that Swiss enchiladas are any enchiladas with cream included among the ingredients?)

Some recipes in this chapter fall into the category of Cajun cookery; most of these were contributed by our moms in East Texas and Louisiana. One Aggie mom, Sally Chow of Lafayette, Louisiana, caught the essence of this cuisine in her recipe for bean soup: "Here in Louisiana we are heavy on the red pepper sauce, so the soup is *hot*." She wasn't talking about temperature.

Shrimp-Crab Gumbo (Galveston Style)

3 slices bacon, cut into small
   pieces
½ cup chopped onion
½ cup chopped celery
3 tablespoons all-purpose flour
salt and pepper to taste
4–6 cups water
1 large can (28 ounces) tomatoes
1 pound shrimp, shelled and
   deveined

½ pound crabmeat
½ pound okra, cleaned and cut
   into small rings
1 clove garlic, minced (optional)
½ green pepper, chopped
   (optional)
½ teaspoon cumin (optional)

Put bacon pieces in skillet and render. Drain off most of the fat. In the rest, sauté onions and celery until soft. Blend in flour; add salt and pepper to taste. Slowly add water, tomatoes, shrimp, crabmeat, and okra. If desired, add garlic, pepper, and cumin at this time. Cook slowly until okra is cooked. *Because my four Aggie sons lived on an island, they would always bring buddies home for spring break. They would always request Galveston-style gumbo for their guests.* SERVES 4 OR 5 "HUNGRY" AGGIES.

—*Carol Greaney, Galveston Island Club*

Cajun Creole Gumbo

½ cup vegetable oil
1 pound diced chicken
all-purpose flour for dredging
1 cup chopped celery
1 cup chopped green onions
½ cup chopped parsley
½ cup sliced green pepper
2 large tomatoes, finely chopped

3 pounds tiny whole shrimp
1 pound diced ham
1 pound cut okra
1½ quarts of boiling water
salt and pepper to taste
1 tablespoon gumbo filé
cooked rice

Heat half (¼ cup) of vegetable oil in large frying pan; roll diced chicken in flour. Brown lightly for 15 minutes; set aside. In large pot with remaining

¼ cup of oil, add celery, green onions, parsley, green pepper, and tomatoes. Sauté a few minutes until tender. Add shrimp, ham, browned chicken, okra, and boiling water. Reduce heat and simmer for 30 minutes. Add gumbo filé and stir in well. Serve over cooked rice. *This recipe, using frozen chicken, shrimp, ham, and okra, was a national winner in a frozen food contest. This is a popular entrée.* MAKES 24–30 SERVINGS.

—*Col. Fred W. Dollar and J. W. Maynard, TAMU Food Services Department*

Seafood Gumbo

1 cup vegetable oil

1 scant cup all-purpose flour

1 cup chopped onion

1 cup chopped green pepper

1 cup chopped celery

1 quart water

1 can (10¾ ounces) cream of celery soup

1 can (10¾ ounces) tomato soup

1 can (10¾ ounces) beef bouillon

1 clove garlic, chopped

2 tablespoons green onion tops

½ teaspoon red pepper

2 tablespoons Worcestershire sauce

dash parsley

salt and pepper to taste

3–4 pounds crabmeat, raw shrimp (shelled and deveined), cooked fish (proportions may vary)

1–2 teaspoons gumbo filé (depending on amount of seafood used)

cooked rice

Make a roux by browning flour in the oil until it is very brown (almost burned), stirring constantly and cooking slowly. Add onion, green pepper, and celery, and cook about 20 minutes. Add water, undiluted soups, garlic, onion tops, red pepper, Worcestershire sauce, parsley, salt, and pepper. Cook over low heat until well dissolved (several hours). Add crabmeat, cut-up shrimp, and flakes of cooked fish. Cook 15–20 minutes more. Stir in gumbo filé. Serve over hot, cooked rice. *This is really good if you are a gumbo eater. Recipe makes a large amount, and taste improves on the second day.* SERVES 10–12. —*Sandra Lark, Matagorda County Club*

Crawfish Supreme

½ cup (1 stick) margarine

¼ cup chef's seasoning

4 small green onions, chopped

2 tablespoons all-purpose flour

1 small can (4 ounces) mushrooms, with liquid

1 cup milk

1 pound crawfish tails

salt, pepper, and red pepper to taste

2 ounces cheddar cheese, grated

Melt margarine; add the chef's seasoning (found in frozen food section) and green onion. Cook at low heat for 15 minutes. Stir in flour, allowing to thicken slightly. Add mushrooms and liquid, milk, and crawfish, and cook about 7 minutes. Season with salt, pepper, and red pepper. Pour into casserole dish, and top with grated cheddar cheese. Bake in 325° oven about 20 minutes, or until bubbly. MAKES 4–5 SERVINGS.

—*Norma Truelove, Lafayette, Louisiana Club*

Jalapeño Shrimp Casserole

1 squeeze tube (6 ounces) jalapeño pepper cheese

1 can (10¾ ounces) cream of mushroom soup, diluted with ¼ can of water

1 small jar (2 ounces) diced pimientos

2 cups diced cooked shrimp

1 cup raw rice, cooked according to package directions

In saucepan, melt cheese, mushroom soup, and water. Add pimientos and diced shrimp. Add all the rice if needed, but don't let the mixture get too dry. Pour into casserole, and bake at 350° for 30–35 minutes, or until bubbly. *This dish is quite hot, but very tasty. If a milder taste is desired, decrease amount of jalapeño cheese (or use a milder cheese for part of the 6 ounces). Good served with tossed green salad and hard rolls or saltine crackers.* SERVES 4–6.

—*Dorothy Skiles, Orange County Club*

Shrimp Loaf

2 envelopes (1 tablespoon each)
  unflavored gelatin

⅓ cup hot water

1 can (10¾ ounces) tomato soup,
  heated, not diluted

1 teaspoon salt

2½–3 cups chopped celery

1 small onion, chopped

1 medium green pepper, chopped

1 pound cottage cheese

1 cup mayonnaise

1 pound cooked shrimp, chopped

Dissolve gelatin in water. Heat undiluted soup and gelatin solution. Stir in salt, celery, onion, green pepper, cottage cheese, mayonnaise, and shrimp. Mix well. Pour into large ring mold or individual molds. Chill. *Easy, elegant dish to serve that special date. Good with crispy garlic rounds or croissants.* MAKES 7 CUPS.   —*Dixie (Mrs. E. Leonard) Copeland, Brazos County Club*

Shrimp Gumbo I

2 tablespoons peanut oil

2 tablespoons all-purpose flour

small amount of water for thinning

3 cups sliced okra

2 onions, chopped

2 additional tablespoons peanut oil

1 can (28 ounces) tomatoes

2 quarts water

1 bay leaf

1 teaspoon salt

3 cloves garlic

red pepper to taste

2 pounds shrimp, shelled and
  deveined

cooked rice

Make a roux (a thickener for the sauce) of 2 tablespoons peanut oil and 2 tablespoons flour in small, heavy skillet. Let brown, then add small amount of water for thin paste; dissolve any lumps. Set aside. Sauté okra and onions in peanut oil. When cooked, add tomatoes, water, bay leaf, salt, garlic, and red pepper. Add shrimp and roux to this mixture; cover and simmer for 30 minutes. Serve over fluffy rice. SERVES 6–8.

—*Harrison County Club*

My Roommate's from New Jersey

Shrimp Gumbo II

⅓ cup vegetable shortening

2 cups sliced fresh okra or 1
    package (10 ounces) frozen
    sliced okra

⅔ cup chopped green onions and
    tops

2 cloves garlic, peeled and mashed

1½ teaspoons salt

½ teaspoon pepper

1 pound fresh or frozen shrimp,
    peeled and deveined

2 cups hot water

1 cup canned tomatoes

2 bay leaves

3 drops Tabasco sauce

1 teaspoon gumbo filé

1½ cups cooked rice, prepared
    according to package directions

Sauté okra in shortening stirring constantly, about 10 minutes, or until okra appears dry. Add green onions, garlic, salt, and pepper. Stir and cook for 2–3 minutes. Remove garlic and discard. Add shrimp; cook about 5 minutes. Add water, tomatoes, and bay leaves. Cover and simmer 20 minutes. Remove bay leaves. Add Tabasco sauce and filé. Stir and remove from heat at once. Place ¼ cup of cooked rice in each of six deep soup plates; fill with gumbo. *This is a meal in itself.* MAKES 6 SERVINGS.

—*Eva Smith, Baytown Club*

Sesame Shrimp

1 tablespoon sesame seeds

2 tablespoons vegetable oil

2 tablespoons sesame oil

1 pound shrimp, shelled and
    deveined

½ cup chopped green onions

½ teaspoon salt

¼ teaspoon pepper

1 tablespoon brown sugar

1 tablespoon soy sauce

Cooked rice, prepared according to
    package directions

Toast sesame seeds in 300° oven until golden brown (about 15 minutes), stirring occasionally. Heat oils in heavy pan over high heat. Add shrimp, green onions, salt, pepper, and brown sugar. Stir-fry for 1–3 minutes. Reduce heat to low; add soy sauce, and stir. Remove from heat, and sprinkle with sesame seeds. Serve hot over rice. *Add a nice salad, bread, and brownies, and you have a delicious meal.* SERVES 8 PEOPLE (OR 4 SHRIMP LOVERS OR VERY HUNGRY PEOPLE).

—*Betty Maskey, Corpus Christi Club*

Crawfish au Gratin

½ cup (1 stick) margarine

1 onion, chopped

3 ribs celery, chopped

1 green pepper, chopped

2 tablespoons all-purpose flour

2 egg yolks

½ can (10¾ ounces) cheddar cheese soup

1 pound crawfish tails

1 teaspoon parsley flakes

½–1 can (12 ounces) evaporated milk

salt and red pepper, to taste

1 block Monterey Jack cheese with jalapeño pepper, grated

Sauté onion, celery, and green pepper in margarine. Add flour and mix well. Stir in beaten egg yolks, cheddar cheese soup, crawfish tails, and parsley flakes. Cook for 10 minutes. Add enough evaporated milk to thicken. Season to taste with salt and red pepper. Pour into casserole dish, and top with grated jalapeño cheese. Bake at 350° for 8–10 minutes, and then bake for additional 15 minutes at 300°. *This recipe can be doubled easily. Shrimp or crab may be substituted for crawfish.* SERVES 6–8.

—*Marian W. Prihoda, Lafayette, Louisiana Club*

One-Dish Shrimp Special

4 teaspoons butter

1 green pepper, diced

1 small onion, diced

1½ cups half and half or
  evaporated milk

¾ cup sauterne

½ teaspoon curry powder

salt and pepper to taste

1 cup uncooked rice

1 package (10 ounces) frozen green
  peas

1½ pounds cooked shrimp, shelled
  and deveined

½ teaspoon paprika

Preheat oven to 350°. Sauté green pepper and onion in butter until soft and golden, in heavy skillet or saucepan. Add half and half, sauterne, curry powder, salt, and pepper, and stir until well mixed. Add uncooked rice, uncooked peas, and cooked shrimp. Mix and spoon into baking dish. Cover and bake at 350° for 30 minutes, stirring occasionally. Uncover, sprinkle top with paprika, and bake an additional 15 minutes, uncovered. *Easy to make for the family, or can be put in individual ramekins for a luncheon or dinner party.* SERVES 6. —*Jesilin Rigano, Titus County Club*

Shrimp Casserole

½ cup (1 stick) margarine

1 cup chopped onion

1 cup chopped green pepper

1 cup chopped celery

4 cups cooked shrimp, shelled and
  deveined

1 can (10¾ ounces) cream of
  mushroom soup

1 can (10¾ ounces) cheddar cheese
  soup

1 cup chopped pimiento, with
  juice

1 cup green onion tops (optional)

¾ teaspoon black pepper

⅓ cup chopped parsley

1 tablespoon Picante sauce

1 teaspoon salt

2 cups rice, prepared according to
  package directions

bread crumbs for topping

butter or margarine for topping

Sauté onion, green pepper, and celery in margarine. Combine remainder of ingredients except for topping (bread crumbs and butter or margarine), and mix well. Spoon into 13-by-9-inch baking dish; sprinkle with bread crumbs and dot with butter or margarine. Bake at 350° for 30 minutes. If mixed ahead of time and refrigerated, increase baking time 10–15 minutes. Extra rice and grated cheese may be added, if desired. *Excellent served with spinach salad with lemon French dressing and hot bread.* SERVES 10–12.

—*Gladys Dvoracek, Lubbock Area Club*

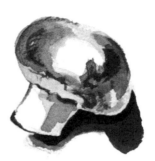

Shrimp and Rice Casserole

3 tablespoons margarine, melted

1 pound raw shrimp, peeled and deveined

1 cup chopped green onions

½ cup chopped green pepper

½ cup chopped celery

1 can (10¾ ounces) cream of mushroom soup

1 can (10¾ ounces) cream of chicken soup

1 teaspoon lemon juice

parsley

garlic salt and black pepper to taste

2 cups rice, cooked according to package directions

1 cup grated cheddar cheese

Sauté shrimp, green onions, green pepper, and celery in melted margarine, cooking until vegetables are limp. Over low heat, add soups, lemon juice, parsley, garlic salt, black pepper, and rice, mixing well. Spoon into greased casserole, and top with grated cheese. Bake at 350° for 30 minutes. This casserole may be frozen before baking. SERVES 6–8.

—*Marie Broussard, Beaumont Club*

Shrimp Etouffé

½ cup vegetable oil

1 cup all-purpose flour

1 medium onion, chopped

1 small green pepper, chopped

½ cup chopped celery

1–1½ cups water

1 clove garlic, minced

2 tablespoons parsley, minced

salt to taste

½ teaspoon black pepper

1 package shrimp-crab boil

2–3 cups water

1–2 pounds fresh or frozen shrimp, shelled and deveined

1 tablespoon gumbo filé

cooked rice

Use large heavy pot or Dutch oven. Brown flour in oil until a dark reddish-brown roux is formed. Add onion, green pepper, and celery, and cook over low heat until tender. Add 1–1½ cups water, stirring until smooth; this may be rather thick. Add garlic, parsley, salt, and pepper; let simmer. In another large saucepan, bring 2–3 cups of water to boil. Add package of shrimp-crab boil, and let boil 2–3 minutes. Add shrimp and return to boil until shrimp are pink (about 5 minutes). Remove spice bag, and add water and shrimp to first mixture. If too thick, add more water. Let simmer another 5 minutes. Add filé. Serve over rice, or add rice to shrimp to make a gumbo. *This recipe is very good with crackers or French bread.* SERVES 4–6.

—*Reba Stacy, Panola County Club*

New Orleans Shrimp Etouffé

½ cup (1 stick) butter

1 medium onion, chopped

2 green onions, finely chopped

3 cloves garlic, minced

¼ cup finely chopped celery

2 tablespoons all-purpose flour

2½ cups water

1¼ cups tomato puree

2 bay leaves

1 tablespoon Worcestershire sauce

4 drops Tabasco sauce

1 teaspoon salt

½ teaspoon sugar

½ teaspoon thyme, crushed

⅛ teaspoon pepper

3 cups cleaned raw shrimp

cooked rice

Sauté onion, green onions, garlic, and celery in butter until tender. Add flour; cook and stir until lightly browned. Add water, tomato puree, bay leaves, Worcestershire sauce, Tabasco sauce, salt, sugar, thyme, and pepper. Simmer uncovered, stirring occasionally, for 25 minutes. Add shrimp; cook 15 minutes more. Prepare rice according to package directions. Serve etouffé over hot rice. *From Brennan's in New Orleans. Crawfish may be substituted for shrimp.* MAKES 4–6 SERVINGS.   —*Anita Kyle, Fort Bend Club*

Quick Shrimp Creole

4 strips bacon

1 cup chopped onion

½ cup chopped celery

½ cup chopped green pepper

1 clove garlic, minced

1 large can (28 ounces) tomatoes

2 bay leaves

salt and pepper to taste

½ teaspoon Tabasco sauce

½ teaspoon Worcestershire sauce

2 cups cooked shrimp

1 teaspoon gumbo filé

rice

Using heavy skillet or Dutch oven, fry bacon until crisp. Remove and break into small pieces. Set aside. Brown onion, celery, green pepper, and garlic in bacon drippings. Add tomatoes and bay leaves. Add seasonings, crumbled bacon, and shrimp. If using larger shrimp, cut into several pieces before adding. Cook over low heat about 10 minutes. Serve over hot rice, prepared according to package directions. *My son's favorite.* SERVES 4.

—*Gail Jordan, Hays County Club*

My Roommate's from New Jersey

Jambalaya

1 tablespoon vegetable shortening
1 tablespoon all-purpose flour
¼ pound ham, cubed
¼ cup chopped green pepper
1 bay leaf
1 sprig thyme
1 sprig parsley

1 onion, sliced
1 clove garlic, minced
salt and pepper to taste
2 cups tomato juice
1 cup rice, uncooked
1 pound shrimp, peeled

Melt shortening in large heavy saucepan over medium heat. Stir in flour, and mix well. Add ham and green pepper. Simmer 5 minutes, stirring constantly. Add bay leaf, thyme, parsley, onion, garlic, salt, pepper, and tomato juice. Bring to a boil. Mix rice into liquid, cover and simmer over low heat for 40 minutes, stirring occasionally. Add shrimp and simmer another 5 minutes. *This is a New Orleans recipe my mother loved to make.* SERVES 6.
—*Lil Blanda, Orange County Club*

Fish Pharr

¼ cup (½ stick) margarine
1 small onion, chopped
1 stalk celery, chopped
1 small green pepper, chopped
1 small can (4 ounces) mushrooms
  or ¼ pound fresh mushrooms,
  sliced
2 tablespoons all-purpose flour
1½ cups milk
1 teaspoon lemon juice

½ teaspoon Worcestershire sauce
1 teaspoon salt
½ teaspoon pepper
¼ teaspoon red pepper
dash Tabasco sauce
2 cans (6 ounces each) white crab
  meat, drained
¼ cup (½ stick) margarine, melted
1–2 pounds fish fillets, seasoned
  with salt and pepper

Sauté onion, celery, green pepper, and mushrooms in ¼ cup margarine until tender. Add flour and milk; stir until thick. Add lemon juice, Worcestershire sauce, salt, pepper, red pepper, Tabasco sauce, and crab meat.

Simmer 5 minutes. Melt additional ½ stick margarine in 13-by-9-inch baking dish. Place fish fillets in dish; broil 10 minutes. Top with crab mixture; cover and bake 30 minutes at 350°. Uncover and broil 5–10 minutes more. *I concocted this dish the first weekend my son came home after freshman corps orientation. He asked what it was, so I named it "Fish" Pharr.* SERVES 6–8.

—Paulette Pharr, Pasadena Area Club

New Orleans Red Beans

2 cups dried kidney beans, washed and sorted

5 cups water

2 tablespoons bacon drippings

2 onions, chopped

2 cloves garlic, minced

½ pound ham, cubed or chunked

1 teaspoon salt

½ teaspoon pepper

dash cayenne pepper

Add water to washed beans; boil 2 minutes. Remove from heat, and let soak for 1 hour. Heat drippings; add onions and garlic, and sauté until tender. Add remaining ingredients and bring to a boil. Reduce heat to low. Cover and simmer 2 hours. During last 20 minutes of cooking, stir frequently, and mash lightly with spoon. May be served with rice, prepared according to package directions. *This is a New Orleans recipe my mother loved to make.* SERVES 4–6.

—Lil Blanda, Orange County Club

Red Beans and Rice

2 cans (15 ounces each) red beans with jalapeño

1 can water

1 pound smoked sausage cut into bite-sized pieces

cooked rice

Simmer red beans, water, and smoked sausage at low heat for 30 minutes. Cook rice according to package directions. Serve bean-sausage mixture over hot rice. *Good served with cornbread.* SERVES 6–8.

—Nell Bauer, Panola County Club

Dirty Rice (Rice Dressing)

1 pound sausage

½ pound chicken livers, chopped

1 large green pepper

1 large onion

5–6 celery stalks

1–2 cloves garlic

parsley

salt, pepper, and Tabasco sauce, to taste

3–4 cups cooked rice

Brown sausage; drain off excess fat. Add chopped livers, and cook thoroughly. Put green pepper, onion, celery, garlic, and parsley in grinder or food processor. Add vegetables to sausage and liver; cook thoroughly. Add salt, pepper, and Tabasco sauce to taste; add a small amount of water, if needed. Cook until done; mix in cooked rice. SERVES 6–8.

—*Mary Ann Markey, Orange County Club*

Green Enchiladas with Chicken

1 breast of chicken, cooked, deboned and shredded (reserve broth)

10–12 green tomatillos

1 tablespoon vegetable oil

⅓ cup finely chopped onion

1 clove garlic, mashed

pinch of ground cumin

salt to taste

3 tablespoons all-purpose flour

2 cups chicken broth

½ cup vegetable oil

1 dozen corn tortillas

½ cup grated Monterey Jack cheese

sour cream for garnish

Cook chicken in sufficient salted water to have 2–3 cups of broth. Debone and shred meat. Set aside. Remove skins from tomatillos; wash and cut into small pieces. Put in blender to make purée. Heat 1 tablespoon oil in skillet; add onion, garlic, cumin, salt, and flour. Sauté, but do not brown. Add tomatillo purée and chicken broth, and bring to a boil. Lower heat, and simmer for about 3 minutes. Cover to keep warm and set aside. Heat ½ cup oil in skillet and add tortillas, one at a time. Remove while still soft and pliable, not crisp. Stack on a plate and set aside. Fill each tortilla with chicken and shredded cheese; roll and place in large baking pan in single layer. Pour a small amount of warm tomatillo sauce over them to keep moist. Cover dish with foil, and keep in warm oven (200°) for 10–15 minutes, or until ready to serve. As you make each serving, add warm tomatillo sauce and a dollop of sour cream. SERVES 4.

—*Belia Tijirina, San Angelo Club*

Chicken Enchiladas I

1 frying chicken (3–4 pounds), reserve broth

1 chopped onion

1 jalapeño pepper, chopped

butter or margarine for sautéeing

1 can (10¾ ounces) cream of mushroom soup

1 soup can milk

½ soup can chicken broth, or more

8 flour tortillas

1 pound longhorn cheese, grated

Cook chicken; debone and chop; reserve some chicken broth. Sauté onion and pepper in small amount of butter or margarine. Add soup, milk, chicken broth, and chopped chicken. If needed, add more chicken broth to get the right consistency—not runny, but not chunky. Grease baking dish and layer with torn tortillas, chicken mixture, and grated cheese. Bake at 350° for 30 minutes. *Recipe can be divided with part frozen for future use.* SERVES 4–6.

—*Jerri Kelley, Grayson County Club*

Chicken Enchiladas II

1 package (12 ounces) soft tortillas

vegetable oil

1 can (10¾ ounces) cream of chicken soup

1 can (4 ounces) diced green chilies

½ pint sour cream

¾ cup grated cheddar cheese

1 whole chicken breast, cooked and cubed

Heat vegetable oil in skillet. Using tongs, dip tortillas in oil one at a time, until barely soft, 5–10 seconds. Turn and remove. Drain on paper towels. Combine soup, chilies, sour cream, and half of cheese. Add chicken to each tortilla, plus a generous tablespoon of soup mixture. Roll up, and arrange with seams down in oblong baking dish. Pour remaining sauce over enchiladas. Sprinkle remainder of cheese on top. Bake at 350° for 20 minutes. SERVES 6–8.

—*Mrs. G. L. Hayes, Matagorda County Club*

Sour Cream Chicken Enchiladas

10 flour tortillas

3 cups cooked chicken, chopped

1 pound Monterey Jack cheese, shredded

1 onion, chopped

SAUCE

½ cup (1 stick) butter, melted

3 tablespoons all-purpose flour

2 cups chicken broth or 1 can (14½ ounces) broth plus ½ can water

1½ cups sour cream

2 cans (4 ounces each) diced green chilies

Assemble chicken, cheese, and onion in tortillas; roll, and place in 13-by-9-inch pan or glass dish. To make sauce, melt butter, stir in flour and chicken broth. Bring to a boil. Fold in sour cream and heat to almost boiling. Add green chilies. Pour sauce over assembled stuffed tortillas. Bake for 20 minutes at 350°. MAKES 10 ENCHILADAS.

—*JoAnn Hollingsworth Moser, Port Arthur Club*

Chicken Tortillas (for slow cooker)

1 fryer, cooked and boned (or leftover turkey may be used)

1 can (10¾ ounces) cream of chicken soup

½ can (½ cup) tomatoes and green chilies

2 tablespoons quick-cooking tapioca

6–8 flour tortillas, torn into pieces

1 medium onion, chopped

2 cups grated cheddar cheese

Cut chicken or turkey into bite-sized pieces. Mix well with soup, tomatoes and green chilies, and tapioca. Line bottom of well-greased slow cooker with tortillas. Add ⅓ of chicken and soup mixture; sprinkle with onion and cheese. Repeat layers of tortillas, chicken mixture, onion, and cheese. Cover and cook on low for 6–8 hours, or on high for 3 hours. Recipe may be doubled, if desired. *I often use this recipe with leftover turkey the day after Christmas.* SERVES 6.

—*Juanita Toronjo, Orange County Club*

Swiss Enchiladas

1 chopped onion

2 tablespoons vegetable oil

1 clove garlic, chopped or crushed

2 cups tomato puree

2 tablespoons diced green chilies (or more to taste)

2 cups cooked, chopped chicken

salt and pepper to taste

vegetable oil to 1 inch in frying pan

1 dozen flour tortillas

2–3 cups half and half or cream

6 chicken bouillon cubes (or 1 cup reserved broth)

½–1 pound Monterey Jack or Swiss cheese, grated

Preheat oven to 350°. Sauté onion in oil until soft; add garlic, tomato puree, green chilies, and cooked chicken. Season with salt and pepper. Simmer 10 minutes. Fry tortillas in 1 inch oil; turn with tongs. Do not allow to become crisp, as they are to be rolled. Heat half and half in saucepan; dissolve bouillon cubes or add broth. Do not boil. Dip each tortilla in mixture, add about 2 tablespoons of chicken mixture, and roll up. Put seamside down in baking dish. Pour remaining cream mixture over, and top with grated cheese. Bake for 30–45 minutes at 350°. *These are wonderful! I usually make extra ones to freeze, since they are messy to make.* MAKES 6–8 SERVINGS.   —*Cecile Ramey, Austin Club, and Jo Ella Wozniak, Rio Grande Valley Club*

Carne Guisado

2–3 pounds round steak, cubed

2 tablespoons vegetable oil

2 tablespoons all-purpose flour

4 tablespoons chopped green peppers

4 tablespoons chopped onions

4 tablespoons chopped tomatoes

2 large cloves garlic, chopped fine

1 jalapeño pepper, chopped fine (optional)

½ teaspoon black pepper

1 can (6 ounces) tomato juice

salt to taste

about ½ cup of water

Brown the cubed steak in oil. After it is brown, coat it with flour, and add the remaining ingredients. Cook about 30–40 minutes, or until the meat and other ingredients are tender and the sauce becomes thick. *Tacos, like enchiladas, can be made with many different fillings. Tacos made with flour tortillas are frequently filled with carne guisado. This mixture is also good over rice.* SERVES 4.   —*Marilyn Putz, Rio Grande Valley Club*

My Roommate's from New Jersey

Mexican Pot Roast

5–6 pound beef roast

2 tablespoons vegetable oil

1 can (8 ounces) tomatoes, cut up

1 can (4 ounces) chopped green
chilies

¼ cup water

½ envelope (2 tablespoons) taco
seasoning mix

2 teaspoons beef bouillon granules

1 teaspoon sugar

¼ cup cold water

2 tablespoons all-purpose flour

Brown meat in oil in large Dutch oven. Add rest of ingredients except the ¼ cup cold water and 2 tablespoons flour reserved for gravy. Mix well and let simmer for 2–2½ hours. Remove meat from pot. Mix water and flour and add to liquid in pot. Stir and cook until thickened. You may need to add more water if too thick. Serve with steamed rice, prepared according to directions. *This is a good change from the "ordinary" pot roast.* SERVES 6–8.
—*Esther Goessler, Washington County Club*

Firecracker Casserole

2 pounds ground beef

1 large onion, chopped

2 tablespoons chili powder

3 teaspoons ground cumin

1 teaspoon salt

1 can (15 ounces) chili-flavored red
beans

8–10 corn tortillas, torn into
pieces

1½ cups shredded Monterey Jack
cheese

1½ cups shredded cheddar cheese

1 can (10¾ ounces) cream of
mushroom soup, undiluted

1 can (10 ounces) tomatoes and
green chilies

Cook ground beef and onion in large skillet until meat is brown and onion is tender; discard drippings. Add chili powder, cumin, and salt; stir well. Cook over low heat 10 minutes. Spoon meat mixture into 13-by-9-inch baking pan. Layer beans, tortillas, and cheeses over mixture. Spread soup on top, and pour tomatoes and green chilies on top of soup. Cover baking pan; refrigerate overnight. Bake, uncovered, at 350° for 1 hour. SERVES 6–8.
—*Loretta Franke, Midland Club*

Aunt Wanda's "Good" Chili

4 pounds ground chili meat

2 large onions, chopped

4 cloves garlic, minced

1 large can (46 ounces) tomato juice

½ teaspoon crushed red pepper

5 teaspoons cumin

8 tablespoons chili powder

3 teaspoons salt

2 tablespoons masa harina, mixed with water

Cook meat, onion, and garlic until brown. Add tomato juice and bring to a boil. Reduce heat to simmer. Add red pepper, cumin, chili powder, and salt. Cook slowly for several hours. You may add water if needed during cooking. Mix masa harina with small amount of water; add for the last 30 minutes. *Good "after the game" meal, and a favorite of my daughter.* SERVES 10–12. —*Margie Harmon, Hays County Club*

Chili Verde

1–1½ pounds round steak, cubed

vegetable oil for sautéeing

1 chopped onion

2 cans (4 ounces each) diced green chilies

2 cloves garlic, chopped or mashed

cumin, to taste

2 cups water

2 bouillon cubes

1 package flour tortillas

1 can (16 ounces) refried beans

Monterey Jack cheese, shredded

Picante sauce, to taste

cheddar cheese, shredded

Cube round steak and sauté in small amount of oil. Add onions; stir until wilted. Add green chilies, garlic, and cumin. Add water and bouillon cubes, mixing well. Bring to a boil, lower heat, and simmer approximately 2½ hours. Add more water if necessary. Before serving, heat refried beans and shredded Monterey Jack cheese together. Steam flour tortillas (one way is to wrap them in foil and use a vegetable steamer over boiling water). Spread bean and cheese mixture over hot tortilla; add meat mixture down center of tortilla; add Picante sauce and cheddar cheese. Fold ends in and roll. *This recipe can be expanded to serve any number, depending on the amount of meat available and the size of appetites. The recipe was given to me by a friend and is so good I never felt the need to change anything.* SERVES 4–6. —*Lois Harrington, Midland Club*

Spanish Rice

2 tablespoons shortening

1 cup rice (uncooked)

2 cups water

1 clove garlic

¼ teaspoon cumin

¼ teaspoon chili powder

Brown rice in hot shortening, stirring frequently, in saucepan. Add water after rice is brown, and cover. Steam until dry (15–20 minutes with most white rice). Add garlic, cumin, and chili powder. SERVES 4.

—*Ruth Lindquist, Brush Country Club*

Tamale and Corn Bake

¾ cup finely crushed corn chips

1 large can (17 ounces) whole kernel corn, drained

¼ teaspoon salt

2 teaspoons chili powder

½ cup chopped ripe olives

1 can (17 ounces) tamales, drained and cut into 1-inch pieces

2 cups grated cheddar cheese

¾ cup crushed corn chips (for topping)

1 cup tomato juice

Picante sauce

Arrange in baking dish step by step as given above. Bake at 350° for 25 minutes, or until bubbly. Serve with Picante sauce. *Casserole may be made and frozen for future use.* SERVES 4–6.   —*Ruby Carpenter, Tyler Club*

Mexican Corn Bread

1½ cups corn meal

¾ cup buttermilk

¾ cup vegetable oil

2 eggs

1 medium can (17 ounces) cream-style corn

1 teaspoon salt

3 teaspoons baking powder

3 jalapeño peppers, chopped

1 cup cheddar cheese, grated

Make batter of all ingredients except cheese; mix well. Pour half of batter into baking dish; sprinkle on half of cheese. Add remaining batter and top with cheese. Bake about 1 hour at 350°. SERVES 6–8.   —*Milam County Club*

Jalapeño Corn Bread

2 eggs

⅔ cup vegetable oil

1 carton (8 ounces) sour cream

1 cup yellow corn meal

1 cup cream-style corn

3 teaspoons baking powder

1½ teaspoons salt

1 small can (7 ounces) jalapeño peppers, chopped fine

1 cup grated cheddar cheese (more if desired)

Mix all ingredients in order, reserving some cheese for top. Pour into well-greased 13-by-9-inch pan. Bake at 350° for 45 minutes. Sprinkle a little cheese on top. SERVES 10–12.   —*From* Hungry Aggie Cookbook, *Kingsville Club*

Mexican Pecan Candy

2 cups sugar

¾ cup milk

½ teaspoon baking soda

2 tablespoons butter or margarine

½ cup pecans

Combine sugar and milk in heavy saucepan; boil to soft-ball stage (240° on candy thermometer). Remove from heat and beat. Add soda, butter or margarine, and pecans. Drop from spoon on waxed paper. Wrap individually and seal tightly when cool. MAKES 1½–2 DOZEN.

—Judy Young, Orange County Club

Chewy Pralines

2 cups sugar

1 pint whipping cream (divided)

½ cup (1 stick) butter or margarine

2 cups light corn syrup

1 teaspoon vanilla

4–5 cups pecans

In heavy saucepan combine sugar, ½ pint whipping cream, butter or margarine, and corn syrup. Cook to soft ball stage (240°) on candy thermometer. Remove from heat; add remaining ½ pint whipping cream and vanilla. Cook to 2° above soft ball. Remove from heat; stir in pecans. Drop on greased cookie sheet or waxed paper. Let set until not sticky. Wrap in plastic wrap. *These are just like the ones you get in a Mexican restaurant.*
MAKES 3–4 DOZEN.   *—Marilyn Anderson, Guadalupe County Club*

My Roommate's from New Jersey

10

Home, Sweet Home

A&M Mothers' Club members treasure—but also enjoy sharing—their favorite dessert recipes. The cakes, pies, and other favorites in this chapter include some family favorites and some classics that make suitable endings to potluck suppers or elegant finales to special meals. Home, sweet home may mean apple pie to some and fudge brownies to someone else.

When you think *dessert*, you frequently think calories. However, there are ways around that. If you're planning to serve a dessert after a heavy meal, select one of the lighter ones or even just fresh fruit, and it will be enjoyed much more. In some recipes, you may adjust caloric and fat content somewhat by substituting ingredients, but you might want to experiment first with half a recipe. Whipped topping mixes and thawed frozen whipped topping can usually be substituted for real whipping cream. Margarine will usually work instead of butter, but be careful about substituting diet or whipped margarines—the volume and water content may be different. Plain yogurt (unflavored) or imitation sour cream will frequently work in a recipe calling for sour cream, but expect the taste to be slightly different.

Sometimes that seemingly ever-present diet goes out the window (just for a little while). "Come for coffee and dessert" is a special invitation to receive, because you know you're going to taste a creation that has been prepared with extra care. This is the time to enjoy every morsel and vow to increase your workout time tomorrow.

Dessert may also mean a special kind of birthday cake for that son or daughter or candles on a pie. Whatever your favorite, serve it with a generous dollop of love.

Cheesecake Cookies

⅓ cup butter or margarine, softened

⅓ cup brown sugar, firmly packed

1 cup all-purpose flour

½ cup chopped walnuts

¼ cup sugar

1 package (8 ounces) cream cheese, softened

1 egg

2 tablespoons milk

1 tablespoon lemon juice

½ teaspoon vanilla

Cream butter with brown sugar in small mixing bowl; mix flour and walnuts and add to butter mixture. Reserve 1 cup mixture for topping. Press remainder into 8-inch square pan. Bake at 350° for 12–15 minutes. Blend sugar with cream cheese until smooth. Add egg, milk, lemon juice, and vanilla. Beat well; spread over crust. Sprinkle with reserved crumb mixture. Bake at 350° for 25 minutes. Cut into bars. Refrigerate. MAKES ABOUT 2 DOZEN SMALL COOKIES. —*Patsy Kavanaugh, Mainland Club*

Chocolate Rollaway Balls

1¼ cups butter or margarine

⅔ cup sugar

1 teaspoon vanilla

½ cup cocoa

2 cups all-purpose flour

⅛ teaspoon salt

1 cup chopped pecans

powdered confectioners sugar

Cream butter or margarine and sugar. Add vanilla. Sift together cocoa, flour, and salt and add to sugar mixture. Add pecans. Mix well. Refrigerate for 6 hours. Roll into walnut-sized balls. Bake at 350° for 20 minutes. Let cool. Roll in powdered sugar. MAKES 3 DOZEN.

—*Mrs. Otto Wehring, Washington County Club*

Chewy Chocolate Chip-Pecan-Oatmeal Cookies

4½ cups all-purpose flour

2 teaspoons baking soda

1 teaspoon salt

2 cups butter, softened, or
vegetable shortening

1 cup sugar

1½ cups brown sugar

½ cup honey

2 teaspoons vanilla

1 teaspoon water

4 eggs

1 package (12 ounces) semisweet
chocolate morsels

4–5 cups chopped pecans

2 cups quick oats

Sift together flour, soda, and salt; set aside. Cream butter, sugars, honey, vanilla, and water in large mixing bowl. Beat in eggs, one at a time, until well blended. Add flour mixture and mix well. Stir in chocolate morsels, pecans, and oats. Drop from tip of teaspoon on lightly greased cookie sheet. Bake in 375° oven for 10–12 minutes. *This recipe makes a large batch. They stay moist and chewy for days or freeze well.* MAKES 8 DOZEN LARGE COOKIES OR 16 DOZEN MEDIUM COOKIES. —*Albina Englert, San Angelo Club*

Coconut Pecan Chocolate Chip Cookies

1 cup vegetable shortening

½ cup sugar

1 cup light brown sugar, firmly
packed

1 teaspoon vanilla

2 eggs

2 cups all-purpose flour

1 teaspoon baking soda

1 teaspoon salt

1 cup chopped pecans

2 cups mini semisweet chocolate
morsels

1 cup shredded coconut

Cream together shortening, sugars, and vanilla. Add eggs and beat well. Sift together flour, baking soda, and salt; add to creamed mixture. Stir in nuts, chips, and coconut. Drop by teaspoonfuls onto greased baking sheet. Bake at 375° for 8–10 minutes. Remove with spatula and cool on rack. *Bake a shorter time (just until light brown) if you want soft cookies. If you want crisp cookies, bake until medium to dark brown.* MAKES 6 DOZEN COOKIES.
—*Nell (Mrs. Richard) Witkowski, San Antonio Club*

Norwegian Butter Cookies

3 cups (6 sticks) sweet (unsalted) butter, softened (no substitute)

1½ cups powdered confectioners sugar, sifted twice

1½ teaspoons salt

5 cups cake flour, sifted twice

1 cup sliced almonds

½ teaspoon almond extract

Cream butter in mixer until white in color and very fluffy. Add powdered sugar, salt, and flour—a little at a time—until all added and smooth. Stir in almonds and almond extract. Drop by teaspoonfuls onto an ungreased cookie sheet. Bake for 10–12 minutes in a 350° oven, or until just turning brown around the edges. Watch closely the last few minutes. *This is a butter cookie which improves in flavor when stored in a tight container for several weeks (this works only if no one knows you have baked them)*. MAKES APPROXIMATELY 9 DOZEN COOKIES. —*Marilyn Putz, Rio Grande Valley Club*

Cut-Out Sugar Cookies

½ cup margarine

½ cup sugar

2 eggs

1 teaspoon vanilla

2 teaspoons baking powder

2¾ cups all-purpose flour

Cream margarine and sugar; beat in eggs and vanilla. Sift baking powder and flour together and add, one cup at a time, mixing well. The dough will be very stiff. Do not chill. Roll out immediately on floured surface to approximately ⅛-inch thickness. Dip cutters in flour before each use. In preheated 400° oven, bake 6–7 minutes, or until golden brown.

ICING

2 tablespoons color flow mix

1 box (16 ounces) powdered confectioners sugar

¼ cup water

paste-type food coloring (added to small amounts of icing)

Beat frosting ingredients on low speed about 5 minutes. Keep in covered bowl. Color small bits and "paint" cookies. It dries out quickly, so keep covered with foil, and work with one color at a time. *Recipe doubles nicely. It is a very good cookie recipe—many bakers consume as many as they frost, so make extras*. MAKES 2 DOZEN. —*Judith Paré, Midland Club*

Santa's Whiskers
(Christmas Cookies)

1 cup butter or margarine,
softened
1 cup sugar
2 tablespoons milk
1 teaspoon vanilla or rum extract

2½ cups sifted all-purpose flour
¾ cup finely chopped red and
green candied cherries
½ cup finely chopped pecans
¾ cup flaked coconut

In large mixing bowl, cream together butter or margarine and sugar; blend
in milk and vanilla. Stir in flour, candied cherries, and nuts. Form into two
rolls, each 2 inches in diameter and 8 inches long. Roll in coconut. Wrap
and chill several hours or overnight. Slice ¼-inch thick; place on ungreased cookie sheet. Bake at 375° oven for 12 minutes, or until edges are
golden. *Even though some of my children do not like candied fruit, they all like
these cookies.* MAKES ABOUT 5 DOZEN.   —*Mrs. Laura Stoffer, Orange County Club*

Pecan Tassies

1 package (3 ounces) cream cheese,
softened
½ cup (1 stick) margarine,
softened

1 cup all-purpose flour

FILLING

1 egg
¾ cup brown sugar
1 tablespoon margarine, softened

1 teaspoon vanilla
1 cup chopped pecans

Mix cream cheese and margarine until well blended. Stir in flour and chill.
Shape into 1-inch balls; place in ungreased miniature muffin tins and pat
into shells. For filling, mix egg, brown sugar, margarine, and vanilla. Add
nuts. Spoon mixture into unbaked shells. Bake at 325° for 20–25 minutes.
A pecan half or a maraschino cherry may be placed on each tassie before
baking if desired. MAKES 2 DOZEN 1½-INCH TASSIES.

—*Harrison County Club*

Finger Cookies

3 cups sifted all-purpose flour

1 pound (4 sticks) butter (do not
substitute)

1 cup sugar

2 eggs, beaten

sugar

nuts, finely chopped

Blend flour, butter, and sugar until well mixed. Pinch off small amount of dough and roll between hands to the size of a finger. Dip into beaten egg, then roll in sugar and chopped nuts. Place on a well-greased cookie sheet. Bake 25 minutes at 325°. MAKES 5–6 DOZEN.

—From Another Hungry Aggie Cookbook, *Kingsville Club*

Kourabiedes
(Powdered Sugar Cookies)

1 pound (4 sticks) unsalted butter,
softened

½ cup sifted powdered
confectioners sugar

1 egg yolk

½ cup finely chopped toasted
almonds

1 teaspoon vanilla

1 jigger whiskey

4 cups sifted cake flour

powdered confectioners sugar for
coating

Beat butter, powdered sugar, and egg yolk until light and creamy (about 10–15 minutes). Add almonds, vanilla, and whiskey. Beating by hand, add cake flour until dough does not stick to the fingers. It will be a soft dough. Pinch off pieces of dough about the size of a walnut, and roll and shape into crescents. Place 1 inch apart on ungreased cookie sheet, and bake in a 350° oven for 20 minutes or until very lightly browned. Carefully remove cookies and place on flat surface that has been sprinkled ½-inch deep with sifted powdered sugar. Sift more sugar over cookies until they are completely covered. Allow to cool. MAKES 6 DOZEN COOKIES.

—Mrs. John Gonzales, Jr., Wichita County Area Club

Tea Cakes

½ cup (1 stick) butter or
    margarine, softened
1 cup sugar
2 eggs
1 teaspoon baking powder
½ teaspoon salt

1 teaspoon vanilla
¼ teaspoon almond extract
    (optional)
¼ cup milk
3 cups all-purpose flour

Cream butter, sugar, and eggs until well mixed. Add baking powder, salt, vanilla, almond, and milk; mix well. Add flour, and mix thoroughly. Chill dough. Using small portions of chilled dough, roll out dough on floured surface to ¼–⅜-inch thickness. *Do not* roll thin. Cut in desired shapes and place on greased baking sheet. Bake at 350° for 10–15 minutes. Important: Bake cookies until lightly brown on the bottom—they will still be white on the top. *This is an old Southern recipe and a favorite in our family for several generations.* MAKES 2½–3 DOZEN. —*Mrs. Bill James III, Eagle Pass Club*

Aggie Nuggets

½ cup (1 stick) butter, melted
3 eggs
1 package (18.5 ounces) yellow
    cake mix
1 package (8 ounces) cream cheese,
    softened

1 box (16 ounces) powdered
    confectioners sugar, sifted
1 cup chopped pecans
1 cup coconut

Combine melted butter with 1 of the eggs and cake mix. Spread thin layer in greased jelly roll pan or 13-by-9-inch pan. Combine cream cheese and sifted powdered sugar. Mix well with remaining 2 eggs. Pour over first layer. Sprinkle with pecans and coconut on top. Bake at 350° for 45–50 minutes, or until golden brown. Cut into squares when cool. SERVES 24.

—*Betty Ann Tolbert, DeWitt–Lavaca County Club*

Gingerbread

1 cup vegetable oil

1 cup cane syrup

3 eggs

1 cup sugar

2½ cups all-purpose flour

2 teaspoons ginger

2 teaspoons allspice

2 teaspoons cinnamon

¼ teaspoon salt

¼ cup water

2 teaspoons baking soda

1 cup boiling water

Combine all ingredients except the boiling water; mix well with mixer. Add boiling water last, and mix again. Bake at 350° for 45 minutes in a greased 13-by-9-inch baking pan.　　*—Janice Ann Rowe, Angelina County Club*

Chewy Bars

2½ cups brown sugar

¾ cup (1½ sticks) butter

2 eggs

1¾ cups sifted all-purpose flour

3 teaspoons baking powder

1 teaspoon vanilla

2 cups chopped nuts

powdered confectioners sugar

Melt brown sugar and butter in double boiler. Let cool. Beat eggs lightly, and mix with brown sugar and butter. Mix in flour, baking powder, vanilla, and nuts. Bake in 15-by-10-inch pan (jelly-roll type) for 25–35 minutes at 300°. When cool, cut into squares and roll in powdered sugar. MAKES 24–30 BARS.　　*—Marian W. Prihoda, Lafayette, Louisiana Club*

Pecan Bars

1 box (16 ounces) light brown
　sugar

2 cups buttermilk baking mix

2 cups chopped pecans

4 large eggs

powdered sugar (for dusting)

Combine brown sugar, baking mix, pecans, and eggs. Mixture will be thick and lumpy. Pour mixture into greased and floured 9-by-12-inch baking pan. Bake 30 minutes at 375°. Cool before cutting into bars. Roll in powdered sugar. *A quick and easy recipe that everyone likes.* MAKES 36–40 BARS.
—Sandra Benski, Mid-Jefferson County Club

Honey Bars

2 cups all-purpose flour

1 cup sugar

1 teaspoon cinnamon

½ teaspoon salt

1 teaspoon baking soda

¾ cup vegetable oil

¼ cup honey

1 egg, well beaten

1 teaspoon vanilla

1 cup chopped nuts

ICING

1 cup powdered confectioners
  sugar

2 tablespoons mayonnaise (no
  substitute)

2 tablespoons water

½ teaspoon vanilla

Mix flour, sugar, cinnamon, salt, and soda together. Add oil, honey, egg, vanilla, and nuts. Dough will be stiff. Press into a 10-by-15-inch jelly roll pan. Cook exactly 18 minutes at 350°. Remove from oven and immediately pour icing over bars. Let set about 8 minutes. Cut into squares. MAKES 3–4 DOZEN BARS.   —*From* Hullabaloo in the Kitchen, *Dallas County Club*

Lemon Bars

3 eggs

⅓ cup vegetable shortening

1 package (18.25 ounces) lemon
  cake mix

½ cup sugar

½ teaspoon baking powder

¼ teaspoon salt

2 teaspoons grated lemon peel

¼ cup lemon juice

powdered confectioners sugar
  (optional)

Combine 1 egg, shortening, and dry cake mix until crumbly; reserve 1 cup of this mixture. Pat remaining mixture lightly into ungreased 13-by-9-inch pan. Bake at 350° for 15 minutes, or until light brown. Beat remaining 2 eggs, sugar, baking powder, salt, lemon peel, and lemon juice with beater until light and foamy. Pour over hot crust; sprinkle with reserved crumb mixture. Bake at 350° for 15 minutes, or until light brown. Sprinkle with powdered sugar, if desired. Cool. Cut into bars. MAKES 15–20 BARS.

—*Marian W. Prihoda, Lafayette, Louisiana Club*

Lemon Squares

1 cup all-purpose flour

½ cup (1 stick) butter or
   margarine, softened

¼ cup powdered confectioners
   sugar

2 eggs

1 cup sugar

½ teaspoon baking powder

2 tablespoons lemon juice

Blend flour, butter or margarine, and powdered sugar thoroughly. Press into 8-inch square pan. Bake 20 minutes at 350°. Combine remaining ingredients, and beat well. Pour over crust and bake an additional 20–25 minutes. Do not overbake. *Filling puffs during baking but flattens when cooled.* MAKES 16 SQUARES.   —*Anne Cassens, Orange County Club*

Mint Bars

2 squares (1 ounce each)
   unsweetened chocolate

½ cup (1 stick) margarine

2 eggs, beaten

1 cup sugar

½ cup all-purpose flour

½ cup almonds, chopped, or ½
   teaspoon almond extract
   (optional)

Melt together chocolate and margarine in saucepan; let cool. Mix remaining ingredients together in order given; add cooled chocolate-margarine mixture. Line 8-inch square pan with foil; grease foil with butter or margarine. Pour in batter. Bake on bottom rack of oven for 20 minutes at 350°; then bake 5 more minutes on middle rack. While first layer is baking, prepare the second layer.

LAYER II

½ cup powdered confectioners
   sugar

3 tablespoons butter, melted

½ tablespoon milk

1 teaspoon peppermint extract

1 square (1 ounce) unsweetened
   chocolate

1½ tablespoons butter

Mix powdered sugar, 3 tablespoons melted butter, milk, and peppermint extract. When first layer is done, and while it is still hot, pour second layer over top. Refrigerate until firm. To make glaze, melt 1 square unsweetened chocolate with 1½ tablespoons butter. Pour over second layer; spread thinly to edges. Refrigerate until firm. After peeling away foil, slice into ½-inch fingers. *These are very rich—a little more trouble but well worth it. You may substitute 3 tablespoons cocoa and 1 tablespoon margarine for 1 ounce chocolate.* MAKES 5 DOZEN BARS.   —*Danita Ruffner, Amarillo Club*

Pecan Pie Surprise Bars

1 package (18.5 ounces) yellow cake mix (reserve ⅔ cup)

½ cup butter or margarine, melted

5 eggs

2 cups chopped pecans

1 cup firmly packed brown sugar

1 cup white corn syrup

1 teaspoon vanilla

Grease bottom and sides of 13-by-9-inch baking pan. In large mixing bowl, combine cake mix (except for ⅔ cup), melted butter or margarine, and 1 egg. Add 1 cup of the chopped pecans. Mix until crumbly; press into prepared pan. Bake at 350° for 15–20 minutes, until light golden brown. Meanwhile, prepare filling. In large mixing bowl, combine reserved cake mix, brown sugar, corn syrup, vanilla, and remaining 4 eggs. Beat at medium speed 1–2 minutes. Pour filling over partially baked crust; sprinkle with remaining 1 cup of pecans. Return to oven and bake for 30–35 minutes, or until filling is set. Cool and cut into bars. *These are very rich, but very good. They were a big hit at a party.* MAKES 36 BARS.

—*Mrs. Bobby J. Osborn, Abilene Club*

Aggie Wine Cake

¾ cup brown sugar, packed

2 tablespoons cinnamon

1 box (18.5 ounces) yellow cake mix

2 small boxes (3½ ounces each) instant vanilla pudding mix

3 tablespoons all-purpose flour

1 teaspoon nutmeg

3 eggs

¾ cup vegetable oil

1¼ cups cream sherry

Mix together brown sugar and cinnamon. Pour one-third of mixture into bottom of well-greased bundt pan. Mix all remaining ingredients at medium speed for 2 minutes. Add one-half of cake batter, one-third of sugar-cinnamon, and remainder of cake batter. Top with remainder of sugar mixture. Bake for 1 hour, 5 minutes, at 350°. SERVES 12–14.

—*Darnell Hanson, Mid-Jefferson County Club*

Italian Cream Cake

½ cup (1 stick) margarine

½ cup shortening

2 cups sugar

5 egg yolks

2 cups all-purpose flour

1 teaspoon baking soda

1 cup buttermilk

1 teaspoon vanilla

5 egg whites, beaten stiff

1 can (3½ ounces) coconut

1 cup chopped pecans

Cream margarine, shortening, and sugar. Add egg yolks. Mix flour and soda; add to creamed ingredients alternately with buttermilk. Add vanilla; carefully fold in beaten egg whites. Fold in coconut and pecans. Pour into 3 greased and floured 8-inch layer cake pans. Bake at 350° for 25 minutes.

ICING

4 tablespoons (½ stick) margarine

1 package (8 ounces) cream cheese, softened

1 box (16 ounces) powdered confectioners sugar

1 teaspoon vanilla

1 cup chopped pecans

Combine all ingredients and frost between layers and on top and sides of cake. Refrigerate. SERVES 12–14. —*Harrison County Club*

Coconut Cake

1 package (18.5 ounces) white cake mix

3 packages (6 ounces each) frozen coconut, thawed

1 cup sugar

1 cup sour cream

1 teaspoon vanilla

Mix cake mix according to package directions for 2 layers; bake. Cool, and split to make 4 layers. Combine remaining ingredients; spread between layers. Cover and refrigerate until the day you plan to serve it, at which time it can be iced with the following.

WHITE MOUNTAIN ICING

½ cup sugar

¼ cup light corn syrup

3 tablespoons water

2 egg whites, stiffly beaten

1 teaspoon vanilla

Combine sugar, corn syrup, and water in saucepan; cook to 242° on a candy thermometer, or until mixture spins a thread when dropped from a spoon. Beat egg whites until stiff. Add hot mixture very gradually, beating constantly, until stiff peaks are formed. Fold in vanilla. Spread on top and sides of cake. Keep in refrigerator. SERVES 14–16.

—Avis Morris, Orange County Club

Cream of Coconut Cake

1 box (18.5 ounces) yellow cake
   mix

¾ cup vegetable oil

3 eggs

1 teaspoon vanilla

1 cup cream of coconut

8 ounces sour cream

Combine all ingredients in turn and mix thoroughly. Bake in three 8-inch or two 9-inch layer cake pans, which have been greased and floured. Cool completely.

ICING

1 box (16 ounces) powdered
   confectioners sugar

1 package (8 ounces) cream cheese,
   softened

½ cup (1 stick) margarine,
   softened

1 teaspoon vanilla

1 can (3½ ounces) angel flake
   coconut

Blend powdered sugar, cream cheese, margarine, and vanilla with mixer. Stir in coconut and spread on cooled cake. SERVES 10–12.

—Ruth Walters, Orange County Club

Home, Sweet Home

Gooey Butter Cake

1 box (18.5 ounces) yellow
    cake mix
1 egg
½ cup (1 stick) margarine
1 box (16 ounces) powdered
    confectioners sugar

2 eggs
1 package (8 ounces) cream cheese,
    softened

Mix cake mix, egg, and margarine. Press into greased 12-by-9-inch pan. Beat remaining ingredients until smooth. Spoon over unbaked first layer. Bake 40–50 minutes at 350°. Sprinkle powdered sugar on top after baking, if desired. MAKES 12–14 SERVINGS.   —*Barbra Mouton, Orange County Club*

Blitzkuchen (Lightning Cake)

4 egg yolks, well beaten
½ cup sugar
½ cup butter, softened
juice and rind of ½ lemon

1 cup all-purpose flour
1¼ teaspoons baking powder,
    sifted with flour
6 tablespoons milk

TOPPING

4 egg whites, beaten stiff
1 cup sugar

½ cup chopped nuts (pecans
    preferred)

FILLING

1 egg
1 cup milk
2 tablespoons all-purpose flour

½ cup sugar
pinch of salt
½ teaspoon vanilla

Add sugar, butter, and lemon juice and rind to well-beaten egg yolks. Sift flour and baking powder together; add alternately with milk to egg mixture. Divide batter into two round layer cake pans, which have been greased and floured. Beat egg whites until stiff; add 1 cup sugar very gradually. Fold in chopped nuts. Spoon carefully over unbaked cake batter. Bake at 350° for 30 minutes. When cooled, place one cake on plate with meringue on bottom. Prepare filling while cake is baking. Combine egg, milk, flour, sugar, and salt. Cook, stirring frequently, until very thick. Add vanilla. Let cool. Put filling between upside-down layer and top layer (with meringue on top). Must be refrigerated after filling is added. *A traditional German dessert. Interesting to look at and eat.* SERVES 12–16.

—*Charlene Fischer, Comal County Club*

Sock-It-To-Me Cake

½ cup sugar

1 box (18.5 ounces) butter-recipe
  yellow cake mix

¾ cup vegetable oil

8 ounces sour cream (or imitation
  sour cream)

2 teaspoons vanilla

4 eggs

2 teaspoons cinnamon

3 tablespoons brown sugar

½ cup chopped nuts

Combine sugar and cake mix. Blend in oil, sour cream, and vanilla. Beat in eggs, one at a time, until well mixed. Set aside. Combine cinnamon, brown sugar, and nuts. Mix until crumbly. Grease and flour a tube pan. Pour half of batter into pan; add half of nut mixture over batter. Pour in remaining batter, and top with remaining nut mixture. Bake for 60–70 minutes at 325°. While cake is still hot, pour the glaze over it.

GLAZE

2 tablespoons margarine, melted

1 teaspoon vanilla

2 tablespoons milk

1 cup powdered confectioners
  sugar

Cool melted margarine slightly; add vanilla to milk; add margarine. Sift in powdered sugar until proper consistency for glaze. Pour over hot cake. SERVES 12–14.   —*From* Hungry Aggie Cookbook, *Kingsville Club*

Oatmeal Cake

1¼ cups boiling water

1 cup quick-cooking oats

½ cup (1 stick) margarine

1 cup sugar

2 eggs

1⅓ cups all-purpose flour

1 cup brown sugar

1 teaspoon baking soda

½ teaspoon cinnamon

ICING

½ cup (1 stick) margarine

¼ cup evaporated milk

½ cup sugar

1 teaspoon vanilla

1 cup angel flake coconut

1 cup chopped pecans (optional)

Pour boiling water over oats and 1 stick margarine; let stand for 20 minutes. Stir in by hand sugar, eggs, flour, brown sugar, baking soda, and cinnamon; do not use mixer. Pour into greased 13-by-9-inch pan, and bake 35 minutes at 350°. While cake is baking, combine icing ingredients. Spread on hot cake and broil until brown. *Cake stays moist for days.* SERVES 20.

—*Barbara Boedeker, East Bell County Club*

Piña Colada Cake

1 box (18.5 ounces) white cake mix

1 can (4 ounces) coconut

1 can (15 ounces) cream of coconut

Mix cake according to package directions, adding coconut. Bake according to directions for oblong cake. Remove from oven; poke holes with fork. Pour cream of coconut over warm cake. Allow cake to cool before icing.

ICING

1 carton (8 ounces) frozen whipped topping, thawed

1 can (4 ounces) coconut

Combine whipped topping and coconut; spread over cake. Refrigerate. SERVES 24.

—*Carol Ireland, Fort Bend Club*

Neiman-Marcus Cake

1 box (18.25 ounces) yellow cake mix

½ cup (1 stick) butter or margarine, melted

2 teaspoons vanilla

4 eggs

1 box (16 ounces) powdered confectioners sugar

1 package (8 ounces) cream cheese, softened

½ cup coconut or 1 package (6 ounces) semisweet chocolate morsels (optional)

½ cup pecans (optional)

Mix together the cake mix, melted butter or margarine, 1 teaspoon of the vanilla, and 2 of the eggs; spread in greased and floured 15-by-10-inch or 13-by-9-inch pan. This mixture will be tacky. For the second layer, combine powdered sugar, remaining 1 teaspoon vanilla, remaining 2 eggs, cream cheese, and coconut, chocolate morsels, or pecans (as desired). Spread over bottom layer. Bake at 350° for 35–45 minutes. Cool before cutting. (Ed. note: This recipe must have more variations than the store for which it was named. Take your choice among the coconut, chocolate morsels, and pecans—or perhaps you can come up with a new variation. Some cooks recommend using only a butter-recipe yellow cake mix, and purists say not to substitute margarine for the butter.) SERVES 20, OR MAKES 30 BITE-SIZED PIECES IN LARGER PAN.

—*Carole Karr, Amarillo Club, Nancy Tiller, Panola County Club,
and Lynda R. Wortham, Montgomery County Club*

Pound Cake

1 cup (2 sticks) butter, softened

2 cups sugar

6 eggs

2 cups all-purpose flour

2 teaspoons vanilla

1 tablespoon grated orange peel

Cream butter; add sugar gradually. Add 4 eggs, one at a time, beating well after each addition. Fold in flour in thirds, using lowest speed on mixer. Add vanilla, last 2 eggs, and orange peel. Beat at highest speed; pour into greased tube or bundt pan. Bake for 1 hour at 350°. *This is an old plantation recipe given to me by a friend who had the recipe handed down to her from her great-grandmother in Alabama.* SERVES 20+.

—*Ruby Lee Brown, Brazoria County Club*

Home, Sweet Home

Jo's Poppy Seed Pound Cake

1 cup buttermilk

1 tablespoon poppy seed

1 cup butter-flavored vegetable
  shortening

3 cups sugar

1 cup eggs (4 large eggs)

3 cups all-purpose flour (measured
  before sifting)

½ teaspoon baking soda

½ teaspoon salt

1 teaspoon vanilla

1 teaspoon almond extract

Combine buttermilk and poppy seed and set aside. Mix together shortening, sugar, and eggs in large mixing bowl. Beat for exactly 10 minutes. While batter is being mixed, sift together flour, soda, and salt. Add vanilla and almond extract to buttermilk–poppy seed mixture. Then add liquid and dry ingredients alternately to creamed batter. Mix thoroughly. Grease large tube pan, add batter, and bake for 1 hour at 350°. Do not open oven door while baking.

GLAZE

½ cup orange juice

1 cup sugar

1 teaspoon almond extract

1 teaspoon butter flavoring

Combine orange juice (reconstituted orange-flavored breakfast beverage crystals may be substituted) and sugar in saucepan. Bring to a boil and add flavorings. Pour over hot cake in pan. MAKES 12–14 SERVINGS.

—*Jo Nell Carter, Deep East Texas Club*

Cream Pound Cake

3 cups sugar

1 cup butter (no substitute),
  softened

6 eggs

3 cups all-purpose flour

½ pint whipping cream

2 teaspoons vanilla

Cream sugar and butter thoroughly. Add eggs, one at a time, beating well after each addition. Add flour and whipping cream alternately, mixing well. Add vanilla last. Pour into greased and floured tube pan. Put cake in cold oven and set for 325°; bake for 1 hour, 15 minutes. SERVES 12.

—*Juanita Toronjo, Orange County Club*

Sour Cream Pound Cake

3 cups all-purpose flour

1 teaspoon salt

¼ teaspoon baking soda

1 cup (2 sticks) margarine,
  softened

3 cups sugar

6 eggs

1 teaspoon vanilla

½ teaspoon lemon extract

¼ teaspoon almond extract

½ pint (1 cup) sour cream

Sift flour, salt, and soda together; set aside. Cream margarine and sugar thoroughly. Add eggs, one at a time, and beat well. Add vanilla, lemon, and almond extracts. Add dry ingredients and sour cream alternately, mixing well. Pour into tube pan that has been coated with nonstick cooking spray. Bake at 325° for 1 hour, or until cake "shrinks" from sides of pan. SERVES 16–20.   —*Kathleen Fish, Bee County Club*

German Chocolate Pound Cake

1 package (4 ounces) German
  sweet chocolate

1 cup vegetable shortening

2 cups sugar

4 eggs

2 teaspoons vanilla

2 teaspoons butter flavoring

1 cup buttermilk

3 cups all-purpose flour

½ teaspoon baking soda

1 teaspoon salt

Melt chocolate in double boiler over hot water. Cream shortening and sugar; add eggs, vanilla, butter flavoring, and buttermilk. Stir flour, soda, and salt together; add to other ingredients, and mix well. Stir in melted chocolate until well blended. Pour into well-greased and floured 9-inch tube pan. Bake at 300° for 1½ hours, checking after 1¼ hours. Remove from pan. While still warm, place under cover until cooled. *Tastes great with or without glaze. Delicious hot with butter. Both my Aggies request this for birthdays, coming home, or any other special occasion.* SERVES 16–20.

    —*Mrs. Ernest (Deanna) Kimbro, Hays County Club, and Sue Park, Liberty County Club*

Buttermilk Pound Cake

3 cups all-purpose flour

2½ cups sugar

¼ teaspoon baking soda

6 eggs

½ teaspoon vanilla

½ teaspoon lemon extract

1 cup vegetable shortening

1 cup buttermilk

Sift flour, sugar, and baking soda into large mixing bowl. Make well in center. Drop in eggs, vanilla, lemon extract, shortening, and buttermilk. Beat slowly with mixer until moistened. Beat at high speed for 3 minutes, scraping batter from sides of bowl often. Bake at 325° for 1½ hours in greased and floured bundt pan. MAKES 12–14 SERVINGS.

—*Susie McCabe, Hays County Club*

Devil's Food Cake

2 cups sugar

½ cup plus 2 tablespoons vegetable shortening

3 eggs, beaten

1 cup sour milk

1 teaspoon baking soda

1 teaspoon salt

⅓ cup cocoa

1 teaspoon vanilla

2 cups all-purpose flour

Cream sugar and shortening in large mixing bowl. Add beaten eggs. Dissolve soda in sour milk. Add to batter. Add remaining ingredients. Mix well. Pour into greased and floured layer cake pans or large sheet cake pan. Bake at 375° for 30–35 minutes, or until done.

ICING

2 cups sugar

¼ cup vegetable shortening

⅓ cup light corn syrup

½ cup milk

2 ounces (2 squares) unsweetened chocolate

½ teaspoon salt

1 teaspoon vanilla

Combine thoroughly, and bring to a boil in saucepan. Boil 1 minute. Beat until smooth; spread between layers and around cake. SERVES 16–20.

—*Doreen Holmstrom, Williamson County Club*

Aggie Cake

1½ cups sugar

½ cup shortening

2 eggs

2 teaspoons vanilla

1 teaspoon salt

¼ cup cocoa

2½ cups all-purpose flour

1 cup buttermilk

3 ounces red food coloring

1 tablespoon vinegar

1 teaspoon baking soda

Cream sugar and shortening; add eggs and vanilla. Beat well. Add salt and cocoa, and beat well. Add flour alternately with food coloring and buttermilk. Dissolve soda in vinegar and fold by hand into batter. Pour into greased and floured jelly roll pan (15 by 10 inches), and bake 25–30 minutes at 350°. Can also be poured into a greased Bundt pan and baked 35 minutes at 350°. Cool in pan.

ICING

1 box (16 ounces) powdered
   confectioners sugar

½ cup vegetable shortening

½ teaspoon salt

1 tablespoon vanilla

½ teaspoon almond flavoring

1 teaspoon butter flavoring

1 tablespoon coffee (optional)

5 tablespoons milk

Mix all icing ingredients in order given; use electric mixer, and beat at least 3 minutes. Spread on cake with spatula. *Many of the Corps of Cadets have eaten and requested this cake during the past six years. During the fall we host an Abbott barbecue on the corps green area for some of the cadets—our menu always includes Aggie Cake.* (Ed. note: Experiment with your red food colorings; some brands are more maroon than others.) SERVES 20 OR MORE.

—*Joanie Abbott, Deep East Texas Club*

Home, Sweet Home

Chocolate Date Cake

1 cup chopped dates

1 cup boiling water

1 teaspoon baking soda

1¾ cups all-purpose flour

2 tablespoons cocoa

½ teaspoon salt

1 cup vegetable shortening

1 cup sugar

2 eggs

1 teaspoon vanilla

1 cup chopped pecans

1 small package (6 ounces)
semisweet chocolate morsels

Add chopped dates to boiling water and soda; stir and let cool. Sift together flour, cocoa, and salt. Cream shortening and sugar. Add eggs and vanilla and stir well. Add the cooled date mixture and mix well. Slowly add the flour mixture, and mix well. Grease and flour a 13-by-9-inch pan. Pour in cake batter; sprinkle pecans and semisweet chocolate morsels on top. Bake at 350° for 35 minutes or until toothpick inserted in cake comes out clean. *Good cake to take to picnics and ballgames.* SERVES 16–20.

—*Mrs. Leonard Gulig, West Bell County Club*

Red Devil's Food Cake

½ cup vegetable shortening

1½ cups sugar

2 eggs

4 tablespoons cocoa

1 teaspoon red food coloring

4 tablespoons hot coffee

1⅞ cups all-purpose flour

1 teaspoon salt

1 cup buttermilk

1 teaspoon baking soda

1 teaspoon vanilla

Combine shortening, sugar, and eggs in large mixing bowl, and mix well. Set aside. Mix together the cocoa, food coloring, and coffee; add to shortening mixture. Combine flour and salt; set aside. Add soda to buttermilk; mix well. Add flour mixture alternately with buttermilk mixture; mix well. Add vanilla. Grease three 9-inch round cake pans; divide batter between them. Waxed paper in the bottom will facilitate removal of layers. Bake at 350° for 25 minutes, or until done.

1½ cups sugar

⅔ cup milk

2 tablespoons butter

1 teaspoon vanilla

Mix sugar, milk, butter, and vanilla together in saucepan; bring to a boil. Cook until mixture is thick enough to spread. You may test by dropping a small amount in cold water to see if it will harden. Remove from heat, and beat until mixture thickens. This is a very old-fashioned icing. *This recipe has been in my family for some 60 years. My mother acquired it at John Tarleton University, and it has been a favorite of all the men in my family all of my life.* MAKES 20 SERVINGS.

—*Zoe Ella Brusenhan, Victoria County Club*

Cookie Sheet Chocolate Cake (Fudge Cake)

½ cup (1 stick) margarine

½ cup vegetable shortening

4 tablespoons cocoa

1 cup water

2 cups sugar

2 cups all-purpose flour

2 eggs, beaten

½ cup buttermilk

1 teaspoon vanilla

1 teaspoon baking soda

Bring margarine, shortening, cocoa, and water to a boil in a saucepan, stirring to blend. Remove from heat, and set aside. Combine sugar and flour in large mixing bowl. Add cocoa mixture and mix well. Add beaten eggs, buttermilk, vanilla, and baking soda. Pour into large cookie sheet with sides (jelly roll pan). Bake at 375° for 20 minutes.

ICING

½ cup (1 stick) margarine

4 tablespoons cocoa

6 tablespoons milk

1 box (16 ounces) powdered
  confectioners sugar

1 teaspoon vanilla

1 cup chopped nuts

Combine margarine, cocoa, and milk in saucepan. Boil 2–3 minutes. Remove from heat; beat in powdered sugar. Stir in vanilla and nuts. Pour on cake while hot. *This may be cut into any size desired—serves well as cake with ice cream on top or cut into brownie-sized pieces.* SERVES 24.

—*Sandra Morgan, Angelina County Club, and Millie Jenkins, Mainland Club*

Cake in a Pan

2½ cups sugar

1 cup vegetable oil

2 eggs

½ teaspoon salt

2 teaspoons baking soda

2½ cups all-purpose flour

½ cup cocoa

1 cup buttermilk

1½ teaspoons vanilla

1 cup boiling water

Mix sugar, oil, and eggs together, and beat well. In another bowl, combine salt, soda, flour, and cocoa. Add dry mixture alternately with mixture of buttermilk and vanilla. Add boiling water all at once. Bake in 13-by-9-inch pan at 350° for 50 minutes.

ICING

½ cup cocoa

2 cups sugar

⅔ cup milk, minus 1 tablespoon

¼ teaspoon salt

½ cup (1 stick) margarine

1 teaspoon vanilla

Combine in saucepan the cocoa, sugar, milk, salt, and margarine. Boil 3–4 minutes, stirring constantly. Cool slightly, beating until glossy and slightly thickened. Add vanilla. Pour over hot cake, pricked with fork, so icing drizzles inside cake. Cool before eating. MAKES 15 SQUARES.

—*Frances Sanders, Victoria County Club*

Mississippi Mud Cake

1 cup (2 sticks) margarine, softened

2 cups sugar

⅓ cup cocoa

4 eggs

1½ cups all-purpose flour

1 teaspoon baking powder

1 cup coarsely chopped nuts

1 jar (7 ounces) marshmallow creme

Mix together margarine, sugar, and cocoa. Add eggs, one at a time, beating well after each addition. Mix in flour, baking powder, and nuts. Bake in 9-by-13-inch pan for 30 minutes at 350°. Spread marshmallow creme on hot cake. Cool in pan.

ICING

½ cup (1 stick) margarine, softened

⅓ cup cocoa

5 teaspoons milk

1 box (16 ounces) powdered confectioners sugar

1 teaspoon vanilla

Mix ingredients thoroughly. Spread on cake. SERVES 24.

—*Carol Ireland, Fort Bend Club*

Best Yet Cake

1 package (18.5 ounces) yellow cake mix

1 small package (3½ ounces) instant vanilla pudding mix

1 package (8 ounces) cream cheese, softened

⅙ of German chocolate bar (4-ounce size), grated

1 package (6 ounces) semisweet chocolate morsels

1 cup chopped pecans

½ cup vegetable oil

½ cup water

4 eggs

Mix all ingredients thoroughly. Pour into bundt pan. Bake at 350° for 50 minutes, or until done. When cool, frost with cream cheese icing if desired.

CREAM CHEESE ICING

½ cup butter or margarine, softened

2 teaspoons vanilla

2 cups powdered confectioners sugar

1 package (8 ounces) cream cheese, softened

Combine all ingredients, mixing well until smooth. Make only half the icing recipe if only a topping is desired. However, the full recipe is recommended. MAKES 12–14 SERVINGS.

—*Betty Rice, Baytown Club*

Lorrie's Carrot Cake

1½ cups vegetable oil or shortening

2½ cups sugar

4 eggs

5 tablespoons hot water

2½ cups all-purpose flour

1½ teaspoons baking powder

½ teaspoon baking soda

¼ teaspoon salt

1 teaspoon nutmeg

1 teaspoon cinnamon

1 teaspoon ground cloves

2–3 cups grated raw carrots

1 cup raisins

Cream together oil or shortening and sugar. Beat in eggs and hot water. Sift together flour, baking powder, baking soda, salt, nutmeg, cinnamon, and ground cloves, and add to first mixture. Stir in carrots and raisins. Bake in bundt pan for 60–70 minutes at 350°. May be frosted or served plain. *Chopped nuts may be added with carrots and raisins if desired.* SERVES 12–14.

—*Loretta Franke, Midland Club*

Carrot Cake

2¼ cups corn oil

5 eggs

12 ounces (1½ cups) fresh grated carrots

2¼ teaspoons vanilla

13½ ounces cake flour

1 tablespoon baking powder

2 teaspoons baking soda

18 ounces (2¼ cups) sugar

¾ teaspoon cinnamon

1 teaspoon salt

Combine corn oil, eggs, carrots, and vanilla in large mixing bowl. Beat at low speed for 2 minutes. Add remaining ingredients, and beat at medium speed for 10 minutes. Pour into large (13-by-9-inch) oblong baking pan which has been greased and floured. Bake at 350° for 45 minutes, or until cake pulls away from sides of pan. When cool, ice.

ICING

8 ounces cream cheese

¼ pound (1 stick) margarine

1 pound powdered confectioners
sugar

1 cup pecans, chopped

¾ cup coconut, grated

1 cup raisins

Cream together margarine and cream cheese. Add sifted powdered sugar, and mix well. Add pecans, coconut, and raisins; mix for 3 minutes on medium speed. *An Aggie favorite.* MAKES 1 SHEET CAKE.

—*Col. Fred W. Dollar and J. N. Maynard, TAMU Food Services Department*

Pecan Pie Cake

1 box (18.25 ounces) yellow cake
mix (reserve ⅔ cup of mix)

½ cup (1 stick) margarine,
softened

1 egg, beaten

Mix cake mix (except for reserved ⅔ cup), margarine, and egg until well blended. Press into greased 13-by-9-inch pan. Bake at 350° for 10–15 minutes. While crust is baking, prepare the filling.

FILLING

reserved ⅔ cup cake mix

½ cup brown sugar

3 eggs

1⅓ cups light corn syrup

1 teaspoon vanilla

1 cup chopped pecans

With mixer at medium speed, combine cake mix, brown sugar, eggs, corn syrup, and vanilla. Pour over crust, and sprinkle with chopped nuts. Bake at 375° for 20 minutes. SERVES 16. —*Marie Sitton, Waller County Club*

Banana Nut Cake

⅔ cup vegetable shortening

1½ cups sugar

5 egg yolks

2 large mashed bananas

2½ cups sifted all-purpose flour

1 teaspoon baking soda

¼ teaspoon salt

1 cup buttermilk

1 teaspoon vanilla

Cream vegetable shortening and sugar; add egg yolks and beat well. Add mashed bananas and dry ingredients alternately with buttermilk. Add vanilla. Pour into two greased and floured layer cake pans. Bake for 30–35 minutes at 350°. When cool, cut each layer in half horizontally, making 4 thin layers instead of 2. Frost with the following icing.

ICING

12 ounces cream cheese, softened

¾ cup (1½ stick) margarine, softened

1½ boxes (24 ounces) powdered confectioners sugar

1½ teaspoons vanilla

bananas, thinly sliced to cover layers

chopped pecans, for topping

Combine cream cheese and margarine; cream until smooth. Add powdered sugar and vanilla; beat until fluffy. Spread bottom layer with icing, and cover with thinly sliced bananas. Continue with cake icing, and thinly sliced bananas until all layers have been covered. Ice top and sides of cake, and sprinkle generously with chopped pecans. SERVES 18–20.

—*Lil Trussell, Brazoria County Club*

Almond Bundt Cake

½ cup butter-flavored shortening

½ cup sugar

3 eggs, beaten

2 cups all-purpose flour

2 teaspoons baking powder

½ teaspoon salt

1 can (8 ounces) almond paste

Cream shortening, sugar, and beaten eggs. Sift together flour, baking powder, and salt. Add to creamed mixture. Mix in almond paste. Pour into greased and floured bundt pan. Bake 50–55 minutes at 350°. Let cool 10 minutes in pan; then complete cooling on rack.

GLAZE

2 cups powdered confectioners sugar

¼ cup margarine or butter, softened

Beat together until smooth. Pour over cake. SERVES 12–16.

—*Blanca C. Volpe, Laredo Club*

Poppy Seed Cake

½ cup poppy seed

1¼ cups milk, scalded

½ cup vegetable shortening

1½ cups sugar

1 teaspoon vanilla

2 cups all-purpose flour, sifted

2 teaspoons baking powder

3 egg whites, beaten stiff

FILLING

1 cup sugar

3 tablespoons cornstarch

2 cups milk

3 egg yolks, beaten

1 teaspoon vanilla

Pour scalded milk over poppy seed and let stand for 3–4 hours. Cream shortening, sugar, and vanilla. Add sifted flour and baking powder alternately with milk–poppy seed mixture. Fold in stiffly beaten egg whites. Bake in two greased and floured 8-inch layer cake pans for 25 minutes at 350°. Cool. To prepare filling, mix sugar and cornstarch. Add to beaten egg yolks and milk. Cook until thick. Stir in vanilla. Spread between layers and on top and sides of cake. SERVES 10–12.

—*Maggie Jahn, Past President of Federation (1985–86), DeWitt–Lavaca County Club*

Easy Upside-Down Cake

1 can (20 ounces) sliced pineapple, drained (reserving ¼ cup syrup)

¼ cup (½ stick) margarine, softened

10 pecan halves

1 jar (10 ounces) strawberry or apricot preserves

1 package (18.25 ounces) yellow cake mix

Thoroughly drain pineapple slices, reserving ¼ cup syrup. Cover bottom of 13-by-9-inch baking pan with margarine. Arrange pineapple slices and pecan halves in pan. Combine reserved pineapple syrup and preserves; spoon over pineapple. Prepare cake mix according to directions on package. Pour batter over all. Bake at 350° for 40–45 minutes, or until toothpick inserted in center comes out clean. Immediately invert on serving plate. *You may want to save all the syrup from the sliced pineapple and use some of it for part of the liquid the cake mix calls for.* SERVES APPROXIMATELY 18.   —*Judy LeBlanc, Mid-Jefferson County Club*

Pineapple Wonder Cake

1 box (18.25 ounces) yellow cake mix

1 can (20 ounces) crushed pineapple, with juice

1½ cups sugar

1 package (8 ounces) cream cheese, softened

1 package (3½ ounces) instant vanilla pudding

1½ cups milk

3 bananas, sliced

1 small carton (8 ounces) frozen whipped topping, thawed

¾ cup coconut

¼ cup chopped pecans

Bake yellow cake as directed on package, using a 13-by-9-inch glass baking pan. Combine pineapple and sugar in saucepan and bring to boil. Spread on cake while hot. When cake has cooled, mix cream cheese, pudding mix, and milk until smooth and spreadable. Do not cook. Spread over pineapple layer. Arrange sliced bananas on top. Frost with whipped topping, and garnish with coconut and pecans. Refrigerate. Better if made 2–3 days in advance. SERVES 16.

—*From* Hullabaloo in the Kitchen, *Dallas County Club*

Pineapple Cake

2 cups sugar

2 cups all-purpose flour

1 teaspoon baking soda

1 teaspoon salt

1 large can (20 ounces) crushed
pineapple, with juice

2 eggs

1 cup vegetable oil

Combine sugar, flour, baking soda, and salt; mix thoroughly. Add pineapple, eggs, and vegetable oil; mix well. Pour into 13-by-9-inch greased pan. Bake at 350° for 45 minutes, or until done.

ICING

1 cup sugar

1 small can (6 ounces) evaporated
milk

¾ cup (1½ sticks) margarine

1 cup coconut

1 cup chopped nuts

Mix sugar, milk, and margarine. Boil 10 minutes, stirring often. Add coconut and nuts. Pour over cake while warm. SERVES 16–20.

—*Mary Lou Perry, Orange County Club*

Summer's Pineapple Cake

1 box (18.25 ounces) pineapple
cake mix

1 box (3½ ounces) instant vanilla
pudding mix

½ cup vegetable oil

1 cup water

4 eggs

FILLING

3 tablespoons reserved cake batter

1 large can (20 ounces) crushed
pineapple

1 cup sugar

½ cup (1 stick) margarine

Grease and flour three 8- or 9-inch cake pans. Combine cake mix, pudding, oil, water, and eggs in large mixing bowl; mix well. Reserve 3 tablespoons of batter for filling. Pour remainder of batter, evenly divided, into the three pans. Bake 25–30 minutes at 350°. Cool. In a double boiler, combine 3 tablespoons batter, pineapple, sugar, and margarine. Cook until thick and clear. Top each layer with cooked filling. SERVES 12–16.

—*Dr. Barbara Flournoy, Angelina County Club*

Home, Sweet Home

Texas Pie

1 can (20 ounces) cherry pie filling

1 can (20 ounces) crushed
  pineapple

1 box (18.5 ounces) yellow cake
  mix (dry)

1½ cups coconut

1½ cups chopped pecans

1 cup (2 sticks) margarine, melted

Layer first five ingredients in a 9-by-13-inch pan. Melt margarine and spoon over layered ingredients. Bake in 350° oven for about 45 minutes. SERVES 20.
     —Mary Kay Rowlett, Brown County Club

Rum Pineapple Coconut Cake

1 package (18.5 ounces) white cake
  mix

1 package (3½ ounces) instant
  coconut cream pudding and pie
  filling

4 eggs

½ cup water

⅓ cup dark rum (80 proof)

¼ cup vegetable oil

Combine all ingredients in large mixing bowl. Beat 4 minutes at medium speed. Pour into two greased and floured 9-inch layer cake pans. Bake at 350° for 25–30 minutes or until cake springs back when lightly pressed. Do not underbake. Cool in pan 15 minutes; remove and cool on racks.

ICING

1 can (8 ounces) crushed
  pineapple, with juice

1 package (3½ ounces) instant
  coconut cream or vanilla
  pudding and pie filling

⅓ cup dark rum (80 proof)

1 container (8 ounces) frozen
  whipped topping, thawed

flaked coconut

Combine pineapple, pudding mix, and rum in a bowl. Beat until well blended. Fold in whipped topping. Spread between layers and on sides and top of cake. Sprinkle with coconut. Chill. Refrigerate leftover cake. MAKES 2 LAYERS.

VARIATION: Substitute 1 package vanilla pudding for coconut cream in the cake. Increase water to ¾ cup, and add 1 cup flaked coconut to batter.

—Marian Prihoda, Lafayette, Louisiana Club

Mandarin Orange Cake

1 box (18.5 ounces) butter-recipe
  yellow cake mix
1 can (16 ounces) mandarin
  oranges, undrained

3 eggs
⅓ cup vegetable oil

In large mixing bowl, combine cake mix, oranges with liquid, eggs, and oil. Mix until smooth. Bake in 3 greased and floured round layer pans for 20–25 minutes at 350°. (If using glass pans, reduce heat to 325°.) Cool and frost.

ICING

1 can (16 ounces) crushed
  pineapple, undrained
1 package (3⅓ ounces) instant
  vanilla pudding (dry)

1 small carton (8 ounces) frozen
  whipped topping, thawed

Mix pineapple and pudding. Gently fold in whipped topping. Spread between layers and on top. Refrigerate. *This is easy to make and always a favorite. Men, especially, seem to like this cake.* SERVES 16.

—Laura Arrington, Brazoria County Club

Strawberry Sour Cream Cake

1 box (18.5 ounces) strawberry
cake mix

1 box (10 ounces) frozen
strawberries, thawed, with juice

8 ounces sour cream (or imitation)

4 large eggs

2 teaspoons strawberry extract

1 teaspoon almond extract

1 teaspoon vanilla extract

½ teaspoon grated lemon peel
(bottled lemon peel may be
used)

2 or 3 drops of pink or red food
coloring for prettier color

ICING

½–1 pound powdered
confectioners sugar

2 tablespoons margarine, melted

strawberry extract

dash of salt

thawed strawberries or milk to
make icing the thickness of
thick syrup

Place all cake ingredients in large mixing bowl. Mix slowly until dry ingredients are moist, then mix on medium speed 1–2 minutes. Mix well, but do not overbeat. Spray bundt or angel food pan with nonstick cooking spray, then grease and flour lightly. (This makes for easy removal and a moist cake that needs no icing.) Bake in preheated 350° oven for 30–45 minutes, or until toothpick comes out clean. Do not overbake. Cool in pan for about 8–10 minutes, loosen sides with knife very carefully, and turn out on plate. Lift pan to be sure it is free from cake, but return pan over cake for cooling. If icing is desired, combine ingredients until well mixed. Packaged butter cream icing may be used in place of powdered sugar and margarine. Spoon over top of cooled cake. Let icing run down sides. Cake may also be baked as cupcakes (15–20 minutes), loaf cake (25–30 minutes), layer cake (30–35 minutes), or sheet cake (25–30 minutes).

VARIATIONS: To appropriate flavor cake mix, add 8 ounces sour cream, 4 large eggs, and fruit, juices, extracts, and peels indicated. Baking instructions are the same as for strawberry.

Spice Cake: spice cake mix, 10 ounces applesauce, grated orange peel, vanilla, and almond extract

Banana Cake: banana or spice cake mix, 10 ounces mashed ripe banana, grated orange peel, vanilla extract, ¼ cup milk

Pineapple Cake: pineapple cake mix, 10 ounces crushed pineapple with juice, lemon peel, vanilla, and pineapple extract

Lemon Cake: lemon cake mix, 1 small can (6 ounces) frozen lemonade, thawed, plus enough milk to make 10 ounces of liquid, 1 tablespoon grated lemon peel, vanilla, and lemon extract   —*Barbara Pittard, Brown County Club*

Fresh Strawberry Cake

1 package (18.5 ounces) white cake mix

1 small package (3 ounces) strawberry gelatin

1 cup vegetable oil

4 eggs

½ cup milk

1 cup angel flake coconut

1 cup chopped pecans

1 cup strawberries (either fresh sliced or frozen)

Combine cake mix and dry gelatin. Add oil, eggs, and milk. Mix well. Gently mix in coconut, pecans, and strawberries. Put waxed paper in three 9-inch round cake pans. Divide batter, and bake at 350° for 20–25 minutes. Cool on wire racks.

ICING

1 box (16 ounces) powdered confectioners sugar

1 package (3 ounces) cream cheese

½ cup (1 stick) butter or margarine

½ cup strawberries (either sliced fresh or frozen)

½ cup chopped nuts

1 cup angel flake coconut

Blend powdered sugar and cream cheese together. Add butter or margarine and mix well. Gently stir in strawberries, nuts, and coconut, and frost cake. MAKES 16 SERVINGS.   —*Audrey Jaschke, Victoria County Club*

Strawberry Torte

¾ cup (1½ sticks) butter or
 margarine, softened

1½ cups sugar

3 eggs, separated

2¼ cups sifted cake flour

3 teaspoons baking powder

1 teaspoon mace

¾ cup milk

FILLING

1 quart fresh strawberries, sliced
 (reserve 6–8 whole berries for
 garnish)

1½ pints whipping cream,
 whipped

½ cup sugar

Cream butter or margarine, adding sugar gradually. Continue creaming until light and fluffy. Add egg yolks; beat well. Sift cake flour, baking powder, and mace together, and add alternately with milk. Beat egg whites until stiff, and fold into batter. Rub bottoms of two 9-inch cake pans with margarine. Pour batter evenly into pans. Bake in a 350° oven for 40–45 minutes. Cool and remove from pans; split each layer lengthwise. Wash and drain strawberries; slice in half lengthwise, reserving 6–8 whole berries for garnish. Whip cream, blending in sugar. Reserve one-fourth of whipped cream for topping; fold sliced berries into remaining whipped cream. Spread strawberry mixture over each layer as they are stacked. Spread plain whipped cream on top, and garnish with whole berries. Refrigerate until serving time. *This delicious strawberry torte is my Aggie's favorite birthday cake—and strawberries are very hard to find in February.*
SERVES 8–12. —*Mrs. John Gonzales, Jr., Wichita County Area Club*

Fresh Apple Cake

4 cups peeled apples, chopped fine

2 cups sugar

1 cup chopped nuts

3 cups all-purpose flour

½ teaspoon nutmeg

½ teaspoon cinnamon

½ teaspoon salt

2 teaspoons baking soda

1 cup vegetable oil

½ teaspoon vanilla

2 eggs, well beaten

Combine chopped apples, sugar, and nuts; mix well and let stand for 1 hour. With mixer, combine flour, nutmeg, cinnamon, salt, baking soda, oil, vanilla, and beaten eggs until smooth. Stir in apple mixture, and mix well. Pour into well-greased and floured Bundt pan, and bake at 350° for 1 hour. *My Aggie son used to get his own apple cake each Christmas to "eat up" as fast or slowly as he chose. We still have fresh apple cake for every holiday (and in between).* SERVES 16–20.   —*Margie Lee, Midland Club*

Fresh Pear Cake I

3 cups all-purpose flour, sifted

2 cups sugar

½ teaspoon nutmeg

½ teaspoon salt

1½ teaspoons baking soda

½ teaspoon mace

½ teaspoon cinnamon

½ teaspoon ground cloves

3 eggs, well beaten

1½ cups vegetable oil

1 teaspoon vanilla

3 cups finely chopped or grated
  fresh pears

1 cup broken pecans

Combine sifted flour, sugar, nutmeg, salt, soda, mace, cinnamon, and cloves. Add beaten eggs, oil, and vanilla. Mix well; stir in chopped pears and pecans. Bake in greased tube pan for 1 hour, 15 minutes, at 350°. *Chopped fresh apples may be substituted for pears.* SERVES 16–20.

—*Ruth Sollock, Past President of Federation (1981–82), Montgomery County Club*

Fresh Pear or Apple Cake II

4 cups grated pears or apples

2 cups sugar

1 cup vegetable oil

3 cups all-purpose flour

2 teaspoons baking soda

½ teaspoon salt

½ teaspoon cinnamon

1 teaspoon vanilla

2 eggs

1 cup each: raisins, chopped nuts, coconut

Combine pears or apples, sugar, and oil. Let stand 1 hour or overnight. Sift together the flour, soda, salt, and cinnamon; mix in raisins, nuts, and coconut, and set aside. Stir eggs and vanilla into pear mixture. Add other ingredients and blend well. Bake in greased and floured tube pan for 1 hour, 15 minutes, at 325°. *Good served with whipped cream or thawed frozen whipped topping. Freezes well.* SERVES 16–20.

—*Christene Richardson, Angelina County Club*

Pumpkin Cake with Cream Cheese Icing

2 cups sugar

4 eggs

1 cup vegetable oil

2 cups canned pumpkin

2 cups all-purpose flour

2 teaspoons cinnamon

2 teaspoons baking soda

½ teaspoon salt

Combine all ingredients, in order given, in large bowl. Turn into 13-by-9-inch greased and floured baking pan. Bake at 350° for 35 minutes, or until toothpick comes out clean. Cool.

ICING

½ cup (1 stick) butter or margarine

1 box (16 ounces) powdered confectioners sugar

1 package (8 ounces) cream cheese, softened

2 teaspoons vanilla

1 cup chopped nuts to sprinkle on top

Combine all ingredients except nuts; beat with mixer. Spread on cooled cake. Sprinkle nuts on top. Refrigerate. SERVES 16.

—*Anne Cassens, Orange County Club*

Home for a Holiday

Lemon Cake

1 box (18.25 ounces) lemon cake
mix

1 small package (3 ounces) lemon
gelatin

¾ cup vegetable oil

¾ cup apricot nectar

4 eggs

1 teaspoon lemon extract

GLAZE

1 cup powdered confectioners
sugar

juice of 1 lemon

Combine cake mix, gelatin, oil, apricot nectar, eggs, and lemon extract.
Beat with mixer for 3 minutes. Pour into greased and floured tube pan.
Bake at 350° for 35 minutes. Cool cake for 15 minutes; invert on cake plate,
and glaze. Mix powdered sugar and lemon juice well with spoon. Drizzle
over cake. SERVES 10–12. —*Mrs. David E. (Joan) Varner, Houston Club*

Pioneer Boulangerie Lemon Cake

1 package (18.25 ounces) yellow
cake mix

1 package (3½ ounces) instant
lemon pudding mix

4 eggs

¾ cup vegetable oil

¾ cup water

GLAZE

1 box (16 ounces) powdered
confectioners sugar

⅔ cup lemon juice

2 tablespoons butter, melted

2 tablespoons water

Combine cake mix and pudding mix with eggs, oil, and water. Beat well for
2–3 minutes with mixer. Pour into ungreased 13-by-9-inch baking pan or
tube pan, and bake at 350° for 30–35 minutes, or until cake springs back
when touched lightly. In another bowl, combine powdered sugar, lemon
juice, melted butter, and water; beat until smooth. While cake is warm,
pierce surface with fork in many places. Pour glaze evenly over top. SERVES
15–18. —*Sandra Lehne, Austin Club*

Spicy Dark Fruitcake

3½ cups (1½ pounds) mixed diced fruits and peels for fruitcake

1¼ cups (8 ounces) dark seedless raisins

1¼ cups (8 ounces) light seedless raisins

1 cup (4 ounces) chopped walnuts

1 cup (4 ounces) chopped pecans

3 cups sifted all-purpose flour

1 teaspoon salt

1 teaspoon baking powder

1 teaspoon cinnamon

1 teaspoon allspice

½ teaspoon nutmeg

½ teaspoon ground cloves

1 cup vegetable shortening

2 cups brown sugar, packed

4 large eggs (1 cup)

¾ cup grape juice

Combine fruits and peels, raisins, walnuts, and pecans. Sift together the flour, salt, baking powder, cinnamon, allspice, nutmeg, and cloves; sprinkle ¼ cup over fruit mixture; mix well. Thoroughly cream shortening and brown sugar; add eggs, one at a time, beating well after each addition. Add remaining sifted dry ingredients alternately with grape juice, beating until smooth after each addition. Pour batter over fruit mixture, and mix well. Line two 8½-by-4½-inch loaf pans with waxed paper, allowing it to extend above all sides. Pour batter into pans, filling three-fourths full. Bake in a very slow oven, 275°, for 3–3½ hours, or until done. Place a pan containing 2 cups of water on bottom shelf of oven—cakes will have greater volume, more moist texture, and a shiny glaze. Batter may also be baked in one 10-inch tube pan, lined with waxed paper, at 275° for 2½ hours. Cool in pan. Store cakes in airtight containers for at least a week. May be wrapped in rum-soaked cheesecloth for 3 weeks. Chill before slicing. *I have made this recipe for 25 years on the Friday after Thanksgiving. Now my first Aggie will carry on the tradition in her home. My family will eat no other fruitcake!* MAKES 6 POUNDS OF FRUITCAKE.

—*Mary C. (Mrs. Mike) Pinson, West Bell County Club*

Home for a Holiday

Fruit Bread

2½ cups sugar

1½ cups ripe bananas, mashed

3 eggs, well beaten

1 small can (8 ounces) crushed
    pineapple, with juice

1 jar (6 ounces) maraschino
    cherries, drained and chopped

¾ cup vegetable oil

2½ cups all-purpose flour

¼ teaspoon salt

¾ teaspoon baking soda

1 teaspoon vanilla

1 cup chopped pecans

Mix sugar, bananas, eggs, pineapple, and cherries. Combine with oil. Combine flour, salt, and soda, and add to fruit mixture. Stir in vanilla and pecans. Pour into greased and lightly floured tube pan, spreading dough evenly. Bake 1 hour, 45 minutes, at 300°. Cool on wire rack. *Fruit bread keeps well or may be frozen.* SERVES 12–14.   —*Milam County Club*

Never Fail Cupcakes

1 egg

½ cup vegetable shortening

1½ cups all-purpose flour

½ cup cocoa

1 cup sugar

½ cup sour milk

1 teaspoon baking soda

1 teaspoon vanilla

½ cup boiling water

Combine all ingredients except boiling water in the order given. (To make sour milk, add 2 teaspoons vinegar to regular milk.) Last of all, add boiling water and mix well. Fill cupcake liners approximately half full. Bake at 350° for 10–15 minutes, or until done. Frost with your favorite icing. These freeze well. MAKES 12 CUPCAKES.   —*Dorothy Lunday, Laredo Club*

Company Cheesecake I (for 100)

12½ cups graham cracker crumbs

1 cup plus 1 tablespoon sugar

2 cups melted butter

12 pounds cream cheese

10 cups sugar

6½ tablespoons grated lemon peel

3 teaspoons vanilla

30 eggs

10 cups sour cream

Company Cheesecake II (for 12)

1¼ cups (about 15 squares) graham cracker crumbs or 1¼ cups finely crushed whole wheat flake cereal

2 tablespoons sugar

3 tablespoons margarine or butter, melted

2 large packages (8 ounces each) cream cheese plus 1 small package (3 ounces), softened

1 cup sugar

2 teaspoons grated lemon peel

¼ teaspoon vanilla

3 eggs

1 cup dairy sour cream or 1 recipe Cherry Glaze

Heat oven to 350°. Mix cracker crumbs, sugar, and melted butter or margarine. Press in bottom of 9-inch springform pan (you'll need 10 for the larger recipe). Bake 10 minutes. Cool. Beat cream cheese in large mixer bowl. Add sugar gradually, beating until fluffy. Add lemon peel and vanilla. Beat in 1 egg at a time. Pour over crumb mixture. Bake at 300° until center is firm, about 1 hour. Cool to room temperature. Refrigerate at least 3 hours but not longer than 10 days. Loosen edge of cheesecake with knife before removing side of pan. Top with sour cream or glaze. (Ed. note: In case you ever need to make 100 servings of cheesecake, the first recipe will help you do just that. On the other hand, if you'd like to make a normal-sized cheesecake to serve 12, use the second recipe, the original version from *Betty Crocker's Cookbook*. Company Cheesecake is one of the very favorite recipes of the athletes who live in Cain Hall). VERSION I YIELDS 100 SERVINGS; VERSION II, 12 SERVINGS.

CHERRY GLAZE (FOR 12-SERVING CAKE)

1 can (10-ounces) pitted red tart
   cherries, drained (reserve syrup)
½ cup sugar

2 tablespoons cornstarch
4 drops red food color

Add enough water to reserved cherry syrup to measure 1 cup. Mix sugar and cornstarch in saucepan. Stir in syrup mixture. Cook, stirring constantly, until mixture thickens and boils. Boil and stir 1 minute. Remove from heat; stir in cherries and food coloring. Cool completely.

—Myrt Davidson, Manager, Cain Hall

Vermont Grandma's Cheesecake

CRUST

1½ cups graham cracker crumbs
   (reserve a few to sprinkle
   on top)

3 tablespoons sugar
½ cup (1 stick) butter, melted

Line 10-inch springform pan with mixture of crumbs, sugar, and melted butter. Press firmly on bottom and sides of pan. Refrigerate.

FILLING

2 packages (8 ounces each) cream
   cheese, softened
1½ pints (3 cups) sour cream
3 eggs

1 cup sugar
¼ teaspoon salt
2 teaspoons vanilla
1½ teaspoons almond flavoring

Using an electric mixer, blend cream cheese and sour cream until smooth. Beat in eggs, one at a time, and sugar, mixing well. Mix in salt, vanilla, and almond. Batter will be quite thin. Pour cheese mix into crumb crust. Sprinkle remaining crumbs on top. Bake at 375° for 35 minutes. Cool on rack. Put in refrigerator overnight. SERVES 12.

—Lucy Vogel, West Bell County Club

Chocolate Almond Cheesecake

1½ cups chocolate wafer crumbs

2 cups blanched almonds, lightly toasted and chopped (reserve ½ cup)

⅓ cup sugar

¾ cup (1½ sticks) butter, softened

3 packages (8 ounces each) cream cheese, softened

1¼ cups sugar

4 eggs

⅓ cup whipping cream, unwhipped

¼ cup almond-flavored liqueur

2 teaspoons vanilla

2 cups sour cream

1 tablespoon sugar

Combine chocolate wafer crumbs, 1½ cups of the almonds, ⅓ cup sugar, and ¾ cup butter. Press on bottom and sides of 9½-inch buttered springform pan. In large bowl, cream together cream cheese and 1¼ cups sugar; beat in eggs, 1 at a time, beating well after each addition. Add whipping cream, almond liqueur, and 1 teaspoon vanilla, and beat mixture until light. Pour batter into shell and bake in preheated 375° oven for 10 minutes. Reduce heat to 275° and bake 1 hour or more until cake is set in middle. Remove from oven and let set for 5 minutes. In bowl, combine sour cream, sugar, and the last teaspoon of vanilla. Spread mixture evenly on cake. Return to oven and bake 5 minutes more. Transfer to rack; cool. Remove sides of pan and press ½ cup toasted almonds around edge and top. SERVES 16–20.   —*From* Hullabaloo in the Kitchen, *Dallas County Club*

Cherry Cheesecake Pie

1 baked pie shell or 9-inch graham
cracker crust
1 package (8 ounces) cream cheese,
softened
1 cup powdered confectioners
sugar
1 teaspoon vanilla

1 cup whipping cream, whipped
1 cup chopped pecans (optional)
½–1 can (21 ounces) cherry pie
filling
¼ teaspoon almond extract

Beat together cream cheese, sugar, and vanilla until smooth. Fold in whipped cream and pecans, if desired. Spoon into pastry shell. Add almond extract to cherry pie filling, and carefully spoon over cream cheese layer. Chill until set. SERVES 8.

—*Libbye Feagins, Titus County Club, and M. M. Lonon, San Angelo Club*

Chocolate Cheesecake I

1 cup all-purpose flour
½ cup (1 stick) magarine, melted
1½ cups finely chopped pecans
1½ cups frozen whipped topping,
thawed
1 cup powdered confectioners
sugar
1 package (8 ounces) cream cheese,
softened

1 large (5⅛ ounces) and 1 small (4
ounces) package instant
chocolate pudding mix
4 cups milk
1 cup frozen whipped topping,
thawed (or more, if needed)
1 bar (1.45 ounces) chocolate,
grated

Combine flour, margarine, and pecans; press into bottom of 13-by-9-inch baking dish. Bake for 15 minutes at 350°. Cool. Mix 1½ cups whipped topping, powdered sugar, and cream cheese. Spread over cooled crust. Mix chocolate pudding and milk at low speed; spread over cream-cheese layer. Spread remaining topping over pudding layer. Garnish with grated chocolate. Chill. Cut into squares. SERVES 12. —*Mary McDonald, Liberty County Club*

Chocolate Cheesecake II

1 package (18.5 ounces) chocolate cake mix (German chocolate or Swiss chocolate preferred)

4 eggs

1 tablespoon vegetable oil

2 packages (8 ounces each) cream cheese, softened

½ cup sugar

1½ cups milk

1 teaspoon vanilla

1 container (12 ounces) frozen whipped topping, thawed

shaved chocolate for garnish, if desired

Measure 1 cup of dry cake mix; reserve. Stir together in the large bowl the remaining dry cake mix, 1 of the eggs, and oil. Press mixture lightly into bottom and ¾ up the sides of a 12-by-9-inch baking pan. Blend cream cheese and sugar in same bowl. Add remaining 3 eggs and reserved 1 cup of cake mix; beat 1 minute at medium speed. Slowly add milk and vanilla at low speed, mixing until smooth. Pour into crumb crust. Bake at 300° for 55–65 minutes, or until center is firm. Cool to room temperature. Spread with whipped topping and shaved chocolate if desired. *This tastes like a rich, complex dessert, but it is very simple to prepare and serve.* MAKES 12 SERVINGS. —*Danisha (Mrs. Bobby) Boyd, Wood County Club*

Party Pie Shells (Miniature) with Apricot Filling

3 cups all-purpose flour

1 cup (2 sticks) margarine

2 eggs, beaten

2 tablespoons water

1 tablespoon vinegar

Mix flour and margarine until crumbly. Add beaten eggs that have been mixed with water and vinegar. (Dough may be mixed in a food processor.) This makes a soft dough; chill in plastic bag. Pinch off pieces of dough about the size of walnuts, and mold into miniature muffin tins. Crust should extend a little above the top of each compartment. Bake in moderate oven (325–350°) until lightly brown, 10–15 minutes.

FILLING

1 can (14 ounces) sweetened
  condensed milk
⅓ cup lime or lemon juice
1 small container (8 ounces) frozen
  whipped topping, thawed

1 can (16 ounces) apricots
1 cup chopped pecans

Mix sweetened condensed milk and lime or lemon juice. Add whipped topping and blend. Add drained, mashed apricots and nuts. Fill cooled shells. MAKES 48–50 TARTS.   —*Geneva (Mrs. W. H.) Gullette, Panola County Club*

Yum-Yums

2 packages (8 ounces each) cream
  cheese, softened
¾ cup sugar
2 eggs

2 teaspoons lemon juice
1 teaspoon vanilla
1 can (21 ounces) cherry pie filling
1 box (12 ounces) vanilla wafers

Combine cream cheese, sugar, eggs, lemon juice, and vanilla; mix well. Put one vanilla wafer in bottom of each cup cake liner in cup cake pan. Fill half full with cheese mixture. Spoon cherry pie filling on top. Bake 12 minutes at 375°. *One can of cherry pie filling is enough for a double recipe of cheese filling.* MAKES 30–36 TARTS.   —*Shirley McCutchen, Milam County Club*

Pecan Pie

1 unbaked pie crust
4 eggs, beaten slightly
1 cup light corn syrup
3 tablespoons vegetable oil

1 cup sugar
⅛ teaspoon salt
1½ teaspoons vanilla
¾ cup pecan halves

Beat eggs slightly. Add corn syrup, oil, sugar, salt, and vanilla, mixing well. Pour into pie crust. Sprinkle pecan halves on top. Bake at 350° about 1 hour. SERVES 6–8.   —*Betty Tiller, Orange County Club*

Dixie Pecan Pie

1 unbaked pie shell	1 cup maple syrup
3 eggs	1½ teaspoons vanilla
2 tablespoons sugar	¼ teaspoon salt
2 tablespoons all-purpose flour	1 tablespoon butter, melted
1 cup light corn syrup	1 cup (or more) pecans

Beat eggs until light. Mix sugar and flour together; add to eggs, and beat well. Add remaining ingredients. Mix again; this cuts the pecans to about the right size. Pour into large unbaked pie shell, and bake at 425° for 10 minutes. Reduce heat to 325°, and finish baking, about 45 minutes more. *This pie is so good it motivates good grades.* SERVES 6–8, OR ABOUT 2 HUNGRY AGGIES. —*Bebe (Mrs. David) Combs, Wichita County Area Club*

Low-Cal Millionaire Pies

2 baked 9-inch pie crusts or 2 graham cracker crusts	1 large carton (10 ounces) frozen whipped topping, thawed
1 package (8 ounces) cream cheese, softened	1 cup chopped pecans
1 box (16 ounces) powdered confectioners sugar	1 can (20 ounces) crushed pineapple, well drained

Combine cream cheese and powdered sugar; beat with electric mixer until smooth. Add whipped topping; beat until peaks are formed. Stir in pecans and pineapple. Pour into pie shells. Chill for several hours. *This is a Weight Watchers recipe.* MAKES 2 PIES; EACH SERVES 6–8. —*Ann Bonner, Bi-Stone Club*

Honey Pecan Pie

1 unbaked pie crust

1 cup honey

4 eggs

¼ teaspoon salt

1 teaspoon vanilla

1 cup pecans

1 tablespoon butter

Pour honey into an iron skillet and bring to a boil. In a large bowl, beat eggs well, and slowly add hot honey, stirring constantly. Add salt, vanilla, and pecans. Pour into pie shell; dot with butter. Bake at 400° for 10 minutes; lower heat to 300°, and bake 20 minutes longer, or until done. *I cover pie with foil the first 20 minutes, and then uncover to brown.* MAKES 6–8 SERVINGS.

—*Dorothy M. Roddam, Orange County Club*

Coconut Pie

2 pie crusts, unbaked

1 small can (4 ounces) angel flake
  coconut

3 cups sugar

1 tablespoon all-purpose flour

¼ teaspoon salt

1 cup (2 sticks) margarine, melted

4 eggs, slightly beaten

½ teaspoon vanilla

1 cup milk

Put half the can of coconut in each pie crust. Combine remaining ingredients and pour over coconut. Bake 10 minutes at 450°; reduce heat to 350°, and bake 30 minutes or more until done. *These pies freeze well.* MAKES 2 PIES; EACH SERVES 6–8.   —*Veda M. Wall, Panola County Club*

Amazing Coconut Pie

2 cups milk

¾ cup sugar

½ cup buttermilk baking mix

4 eggs

¼ cup butter or margarine,
  softened

1½ teaspoons vanilla

1 cup coconut

Combine milk, sugar, baking mix, eggs, butter, and vanilla; blend well. Pour into greased 9-inch pie pan. Let stand about 5 minutes. Sprinkle with coconut. Bake at 350° for 40 minutes. This pie makes its own soft crust. SERVES 6–8.   —*Dorothy M. Roddam, Orange County Club*

Banana Split Pie

3 cups graham cracker crumbs

¾ cup (1½ sticks) margarine, melted

2 eggs

1 cup (2 sticks) margarine, softened

2 cups powdered confectioners sugar

1 teaspoon vanilla

1 large can (20 ounces) crushed pineapple, drained

3 or 4 bananas, sliced

1 large container (12 ounces) frozen whipped topping, thawed

diced maraschino cherries and chopped nuts for garnish

Combine graham cracker crumbs and melted margarine. Press into bottom and sides of 13-by-9-inch baking pan. Combine eggs, softened margarine, powdered sugar, and vanilla in large mixing bowl. Beat with mixer for 15–20 minutes. Spread over crumb mixture. Sprinkle drained pineapple over this. Place sliced bananas in rows over pineapple. Spread with whipped topping. Sprinkle with diced cherries and chopped nuts. Refrigerate until ready to serve. SERVES 15. —*Joan Ketterer, San Antonio Club*

Mountain Mama's Mudslide Pie

1 cup all-purpose flour

1 cup chopped pecans

½ cup (1 stick) margarine or butter, melted

Combine flour, pecans, and melted margarine or butter. Spread in 13-by-9-inch pan, and bake at 325–350° for 20 minutes. Cool.

LAYERS

2 small cartons (8 ounces each) frozen whipped topping, thawed

1 package (8 ounces) cream cheese, softened

1 cup powdered confectioners sugar

2 packages (4 ounces each) instant chocolate pudding

2½ cups milk

chocolate shavings, or ¼ cup toasted pecans (optional)

Make Layer I by mixing together 1 carton whipped topping, cream cheese, and powdered sugar. Spread on cooled crust. For Layer II, mix pudding and milk, and spread on first layer. Make Layer III by stirring chocolate shavings or pecans into remaining carton of whipped topping. Refrigerate at least 4 hours before serving. *This is also known as Died and Gone to Heaven Cake, or Sweet Cream Pie.* SERVES 15.

VARIATION: For layer II, substitute 1 package (3½ ounces) instant vanilla pudding for 1 package chocolate pudding.

—Beverly Bright and Mildred Johnston, Victoria County Club, and
Vicki Spink, Kingwood Club

Oatmeal Pie

4 eggs	½ cup margarine, melted
5 ounces sugar	¾ teaspoon salt
8 ounces brown sugar	1 teaspoon vanilla extract
1 cup quick-cooking oats	1 pie shell, unbaked
1 cup grated coconut, not packed	

Mix eggs and sugars at medium speed for 2 minutes. Add oatmeal, coconut, margarine, salt, and vanilla. Stir until well mixed. Ladle mixture into unbaked 10-inch pie shell. Bake at 350° for 15 minutes. Reduce heat to 300° and bake 45 minutes or until golden and firm. Cool thoroughly before serving. MAKES 1 PIE; SERVES 6–8.

—Col. Fred Dollar and J. W. Maynard, TAMU Food Services

Chocolate Marshmallow Cream Pie

16 graham crackers, crushed	½ large (7.25 ounces) chocolate
¼ cup butter, melted	candy bar
32 large marshmallows	½ pint whipping cream, whipped
½ cup milk	

Combine graham cracker crumbs and melted butter; press into pie plate. Refrigerate for 10 minutes. Melt marshmallows with milk in double boiler. Add chocolate bar and continue melting. Cool. Whip cream and combine with marshmallow mixture. Pour into crust. Chill for 2 hours. *Rich and delicious.* SERVES 6–8.

—Betty P. Zubko, Deep East Texas Club

Kentucky Derby Pie

1 unbaked pie shell

¼ cup (½ stick) butter, softened

1 cup sugar

3 eggs

¾ cup light corn syrup

¼ teaspoon salt

1 teaspoon vanilla

½ cup semisweet chocolate morsels

½ cup chopped pecans

2 tablespoons bourbon

Cream butter and sugar; add beaten eggs, corn syrup, salt, and vanilla. Stir in morsels, nuts, and bourbon; mix well. Pour into unbaked pie shell. Bake at 375° for 40–50 minutes. Serve warm topped with ice cream. SERVES 6–8.

—Jean Patterson, Tyler Club

Chocolate Pie Dessert

1 cup all-purpose flour

1 cup margarine, melted

1 cup chopped nuts

1 package (8 ounces) cream cheese, softened

1 cup powdered confectioners sugar

1 large container (12 ounces) frozen whipped topping, thawed

2 packages (4 ounces each) instant chocolate pudding mix

3 cups milk

Combine flour, margarine, and chopped nuts. Press into pie pan, and bake at 350° for 15 minutes, or until lightly browned. Cool. Combine cream cheese, powdered sugar, and whipped topping until well mixed. Spread on cooled crust. Refrigerate. Mix chocolate pudding mix and milk together; spread on top of chilled cream cheese mixture. Cover and refrigerate. SERVES 6–8.

—Jo Frances Chastain, President of Federation (1986–87), Rio Grande Valley Club

Shawn's Christmas Mint Pie

32 large marshmallows
½ cup milk
¼ cup green crème de menthe
3 tablespoons crème de cacao
1½ cups whipping cream, whipped

few drops green food coloring, if desired
1 chocolate cookie crumb crust (purchased or made)

Heat marshmallows and milk over medium heat, stirring until marshmallows melt. Chill until thickened; blend in crème de menthe and crème de cacao. With electric mixer and a previously chilled bowl, beat cream until stiff. Fold chilled marshmallow mixture into whipped cream. You may also fold in a few drops of green food coloring, if desired, for a darker green color. Pour into crumb crust. Chill 3 hours. *This dessert is a favorite at Thanksgiving or Christmas. It's very light after a heavy dinner. Pie may be frozen and partially thawed before serving.* SERVES 6. —*Anita Kyle, Fort Bend Club*

Rhubarb Cream Cheese Pie

1 9-inch unbaked pie crust
4 cups rhubarb, cut into 1-inch pieces
3 tablespoons cornstarch
¼ teaspoon salt
1 cup sugar

1 package (8 ounces) cream cheese, softened
2 eggs
½ cup sugar
1 cup sour cream
½ cup sliced almonds

In 2-quart saucepan over medium heat, cook rhubarb, cornstarch, salt, and 1 cup sugar, stirring often, until mixture boils and thickens. Pour rhubarb mixture into pie crust. Bake 10 minutes at 425°; remove from oven. Meanwhile, in small bowl, with mixer at medium speed, beat cream cheese, eggs, and ½ cup sugar until smooth. Pour over rhubarb mixture. Reduce heat to 350°. Bake 30–35 minutes, until set. Cool on wire rack. Put into refrigerator to chill. Before serving, spread with sour cream and sliced almonds. *Apples may be substituted for rhubarb.* SERVES 6.
—*Betty Maskey, Corpus Christi Club*

Dewberry Cobbler

½ cup (1 stick) margarine, melted

1 quart dewberries

1 cup sugar

1 cup buttermilk baking mix

½ cup sugar

1 cup milk

Melt margarine in 9-inch square pan you plan to use for baking cobbler. Add berries; sprinkle sugar on top. Mix together the buttermilk baking mix, ½ cup sugar, and milk. Pour over berries. Bake at 350° for 1 hour. SERVES 8–9. —*Milam County Club*

Rhubarb Crunch

1 cup all-purpose flour

1 teaspoon cinnamon

¾ cup quick-cooking oats

1 cup brown sugar

½ cup melted butter

1 cup sugar

2 tablespoons cornstarch

1 cup water

1 teaspoon vanilla

4 cups cubed rhubarb

Combine flour, cinnamon, oats, brown sugar, and melted butter, and press half of mixture into a 9-inch square pan. Set aside. Combine sugar, cornstarch, and water in saucepan. Cook until clear and slightly thickened. Add vanilla. Cool slightly. Mix with cubed rhubarb, and pour over crust. Press remaining half of crumb mixture on top. Bake 1 hour at 325–350°. *The family can't wait for the first batch of rhubarb to enjoy. This recipe is best served warm with ice cream on top.* SERVES 9. —*Vicki Spink, Kingwood Club*

Pat-a-Pie Crust

2 cups all-purpose flour

1 tablespoon sugar

1¼ teaspoons salt

⅔ cup vegetable oil

3 tablespoons milk

In an 8-inch or 9-inch pie plate, mix together flour, sugar, and salt. Combine oil and milk in measuring cup; whip together with fork. Pour over flour mixture, and mix with fork until all flour is dampened. Reserve about one-third of dough for top "crust." Press remaining dough evenly against bottom and sides of pie plate. Crimp edges. Fill with any fruit or custard pie filling. For topping, crumble reserved dough and sprinkle over filling. Bake as directed in pie recipe. *Fast and easy pie crust with no rolling! A perfect crust with no mess or fuss.* MAKES CRUST AND TOPPING FOR 1 PIE.

—*Vicki Spink, Kingwood Club*

Apple Crisp

4–5 tart apples, pared and sliced

½ cup sugar

5 tablespoons water

½ cup (1 stick) butter, melted

½ cup brown sugar

1 cup flour

Peel and slice apples into pie plate. Pour sugar and water over apples. Combine brown sugar and flour with melted butter. Spoon over apples. Bake at 350° for 1 hour. *Good with ice cream on top.* MAKES 6–8 SERVINGS.

—*Geneva Miller, Orange County Club*

Peach Cobbler

3 cups all-purpose flour

1 teaspoon salt

1¼ cups shortening

1 egg

6 tablespoons water

1 teaspoon vinegar

1⅓–1½ cups sugar

4 tablespoons all-purpose flour

⅛ teaspoon cinnamon

6½ cups sliced fresh peaches

4 tablespoons butter

To mix crust, combine flour, salt, shortening, and beaten egg. Add water and vinegar, and mix well with hands until crust falls loose from sides of bowl and forms a ball. Refrigerate 2 hours before rolling out. To mix filling, combine sugar, flour, and cinnamon. The amount of sugar to use depends on the tartness of the peaches and your family's taste. Sprinkle sliced peaches in bowl; toss to coat peaches evenly. Divide chilled dough for crust in half. Line oblong baking dish with one half of pie crust. Add peaches; dot with butter. Cover with top crust; cut slits to allow steam to escape. Bake at 425° for 35–45 minutes. *This pie crust recipe has been in my family for 40 years. You will enjoy using it for all types of pies, quiches, and tart shells. It can be frozen. I usually triple the recipe and make several pie shells to freeze for later use.* ONE RECIPE MAKES 14–16 SERVINGS.

—*Kathleen Brown, Bi-Stone Club*

Old-Fashioned Peach Cobbler

2 packages (16 ounces each) frozen
   peaches, thawed, or 8 cups
   sliced fresh peaches
2 cups sugar

½ cup water
¾ cup (1½ sticks) butter

Combine ingredients and bring to a boil. Cook over low heat until peaches are tender and mixture thickens. Pour into a lightly buttered 13-by-9-inch pan. Set aside.

CRUST

1½ cups all-purpose flour
¾ teaspoon salt

½ cup vegetable shortening
¼ cup plus 1 tablespoon cold water

Combine flour, salt, and shortening until well blended. Add water and shape into a ball. Roll out pastry to ⅛-inch thickness on lightly floured board. Cut into 1-inch strips, and arrange half of strips in lattice design over peaches. Bake at 350° for 35 minutes. Remove from oven, and gently press baked pastry into peach mixture. Repeat lattice design over peaches with remaining pastry. Return to oven, and bake an additional 40 minutes. SERVES 14–16.

—*Betty Tiller, Orange County Club*

Crème d'Ange

1 can (14 ounces) sweetened
   condensed milk
½ pint whipping cream, whipped

1 tablespoon sugar
chopped pecans for garnish

Pour sweetened condensed milk into 8-inch pie plate. Cover with foil. Place in larger shallow pan containing about ¼ inch of hot water. Bake at 425° approximately 1 hour, 20 minutes, or until milk is thick and caramel-colored. (Add hot water to pan as needed.) Chill at least 2 hours. Whip cream until stiff; fold in sugar. Garnish each serving with dollop of whipped cream; sprinkle with chopped pecans. SERVES 5–6.

—*Jamie Lipsey, Baytown Club*

Chocolate Lush Dessert

1 cup all-purpose flour

¾ cup sugar

2 tablespoons cocoa

2 teaspoons baking powder

½ teaspoon salt

½ cup milk

2 tablespoons vegetable oil

1 teaspoon vanilla

½ cup chopped nuts (walnuts or pecans)

¾ cup brown sugar, firmly packed

1¾ cup hot water

¼ cup cocoa

Sift flour with sugar, 2 tablespoons cocoa, baking powder, and salt into mixing bowl. Add milk, oil, vanilla, and nuts; mix until well blended. Spread in ungreased 8-inch or 9-inch square pan. Combine brown sugar, hot water, and ¼ cup cocoa, and pour over batter in baking dish. (This is an awful-looking mess, but it turns out fine.) Bake at 350° for about 45 minutes. Serve warm or cold, topped with ice cream, whipped cream, or whipped topping. SERVES 6–8.　　　　　—*Maureen Thode, Fort Bend Club*

Fruit Supreme

1 can (17 ounces) fruit cocktail, drained

1 small can (8 ounces) pineapple chunks, drained

3 tablespoons cottage cheese

½ small package (3 ounces) strawberry gelatin

2 tablespoons raisins

1 carton (12 ounces) frozen whipped topping, thawed

fresh fruits: strawberries, seedless grapes, etc.

miniature marshmallows

chopped pecans

shredded coconut

Combine fruit cocktail, pineapple, cottage cheese, dry gelatin, and raisins. Fold in whipped topping, fresh fruits, marshmallows, pecans, and coconut. Refrigerate for four hours. *Amounts of ingredients may vary.* WILL SERVE AT LEAST 6—THE MORE FRESH FRUIT, THE MORE SERVINGS.

—*Rosa M. Silva, Laredo Club*

Lemon Fluff

1 large can (12 ounces) evaporated
  milk, chilled
1 package (3 ounces) lemon gelatin
1½ cups boiling water

½ cup lemon juice
1 cup sugar
2½ cups vanilla wafer crumbs
chopped nuts for topping

Chill unopened can of evaporated milk until icy cold (overnight is best).
Also chill large mixing bowl and beaters. Dissolve gelatin in boiling water,
and chill until partially set (thick syrupy). Whip gelatin until light and
fluffy; add lemon juice and sugar and mix well. Whip the evaporated milk
in chilled bowl until thick, and fold into gelatin mixture. Line a 9-by-13-
inch pan with 2 cups of the vanilla wafer crumbs, and pour in gelatin mixture. Cover with remaining crumbs and chopped nuts. Chill until firm.
Cut into squares, and top with a maraschino cherry if desired. *This is a
very old recipe—one of my mother's favorites. A refreshingly light dessert.*
SERVES 15.   —*Rita Wolff, Fort Worth/Tarrant County Club*

Banana Pudding

2 packages (3½ ounces each)
  instant vanilla pudding mix
4 cups milk
½ pint (1 cup) sour cream
1 container (12 ounces) frozen
  whipped topping, thawed

1 small box (12 ounces) vanilla
  wafers
4 or 5 bananas, sliced

Combine pudding mix and milk; beat lightly until it begins to thicken.
Add sour cream and whipped topping, stirring until well blended. Line
serving dish with vanilla wafers. Cover with sliced bananas. Pour pudding
over bananas, covering completely to prevent discoloration. Refrigerate.
Vanilla wafer crumbs may also be sprinkled on top if desired. *This dessert
can be made with fewer calories, using sugar-free pudding, lowfat milk, sugar-
free vanilla wafers, and sugar-free whipped topping.* (Ed. note: One version
uses 2 cups of milk instead of 4, which would give a firmer pudding. Plain

yogurt can sometimes be substituted for sour cream, especially for those who must avoid fats.) SERVES 8–10.

—Doris Bloodworth, Brazos County Club, and Mrs. Ken (Esther) Goessler,
Washington County Club

No-Name Dessert

½ cup (1 stick) margarine, melted

½ cup sugar

½ cup all-purpose flour

1 teaspoon baking powder

½ cup milk

1 teaspoon vanilla

1 small can (17 ounces) fruit cocktail, with juice

Melt margarine in baking dish. Make a batter of sugar, flour, baking powder, milk, and vanilla. Pour into pan with melted margarine. Pour fruit cocktail and juice on top of batter; do not mix. Bake approximately 35 minutes in 375° oven. *Quick and easy and popular with all ages. Recipe may be easily doubled.* SERVES 4–5. *—Pat Braddick, Mid-Jefferson County Club*

Brandy Fruit

1 can (11 ounces) mandarin oranges, drained

1 can (13¼ ounces) pineapple chunks, drained

1 large can (29 ounces) pear halves, partially drained

1 can (20 ounces) cherry pie filling

1 can (20 ounces) apple pie filling

1 large can (29 ounces) sliced peaches, drained

1 package (12 ounces) pitted prunes

¼ cup blackberry or peach brandy

pinch of salt

¼ cup butter or margarine

Combine all fruit and brandy in 13-by-9-inch baking dish. Sprinkle with a little salt; dot with margarine. Bake at 350° for 1 hour or until bubbly. Serve hot, warm, or cold. May be served with cream. *Any flavor of brandy is good. Apricots may also be added or substituted.* SERVES 12–15.

—Norma River, Liberty County Club

Cream Puffs

¼ pound (1 stick) butter or
  margarine

1 cup boiling water

5 ounces (approximately 1¼ cups)
  all-purpose flour

¼ teaspoon salt

4 eggs (at room temperature)

Melt butter in boiling water in large saucepan. Add flour and salt all at once. Beat vigorously. Remove from heat as soon as mixture leaves sides of pan. Cool slightly. Add eggs, one at a time, beating vigorously after each addition, until dough no longer looks slippery. Drop batter with dipper, or use cake decorating tube, onto greased baking sheet. Bake 15 minutes at 425°, then 30 minutes at 325°.

FILLING

3 ounces cornstarch

½ pound sugar

¼ teaspoon salt

1 cup milk, cold

1¼ cups milk, hot

5 eggs, beaten

1 teaspoon vanilla

Combine cornstarch, sugar, and salt; add cold milk, and stir until smooth. Heat 1¼ cups milk in top of double boiler. Add cold milk mixture, stirring constantly, and cook over hot water until thick. Add eggs gradually to thickened mixture. Cook 7 minutes; remove from heat, and add vanilla. Cool. Cut top off each cream puff pastry; fill with custard, and replace top. Top with chocolate sauce.

SAUCE

6 ounces sugar

1 ounce cornstarch

½ teaspoon salt

1½ ounces cocoa

½ cup water, cold

1¾ cups water, boiling

3 ounces butter or margarine

Combine dry ingredients in heavy saucepan; add cold water gradually to form a smooth paste. Add boiling water slowly, stirring constantly. Boil 5 minutes or until thickened. Remove from heat. Add butter or margarine; stir to blend. Drop spoonful on top of each cream puff. *This was a prize-winner at a county fair bake-off, with auction money going to the Mothers' Club scholarship fund.* MAKES 12–14 CREAM PUFFS.

—*Hazel Mondin, Guadalupe County Club*

Cherry Pizza

1 cup all-purpose flour	⅔ cup butter or margarine
3 tablespoons sugar	½ cup finely chopped nuts

Combine flour and sugar. Cut in butter until mixture resembles coarse crumbs. Stir in finely chopped nuts. With hands, shape pastry into ball. Place in 12-inch pizza pan, patting to cover bottom and sides of pan. Bake 15 minutes at 350°. Cool.

TOPPING

1 package (8 ounces) cream cheese, softened	2 cups frozen whipped topping, thawed
1 cup powdered confectioners sugar	1 can (20 ounces) cherry pie filling

Beat cream cheese and powdered sugar until smooth. Fold in whipped topping. Spread on cooled crust. Cover with cherry pie filling, leaving about ½ inch of cream cheese mixture uncovered on outer edge. Pizza will cut better if chilled for at least 1 hour in refrigerator. *This dessert looks pretty and never lasts long.* SERVES 8.

—*Carol Bierwirth, East Bell County Club*

Fruit Pizza

1 sugar cookie roll (18 ounces)

1½ tablespoons cornstarch

½ cup sugar

⅜ cup water

½ cup orange juice

⅛ cup lemon juice

1 package (8 ounces) cream cheese, softened

1 teaspoon vanilla

¼ cup sugar

ascorbic acid or fruit protector, used according to directions

2 cups (or more) fresh fruits: peaches, bananas, strawberries, blueberries, pineapple, kiwi—or any combination of these fruits

Cut the cookie roll in ⅛-inch slices and completely line pizza pan, pressing together. Bake for 10 minutes at 350°. Let cool. In a saucepan, combine the cornstarch and sugar. Add water and orange and lemon juices. Bring to a boil and cook 1 minute. Cool and set aside to use as glaze. In a bowl combine cream cheese, vanilla, and sugar. Mix until creamy; spread over cooled cookie dough. Arrange slices of fruit over cream cheese mixture. Ascorbic acid should be mixed with fruits such as peaches and bananas to keep them from turning brown. Spread cooled glaze over fruit, and refrigerate until ready to serve. Cut into pie-shaped wedges. SERVES 6–8.

—*Shirley Neal, Houston Club*

Date Dessert

12 chocolate, creme-filled sandwich cookies, crushed

1 cup chopped dates

¾ cup water

¼ teaspoon salt

2 cups miniature marshmallows

½ cup chopped walnuts

1 cup whipping cream, whipped

½ teaspoon vanilla

Spread half of crushed cookies in 9-by-13-inch dish. Combine dates, water, and salt; bring to boil. Reduce heat and simmer for 3 minutes. Remove from heat; add marshmallows and stir until melted. Cool to room temperature, add walnuts, and spread over cookie crumbs. Spread unsweetened whipped cream and vanilla on top. Add remaining cookie crumbs. Refrigerate. SERVES 8.

—*Carol Ireland, Fort Bend Club*

Crème de Menthe Dessert

1 small package (16 ounces)
chocolate, creme-filled sandwich
cookies

½ gallon vanilla ice cream,
softened slightly

½ cup green crème de menthe

Crush cookies to crumblike texture. Place half of crumbs in bottom of 13-by-9-inch pan. Mix softened ice cream and crème de menthe; place mixture over crumbs. Add remainder of crumbs on top. Freeze for several hours before serving. *This recipe is a family favorite, often requested in lieu of a birthday cake. A food processor is useful for making the crumbs.* MAKES 12 SERVINGS.
—Suzy Burt, Deep East Texas Club

Cherry-Banana-Nut Ice Cream

3 eggs

2 cups sugar

½ teaspoon salt

3 tablespoons all-purpose flour

3 small packages (3½ ounces each)
instant banana pudding mix

3 large cans (12 ounces each)
evaporated milk

1½ quarts milk

1 tablespoon vanilla

1 small bottle (1 ounce) almond
extract

1 large (10 ounces) and 1 small jar
(6 ounces) of maraschino
cherries, chopped

1½ cups chopped pecans

2 large bags ice

4 cups rock salt

Combine eggs, sugar, salt, flour, pudding mix, and evaporated milk in a large, heavy saucepan. Cook on medium heat, stirring often, until thick—20 minutes is about long enough. Allow to cool in refrigerator for several hours or overnight. When ready to freeze, mix in milk, vanilla, almond extract, cherries, and pecans. Pour into 6-quart ice cream freezer canister and freeze. The ice cream takes 35–40 minutes and a lot of rock salt in an electric freezer. When frozen, remove dasher and cover cannister top with waxed paper and the lid. After wiping salty water from cannister, place canister into a plastic bag, and tie top securely. Replace in freezer with additional ice. This keeps the ice cream from becoming icy. MAKES 6 QUARTS.
—Grace Sneed, Deep East Texas Club

Milky Way® Ice Cream

12 Milky Way® candy bars (2.10 ounces each)

1 can (14 ounces) sweetened condensed milk

1 pint half and half

1½ pints whipping cream

whole milk to fill freezer to specified mark

Melt candy bars. This may be done in a microwave, setting timer for 30 seconds, stirring, and then setting for 30 more seconds. Combine sweetened condensed milk, half and half, and whipping cream with mixer in large bowl. Slowly mix in melted bars. Pour into ice cream freezer container, and fill to specified mark with whole milk (usually ⅔ or ¾ full). Freeze according to freezer instructions, and stand back and take the praise! *This is a not a chocolate ice cream, but is fantastically rich and delicious. Very easy to make.* SERVES ABOUT 15—MAKES 4 QUARTS.

—*Doris Smith, Amarillo Club*

Triple Treats

1 package (11½ ounces or 2 cups) milk chocolate morsels

2 tablespoons vegetable shortening

30 vanilla caramels

3 tablespoons butter

2 tablespoons water

1 cup coarsely chopped peanuts

Melt milk chocolate morsels and shortening over hot (not boiling) water. Stir until chips are melted and mixture is smooth. Remove from heat. Pour half of mixture into an 8-inch foil-lined pan; spread evenly. Refrigerate until firm (about 15 minutes). Combine caramels, butter, and water; melt over boiling water, stirring until caramels melt and mixture is smooth. Stir in nuts until well blended. Pour into chocolate-lined pan, and spread evenly. Refrigerate until tacky, about 15 minutes. Top with remaining melted chocolate (re-melt if necessary), and refrigerate until firm (about 1 hour). Cut into squares. Refrigerate until ready to serve. *Delicious! Just like a well-known candy bar.* MAKES ABOUT 2½ DOZEN PIECES.

—*Kathy Radulovich, Midland Club*

Peanut Butter Puffs

2 egg whites

¼ teaspoon salt

¾ cup sugar

½ cup peanut butter, softened

Beat egg whites with salt until soft peak forms; add sugar very gradually. Beat until stiff peaks form. Beat peanut butter to soften; fold into meringue. Drop by teaspoonfuls 1-inch apart on greased cookie sheet. Bake at 325° for 20 minutes, or until light brown. MAKES 24 PIECES.

—*Mary Lou Perry, Orange County Club*

Pralines

1 small package (3⅛ ounces) butterscotch pudding mix (not instant)

1 cup sugar

½ cup brown sugar

1 tablespoon margarine

½ cup evaporated milk

½ cup chopped pecans

Combine all ingredients in heavy saucepan, stirring until sugars dissolve. Cook over low heat to soft-ball stage (240° on candy thermometer). Remove from heat. Beat until mixture starts to thicken. Drop by tablespoonfuls onto waxed paper. Allow to cool. MAKES 2 DOZEN OR MORE.

—*Gerry Allen, Garland Club*

No-Cook Divinity

1 package fluffy white frosting mix

⅓ cup light corn syrup

1 teaspoon vanilla

½ cup boiling water

1 package (16 ounces) confectioners powdered sugar

1 cup nuts, chopped

In small bowl, combine frosting mix, corn syrup, vanilla, and boiling water. Beat on highest speed until stiff peaks form, about 5 minutes. Transfer to large mixer bowl; on low speed gradually blend in powdered sugar. Stir in chopped nuts. Drop mixture by teaspoonfuls onto waxed paper. When outside of candy feels firm, turn over. Dry at least 12 hours. Store in airtight container. MAKES 3–4 DOZEN PIECES OF CANDY.

—*Paula Perkins, Orange County Club*

Texas Chocolate Bar

1 cup (2 sticks) margarine, softened

2 cups brown sugar

2 eggs

2 teaspoons vanilla

2½ cups all-purpose flour

1 teaspoon salt

1 teaspoon baking soda

3 cups quick-cooking oats

Cream margarine and brown sugar. Beat in eggs and vanilla. Sift flour, salt, and soda and add to creamed mixture. Stir in oats. Put two-thirds of mixture in well-greased 13-by-9-inch baking pan with 2-inch sides. Prepare filling.

FILLING

1 can (14 ounces) sweetened condensed milk

2 cups semisweet chocolate morsels

2 tablespoons margarine

½ teaspoon salt

2 teaspoons vanilla

1 cup chopped pecans

Combine condensed milk, chocolate morsels, margarine, and salt in heavy saucepan. Melt over very low heat, stirring until well blended. Remove from heat; add vanilla and pecans. Spread filling over oat layer. Crumble remaining one-third of oat mixture over top. Bake at 350° for 30–35 minutes. Cool briefly and cut into desired shape. (May be cut into shape of Texas.) MAKES 16–20 SERVINGS. —*Joyce Simpson, Titus County Club*

Fireside Coffee

2 cups chocolate mix

2 cups non-dairy creamer

1 cup instant coffee

1 teaspoon cinnamon

1 cup powdered confectioners sugar

Mix chocolate mix, non-dairy creamer, coffee, cinnamon, and powdered sugar until well blended; store in air-tight container. Use 2 or 3 tablespoons per mug with boiling water. You may add 1 or 2 teaspoons coffee-flavored liqueur if you wish. Nice fireside drink. —*Dorothy Lunday, Laredo Club*

Index

Bread, 52; Yummy Pizza Loaves, 110; White Yeast Bread, 103

Muffins: (with variations), 109; Whuffins, 41

Rolls: Bran Refrigerator Rolls, 118; Buttermilk Rolls, 119; Cottage Cheese Rolls, 106; Extra Special Rolls, 105; Kraut Runzas, 104; Swedish Butterhorns, 105

Breakfast Casserole, 39
Broccoli and Cheese Dip, 74
Broccoli Casserole, 184
Broccoli Salad, 97
Brownies: Double Chocolate, 14; Special, 14
Brown Sugar-Chip Bars, 15
Buffalo Chips, 6
Burgundy Beef Stew, 157
Burritos, 35
Butter Cake, Gooey, 224
Buttermilk Fried Rabbit, 178
Buttermilk Pound Cake, 230
Buttermilk Rolls, 119
Buttermilk Salad, 94
Butterscotch Noodle Candy, 44

Cabbage Salad, Chef's, 99
Cajun Creole Gumbo, 190
Cake in a Pan, 234
Cakes: Aggie, 231; Aggie Wine, 221; Almond Bundt, 238; Banana Nut, 238; Best Yet, 235; Blitzkuchen, 224; Cake in a Pan, 234; Carrot, 236; Chocolate Cookie Sheet (Fudge Cake), 233; Chocolate Date, 232; Coconut, 222; Cream of Coconut, 223; Devil's Food, 230; Easy Upside-Down, 240; Fresh Apple, 247, 248; Fresh Pear, 247, 248; Fresh Strawberry, 245; Fruit Bread, 251; Gingerbread, 218; Gooey Butter, 224; Italian Cream, 222; Lemon, 249; Lorrie's Carrot, 236; Pioneer Boulangerie, 249; Mandarin Orange, 243; Mississippi Mud, 234; Neiman-Marcus, 227; Never Fail Cupcakes, 251; Oatmeal, 226; Pecan Pie, 237; Piña Colada, 225; Pineapple, 241; Pineapple Stir, 42; Pineapple Wonder, 240; Poppy Seed, 239; Pumpkin, 248; Red Devil's Food, 232; Rum Pineapple Coconut, 242; Sock-It-To-Me, 226; Spicy Dark Fruitcake, 250; Strawberry Sour Cream, 244; Strawberry Torte,

246; Summer's Pineapple, 241; Texas Pie, 242. *See also* Cheesecakes; Pound Cakes

Candies: Butterscotch Noodle, 44; Caramel, 24; English Toffee, 26; Leche Pogada, 151; Mexican Pecan Candy, 209; Microwave Peanut Brittle, 150; Microwave Peanut Butter Fudge, 150; No-Cook Divinity, 275; Peanut Patties, 25; Peanut Brittle, 26; Triple Treats, 274. *See also* Pralines

Candy Orange Slice Bar Cookies, 15
Caramel Candy, 24
Caramel Corn, 150, 151
Caramel Fudge Bars, 16
Carne Guisado, 205
Carrot Cake, 236; Lorrie's, 236
Carrots, Marinated, 57
Casseroles: Breakfast, 39; California Baked Rice, 186; Crawfish au Gratin, 195; Crawfish Supreme, 192; Easy Hot Dish, 33; Fiesta Spaghetti, 132; Firecracker, 206; Ham and Broccoli, 177; Ham and Spaghetti, 178; Hamburger, 34; Hungarian Goulash, 133; Jalapeño Shrimp, 192; Microwave Rice Pilaf, 146; Monterrey, 34; Mother's, 33; One-Dish Macaroni-Beef, 141; Rice, 145; Rice and Broccoli, 123; Sausage and Cheese Bake, 52; Sausage and Rice, 178; Spaghetti Delight, 131; Tamale and Corn Bake, 208; Tex-Mex Cornbread I, 159, 160. *See also* Meats; Pasta; Rice

Chicken: Baked Chicken Salad, 171; Baked Chicken with Rice, 167; Chicken Casserole, 31, 170; Chicken and Dressing, 165; Chicken and Rice, 32, 130; Chicken Broccoli, 32; Chicken Crunch, 175; Chicken, for Company, 170; Chicken Gourmet, 129; Chicken Spaghetti, 165; Chicken Spectacular, 129; Chicken Spinach, 128; Chicken Tetrazzini, 130; Hot Chicken Salad, 172; King Ranch, 174; Wild Rice Chicken, 171

Vegetable: Baked Corn, 123; Broccoli, 184; Corn, 184; Easy Potato, 187; Fresh Vegetable, 183; Green Bean-Corn, 185; Green Beans Oregano, 185; Hominy, 123, 183; Mexicali Corn, 147; Mom's Yummy Potatoes, 181; Potato Supreme, 187; Squaw Squash, 182;

Index

Sweet-Sour Sauce, 64
Swiss Enchiladas, 205

Taco Dip, 71
Taco Salad, 99
Tailgating Tips, 48
Tamale and Corn Bake, 208
Tea Cakes, 217
Teriyaki Chicken, 166
Texas Chocolate Bar, 276
Texas Crab Grass, 69
Texas Pie, 242
Texas Squash, 182
Tex-Mex Cornbread Casserole, 159, 160
Tex-Mex Layered Dip, 70
Toffee, English, 26
Tomato-Zucchini Bake, 180
Too Easy to Be Good Coffee Cake, 41
Tortilla Cheese Roll-Ups, 66
Triple Treats, 274
Tuna Ball, 79
TV Niblets, 23
Two-Crust Pastry, ix

Ukrainian Borsch, 126
Unbaked Cookies, 43
Upside-Down Cake, Easy, 240

Vegetable Burgers, 35
Vegetable Casserole, Fresh, 183
Vegetable Garden Dip, 74
Vermicelli Salad, 91

White Mountain Icing, 223
White Yeast Bread, 103
Whuffins, 41
Wild Rice Chicken, 171

Yum-Yums, 257

Zucchini Bisque, 89
Zucchini Bread, 19
Zucchini Salad, 98